MW00773834

Reluctant Raiders

The Reluctant Raiders

The Story of United States Navy Bombing Squadron VB/VPB-109 During World War II

Alan C. Carey

Schiffer Military History
Atglen, PA

ACKNOWLEDGMENTS

This book is the final result of some five years of research pouring over microfiche, photographs, personal flight logs, letters, and interviews. The National Archives, the Navy Historical Center, and the library at the University of Texas provided official information on the United States Navy's role in the Pacific War. However, it is the people who served in Navy land-based squadrons that provide personal perspectives on the war. Therefore, I would like to thank the following former members of VB/VPB-109 who made this book possible: Roy Balke, Jack Biggers, Robert Carey, Thomas Delahoussaye, George Fairbanks, Andrew Halasz, Wayne Turner, George Murphy, Oden Sheppard, and Mrs. Robert Tovey. I would also like to thank Ron Sathre and the International PB4Y Association who made it possible for this writer to meet and interview those men who flew the PB4Y-1 and PB4Y-2. Finally, I would like to thank my wife, Connie, for her support and willingness to help me in accomplishing my dream.

Book Design by Ian Robertson.
Copyright © 1999 by Alan C. Carey.
Library of Congress Catalog Number: 98-89153

Printed in China
ISBN: 0-7643-0757-6

We are interested in hearing from authors with book ideas on related topics.

Published by Schiffer Publishing Ltd.
4880 Lower Valley Road
Atglen, PA 19310
Phone: (610) 593-1777
FAX: (610) 593-2002
E-mail: Schifferbk@aol.com.
Visit our web site at: www.schifferbooks.com
Please write for a free catalog.
This book may be purchased from the publisher.
Please include $3.95 postage.
Try your bookstore first.

In Europe, Schiffer books are distributed by:
Bushwood Books
6 Marksbury Road
Kew Gardens
Surrey TW9 4JF
England
Phone: 44 (0)181 392-8585
FAX: 44 (0)181 392-9876
E-mail: Bushwd@aol.com.

Try your bookstore first.

Contents

Dedication 6
Introduction: Formation of U.S. Navy Bombing
Squadrons 8

Chapter 1   Formation of VB-109 14
Chapter 2   Apamama 18
Chapter 3   Operations from Apamama 24
Chapter 4   Missing in Action 29
Chapter 5   Long Patrols 36
Chapter 6   Operations from Kwajalein 51
Chapter 7   Operations from Eniwetok 64
Chapter 8   Supporting the Marianas Invasion 78
Chapter 9   Operations from Saipan 89
Chapter 10   Last Missions 105
Chapter 11   Reformation of VB-109 as VPB-109 113
Chapter 12   Palawan, Philippines 117
Chapter 13   Okinawa 132
Chapter 14   Tinian and Iwo Jima 149
Chapter 15   Finals at Okinawa 155

Appendix A: Tactical Organization VB-109 (31 December 1943-15 August 1944) 164
Appendix B: Japanese Naval and Merchant Shipping Losses by VB-109 165
Appendix C: Enemy Aircraft Engaged by VB-109 169
Appendix D: List of Air Crews and Individual Combat Records for VB-109 171
Appendix E: Missions and Flying Hours per Patrol Plane Commander 194
Appendix F: PB4Y-1 Aircraft Assigned to VB-109 195
Appendix G: Tactical Organization VPB-109 197
Appendix H: Japanese Naval and Merchant Shipping Losses by VPB-109 198
Appendix I: List of Air Crews and Records of VPB-109 202
Appendix J: Missions and Flying Hours per Patrol Plane Commander 229
Appendix K: Aircraft Assigned to VPB-109 230
Appendix L: List of Personnel Killed in Action 231
Appendix M: Ground Personnel 233

Notes 234
Bibliography 237

DEDICATION

*This book is dedicated to the following men from VB/
VPB-109 who gave their lives in the Pacific:*

Raymond W. Devlin, ARM2c
Benjamin W. Anderson, AOM(T)1c
Ensign Henry Baier Jr.
Robert J. Bennington, AMM1c
Alexander J. Boyd, ARM1c
Sterling T. Brown, AMM2c
James R.T. Carswell, AFC2c
Lieutenant Samuel E. Coleman
Lawrence R. Conroy, AOM3c
Harry F. Donovan, ARM2c
Daniel J. Dujak, ARM2c
Aern R. Durgin, S1c
Ensign Keith E. Ellis
Bobby W. Fickling, AOM3c
Hale D. Fisher, AMM1c
Ensign Leslie E. Fontaine
Richard D. Frye, ARM2c
Paul J. Graham, AOM3c
James T. Heasley, AOM2c
Lieutenant (jg) Charles M. Henderson Jr.
Lieutenant (jg) John H. Herron
Ensign Warren A. Hindenland
Peter G. Ilacqua, ARM2c
Victor B. Jones, AOM2c

William J. Krier, ARM1c
Joe W. Kasperlik, AMM2c
Lieutenant Elmer H. Kasperson
Lieutenant John D. Keeling
Lieutenant Leo E. Kennedy
Hugo L. Kluge, ARM2c
Joseph W. Komorowski, AMM1c
Frank R. Kramer, AMM1c
James E. Krieger, AMM3c
William J. Krier, ARM1c
Ensign Nelson T. O'Bryan
Lou C. Petrick, S1c
Ensign Keith W. Radcliffe
Melvin M. Rager, AMM2c
Louis E. Sandidge Jr.
William F. Schneider, AOM2c
Lieutenant(jg) Leroy A. Shreiner
Warren B. Simon, AMM2c
Truman Steele, AOM2c
Allen K. Stinger, AOM3c
John E. Tusha, S1c
Richard C. Vancitters, AOM3c
William L. Willocks Jr.
Clarence H. Ziehlke, AMM3c

Squadron Song

(Bowdlerized Version) To the tune of "Abdul El Bulbul"

O, the men of ONE O NINE are brave men and bold,
And quite unaccustomed to fear,
And they sing what they think
As they wing o'er the drink;
"Let's get the hell out of here."
Up stood the Skipper in front of the crew,
The men were filled with Suspense.
He pulled out a dispatch
From ComAirCinPac,
And said to them, "No foolin', gents-
Our tour's been extended, the food will get worse,
And the hope will get longer, I guess.
Once we were hot,
But now we're forgot-
It looks like one hell of a mess."
But the men of ONE O NINE are brave men and bold,
And quite unaccustomed to fear,
And they sing what they think
As they wing o'er the drink;
"Let's get the hell out of here."
The men turned away with a tear in each eye,
And said, "It is worse than we think,
Once it was fun-But now we're all done.
Let's go out and get drunk.
For, our Skipper is eager, and don't give a damn
For our curses and prayers and groans.
He leads our old wrecks
Right in on the decks-
We'll never get back to our homes."
But the men of ONE O NINE are brave men and bold,
And quite unaccustomed to fear,
And they sing what they think
As they wing o'er the drink;
"Let's get the hell out of here."

INTRODUCTION:
Formation of U.S. Navy Bombing Squadrons

During the first two years of the Pacific War, the vast Pacific Ocean posed a formidable barrier for American aerial reconnaissance of Japanese-held territory. Patrol aircraft in the Navy's inventory, such as the PBY Catalina and PV-2 Ventura, were inadequate for extensive patrolling of Japanese sea lanes and installations. What the Navy needed was an aircraft capable of staying in the air for an extended duration of time and still be capable of inflicting damage on the enemy.

The only suitable aircraft capable of extended patrols and capable of defending itself and inflicting damage was the Consolidated B-24 Liberator. With a range of 2,960 miles, a cruising speed of 200 miles per hour, and a bomb load of 8800 pounds, it was well suited for the Pacific. In July 1942, the Army agreed to the Navy receiving a quantity of B-24Ds, redesignated as the PB4Y-1, and the first Liberators were given to the Transitional Training Squadron in San Diego the same year.[1]

The first Navy Liberators sent to the Pacific varied little from the Army B-24s. But, as it proved in Europe and the Pacific, the armament in the bulbous plexiglass nose proved inadequate against frontal attacks by enemy aircraft. The distinctive Navy version of the Liberator was introduced when B-24s were modified with the Erco 250SH-1 bow turret in the nose. The bow turret's twin 50 caliber guns carried twice the ammunition supply than other turrets, 800 versus 400. Its armor plating in front afforded the pilots additional protection.[2] This modification extended the aircraft by an additional three feet and, by the end of the war, a total of 977 PB4Y-1 Liberators were received by the Navy. As PB4Y-1s were seeing action in the Pacific and European Theaters of War, the Navy was already planning to replace the Liberator with a four-engine patrol bomber designated as the PB4Y-2 Privateer.

Consolidated-Vultee Aircraft Company began work on the prototype of the Privateer in September 1942. The first prototypes were converted from B-24s by replacing the twin-tail assembly with a tall single fin. By the time production began, the Privateer was seven feet longer then the Liberator, and superchargers were deleted from the Pratt and Whitney Wasp engines. The belly turret was deleted, and waist blisters with twin 50 caliber guns were installed.

The Erco 250TH waist blister consisted of a teardrop outer shell that rotated vertically. A slit in the teardrop allowed the two 50 caliber guns to move laterally, and guns and gunner were enclosed in an inner ball inside the teardrop. This ball rotated laterally and independently of the outer shell. Bullet proof glass and armor plate in front of the gunner moved with him as he manned the guns, thereby protecting him from whatever he was aiming at.[3]

Privateers were extensively equipped for Electronic Counter Measures with radiodomes housing an APA-17HF/DF; an AS-124/APR intercept receiver; an AS-6/APQ-2B for radar jamming; and a bulge below the fuselage under the engines housed an APS-15 surface search radar.[4]

A total of 736 Privateers were produced between 1944 and 1945 and, by the end of the war, some twenty Navy land-based bombing squadrons (VB), later redesignated in October 1944 as Navy patrol and bombing squadrons (VPB), had been equipped with PB4Y-1 Liberators and PB4Y-2 Privateers.

Commander Norman Miller's PB4Y-1 "Thunder Mug" in flight. *Courtesy of Thomas Delahoussaye.*

A flight of PB4Y-2 Privateers. *Courtesy of the National Archives.*

A Consolidated-Vultee PB4Y-2 Privateer in flight with a "Bat" air to ground, radar-guided missile. *Courtesy of the National Archives.*

Beginning in January 1943, when VB-101 became the first Navy land-based squadron to see action in the Pacific, Navy land-based bomber squadrons conducted daily reconnaissance missions, anti-submarine patrols, and bombing missions against the Japanese throughout the Pacific area from as far north as Shemya Island in the Aleutians to as far south as the Solomons. One of the squadrons to see combat was VB-109, which began operations under Task Force 57, Fleet Air Wing 2, in the Central Pacific in January 1944.

Under the command of Commander Norman "Buzz" Miller, VB-109 conducted raids against the Japanese in the Gilbert, Caroline, Marshall, Mariana, Kazan, and Bonin Islands. Throughout its combat tour, the primary mission of the squadron was long-range search, patrol, and armed reconnaissance. Search planes were to attack submarines and small enemy craft, but attacks upon ships, planes, and land installations were secondary and to be made, when in the Patrol Plane Commander's judgement, the results to be achieved seemed worth the risk involved.

Searches normally covered a 900-mile long, nine-degree wide sector of pie-shaped ocean, assigned by higher commands, and the sectors extended progressively westward in the war zone. Early on, daily reconnaissance of enemy-held bases was added to the routine activities. Special searches, patrols, and strikes often exceeded the routine patrols in number of planes employed and number of hours flown.

Air Strikes were often carried out by solitary aircraft flying at masthead altitudes ranging from 50 to 200 feet. Bombing attacks at higher altitudes were rare unless specifically ordered by higher commands. Aggressiveness was always encouraged in the squadron and, consequently, pilots were trained in low level bombing and strafing tactics, making VB-109 the first of such squadrons to exploit fully the deadly effectiveness of the minimum altitude attack.

In a prolonged minimum altitude attack, a plane approaching an enemy target flew 20 to 50 feet off the water to escape radar detection. Once over the target, the general pattern was to pull up to 200 feet altitude over the target for a bombing and strafing run. When VB-109's first tour of duty ended in August 1944, the squadron had flown a total of 353 bombing and strafing attacks, resulting in the sinking or damaging of 134 Japanese merchant and naval ships, four enemy aircraft shot down in the air, and another 20 enemy aircraft destroyed on the ground.

In late April 1945, the squadron paid a return visit to the Pacific as VPB-109 and were equipped with PB4Y-2 Privateers. Under the command of Lieutenant Commander George L. Hicks, the squadron marked the first combat employment of a guided air to ground missile, the SWOD Mark 9 "Bat." Based at Palawan, in the Philippines, and later Tinian and Okinawa, the squadron continued to deploy the low level tactics perfected during the squadron's first tour. The use of the SWOD, Mark 9, by VPB-109 marked the first combat employment by the U.S. Navy of a guided missile. A late arrival, it was installed on squadron planes immediately proceeding the departure for the combat zone, and its employment by the squadron was in effect an operational evaluation of the instrument. Because the weapon was never operated under satisfactory conditions, only four of seventeen attacks made were successful.

The use of Radar Counter Measure (RCM) equipment at Palawan, Iwo Jima, and Okinawa, enabled the squadron to locate some 127 new enemy radar stations electronically and visually, reported to CINPAC and all units concerned by dispatch, and over 300 enemy radar stations were verified. Of those located, the squadron bombed a good number from Palawan and worked in conjunction with the Tactical Air Force and the Tenth Army attacking new locations from Okinawa. In only 61 days of operations, a total of 118 ships were sunk or damaged, 46 strikes were made against enemy ground installations, six enemy planes were shot down in the air, one destroyed on the ground, and another eight were damaged.

This is the history of VB-109 from its commissioning in August 1943 until it ceased combat flights against the Japanese in August 1945.

Extreme effort has been made to substantiate the record of VB/VPB-109 through the squadron's combat history, After Action Reports, and individual crew records

Close-up view of the starboard Erco 250TH waist blister showing the twin 50. caliber machine guns. Also note after dorsal turret. *Courtesy of the National Archives.*

of the squadron. While researching this book, I wanted to verify the accuracy of the squadron's record through reliable sources on the subject. Discrepancies were found concerning the squadron claims on enemy ships sunk with the information gathered primarily from the following sources: *Japanese Naval and Merchant Shipping Losses During World War II* by The Joint-Navy Assessment Committee (1947) and Masanori Ito's, *The End of the Japanese Imperial Navy* (1962). Therefore, specific shipping losses attributed to the squadron are derived from information provided by the cited resources.

1

Formation of VB-109

On the morning of August 2, 1943, twenty-nine naval officers and two enlisted men gathered in Hangar Five at Naval Air Station, San Diego, California, for the commissioning of a new bomber squadron. Lieutenant George Leighton Hicks, USNR, a native of Three Rivers, California, called the group to attention, and Lieutenant Commander Norman Mickey Miller, U.S.N., began reading his orders in connection with the fitting out and commissioning of Bombing Squadron One Hundred Nine.

A soft spoken man with dark Indian features and leathery tanned skin, thirty-six year old Commander Miller was a graduate of Annapolis and a veteran Naval aviator, but this would be his first command of a heavy bomber squadron.[1] Miller would become well respected by the officers and men alike. The officers respected him for his tenacity in action and his sense of fair play. He did not expect his men to fly dangerous missions if he was not willing to do so himself; this was proven in the months to come when he flew some of the most dangerous combat missions himself. Commander Miller involved his patrol plane commanders in planning and coordinating strikes. Miller trusted his officers' judgement and expected them to fulfill their duties in the combat zone. The enlisted personnel respected Miller because he understood them, having entered Annapolis from the ranks himself. He was the type of officer enlisted personnel could trust by not endangering their lives needlessly.

After formally declaring the squadron commissioned, Commander Miller welcomed the officers and men and, with Lieutenant Hicks as executive officer, held a brief inspection. After dismissing the formation, the small group moved outside the hangar for an informal photograph in front of the plexiglass nose of a PB4Y-1 Liberator to commemorate the occasion. With small ceremony and little fanfare,

Bombing Squadron One Hundred Nine came into existence as a part of the air arm of the United States Navy.

VB-109 was designated as a stream-lined Navy Bomber Squadron (VBH), with 15 PB4Y-1 Liberator aircraft assigned and a personnel complement of 87 officers and 148 enlisted organized into eighteen flight crews. It was intended that the squadron would be a highly mobile fighting outfit with all maintenance provided by other units under the Hedron and Casu system (Carrier Aircraft Service Unit). Four ground officers and enlisted men were allowed under the compliment to handle administrative details and maintenance liaison.

A majority of the Patrol Plane Commanders assigned to the squadron at commissioning and, in the following weeks, were veteran pilots, with the exception of Commander Miller, who had some 70 hours flying time in Army B-24s at Hawaii, none had any time in Liberators. A few of the pilots, such as Lieutenant William Bridgeman and Lieutenant Oden Sheppard, were former PBY Catalina flying boat pilots. One officer, Lieutenant Amos Shriener, had 21 operational flights with the Royal Air Force over Europe.[2] Because none of the officers and very few of the enlisted men had never even set foot inside a B-24, Commander Miller ordered all flight personnel to attend the Transition Landplane Unit at North Island for familiarization with the Liberator.

Initially, squadron organization was considerably hampered and delayed by a period of six weeks spent at the Training Landplane Unit. Pilots reporting to the squadron were sent directly to the Training Landplane Unit for temporary duty. It was mid-October before they returned to the squadron for duty. During training pilots received a minimum of ten hours instruction in take-offs and landings, four dual instrument instruction flights, ten hours of solo, and one period of night flying. Pilots also completed two weeks of ground school run by Consolidated Aircraft Company on piloting the B-24 and covering the various systems of the plane. Enlisted flight personnel completed six weeks of ground school run by Consolidated on the mechanics and maintenance of the B-24.

The officers and men of VB-109 at San Diego, California prior to their departure for the Central Pacific. *Courtesy of Robert Carey.*

While most of the personnel were away, the squadron began receiving PB4Y-1 Liberators. In late September, the first aircraft arrived, but it wasn't until late November before the last of the fifteen aircraft was received.

From commissioning until 4 November, the squadron was technically in a training status under Fleet Air Wing Fourteen at Naval Air Station, San Diego. Serious training continued to be delayed because of personnel and equipment problems, with personnel problems continuing unrelieved until the squadron left the States. The last twelve enlisted men who were left behind by VD-4 (Navy Photographic Squadron Four) were assigned to the squadron only eight days before it left the States. By 8 October, the majority of the pilots had reported back to the squadron, and training began under Fleet Air Wing Fourteen. However, the program was further delayed when five pilots, including Commander Miller, were ordered to ferry B-24s from the Army modification Center at Tucson to Commander Air Force, Atlantic Fleet at Norfolk, a trip involving an absence of approximately a week and a half from the squadron. When actual training began, all flight personnel completed a ground school course of one week of radar instruction and two weeks of navigation. Actual flight training consisted of some familiarization flights, practice in low altitude bombing, night flights, and three to four instrument flights per crew. Ten high altitude bombing flights from 8,000 to 14,000 feet were made by dropping water-filled bombs on the barren Salton Sea, and each crew managed six or eight gunnery flights.

On 4 November, orders arrived transferring control of the squadron from Commander Fleet Air Wing Fourteen to Commander Fleet Air Wing Two under Rear Admiral John D. Price. A week earlier, Lieutenant Joseph Jobe with his co-pilot and plane captain flew the first plane of the squadron to Kaneohe, Hawaii, followed by two planes on 6 November, two on 8 November, six on 10 November, three on 12 November, and one on 26 November. Most enlisted personnel left the States aboard the U.S.S. Miller (DD-535) and the S.S. Orson D. Mudd, reaching Kaneohe on 22 November. Upon arrival at Kaneohe, the major part of the squadron's training was accomplished under Fleet Air Wing Two from 4 November to 27 December. Training flights during this period concentrated primarily on gunnery and bombing practice. Fighter groups based at Kaneohe and Maui flew fighter opposition against squadron planes for gunnery practice. Target sleeves were towed by Grumman F6F fighters and SBD Dauntless dive bombers from the aircraft carrier U.S.S. *Independence* for firing. Because the gunnery sleeve had a tendency to come off when the F6F made runs on the PB4Y-1, and the SBD proved too slow to make attacking runs, emphasis was placed upon dry runs of the fighter groups.

High and medium altitude bombing flights were made, and masthead height bombing and strafing tactics were particularly emphasized. Three plane section take-offs were made, and considerable time was spent on night flying and radar flights. Instruction on the ASE Radar was conducted by Lieutenant McCarthy, and each crew made two or three radar flights around the Hawaiian Islands.

The ASE Radar was a piece of air to ground electronics gear capable of locating targets, particularly surface craft on the water up to 15 miles away, even through adverse weather conditions. The unit housed a cathode ray tube which would display green lines, called "grass" by the operator, across the screen. A radar contact would be confirmed when one of the green bands became larger than the others. After making a contact, the radioman, who operated the system, would guide the pilot in for an attack.

After two months in Hawaii, Commander Miller had formed a new squadron into a capable fighting unit. Now it was time to see whether they would perform as well in combat as they had in training.

The officers of VB-109 taken in front of a B-24D model Liberator in San Diego. *Courtesy of Oden Sheppard.*

2

Apamama

On December 27, operational control of the squadron was transferred from Commander Fleet Air Wing Two to Rear Admiral John H. Hoover, Commander of all land-based aircraft in the Central Pacific. Between 28 December and 3 January 1944, squadron aircraft flew from Kaneohe to Canton, in the Ellice Islands before flying east approximately 800 miles to base permanently at O'Hare Field, Apamama, in the Gilbert Islands.

The Gilbert Islands consist of fifteen atolls that run north to south and cover a total land area of 166 square miles.[1] A British possession, the Japanese occupied the islands at the outbreak of hostilities and began fortifying the larger atolls, especially Tarawa and Makin. In November 1943, the Gilberts were invaded by U.S. Naval Forces under the code-name of Operation Galvanic. One of the islands, Tarawa, was the scene of one of the bloodiest battles of the Pacific War.

Apamama lies 75 miles southwest of Tarawa. The island is approximately 15 miles in diameter, shaped like the letter "C," and covered with lush coconut trees.[2] Unlike most of her island sisters, Apamama was spared from complete destruction during Operation Galvanic. Marines who landed on the island found that the 24 Japanese troops garrisoned on the island had committed suicide. The only people to greet the Marines when they landed were the Gilbertese inhabitants, who were extremely happy to see them.

O'Hare Field was named after "Butch" O'Hare, the "Enterprise" fighter pilot and recipient of the Congressional Medal of Honor who was killed during the Gilberts operation. The 8,000-foot coral runway was built by the 95th Seabees, and by 1 February, 5,000 men and 112 planes would be based at the field.[3] In addition to native villages, which were out of bounds to service personnel, there were five separate American military establishments on the island. The Army Defensive Fighter

Group of P-40s was based north of the strip and a second army camp housed the 47th and 48th Medium Bombardment Group of B-25 Mitchells, while the Navy Bomber Camp consisted of VB-108 and a sister unit of VB-109 and VD-3, a Navy photographic squadron.

Even before VB-109's arrival, the bomber camp was already overcrowded, and the addition of another squadron just made living conditions worse. Officers ate in the VD-3 Officers' Mess, but facilities were too inadequate to accommodate VD-109 enlisted personnel and they ate with the ACORN unit (a mobile air station). Living quarters were primitive, with officers' tents having concrete decks and ply-wood half-walls with canvas tops; 6-7 officers slept to a tent. Enlisted men slept 8 to a tent, and the tents had no decking or walls. A couple days after the squadron arrived, electricity became available, which supplemented gasoline lanterns. Bathing facilities on Apamama, other than the ocean, were non-existent, and fresh water was very scarce. The little water available was utilized largely by VD-3 for photographic development. The bomber camp's one shower was reserved for the senior officer present, Commander E. C. Renfro, Commanding Officer of VB-108. Laundry was no problem, however, for the natives did the washing. Relations with the natives were always friendly. They worked as laborers and cleaners in the camp and entertained the camps at feasts on several occasions. The natives took both

Living conditions were primitive on Apamama. *Courtesy of Oden Sheppard.*

officers and men fishing with them in their boats, which supplemented the meager recreational diversions of ocean bathing and shell gathering.

Aircraft maintenance was provided by CASU (Carrier Air Service Unit), a group of approximately 100 men transferred from the CASU unit at Nuku Fetau in the Ellice Islands. It was on-the-job training for these men, because they had little prior training in PB4Y maintenance except for a month with VB-108 at Nuku Fetau. Maintenance problems would grow and multiply throughout the squadron's stay at Apamama, with neither proper equipment or spare parts obtainable. The only available spares would be provided by Lieutenant (jg) John H. Herron's plane, which was destroyed after it struck a tree and hit three parked P-40s in a night landing on the unlit, narrow runway on 3 January.

A few weeks before VB-109 arrived, Admiral Chester W. Nimitz, Commander Pacific Fleet, informed Hoover of the impending Marshalls invasion, code-named Operation Flintlock and Catchpole, that was to begin in February. The operation would consist of two phases: the first, "Flintlock," would begin on 31 January with the invasion of Kwajalein, followed by "Catchpole," the invasion of Eniwetok, on the 17th.

The Marshalls were a former German possession given to the Japanese by the Treaty of Versailles after World War One. The archipelago is one of four groups that make up Micronesia. The other three being the Gilberts, Carolines, and the Marianas. The Marshalls consist of 33 coral atolls containing some 1,100 islands, which extend 800 miles from the southeast to the northwest.[4] In the 1920s, the Japanese began fortifying the larger islands and, by the beginning of the Pacific War, Kwajalein had become one of the most important enemy bases in the island group. The atoll is comprised of three major islands and some 90 other smaller islets, all of which surrounds one of the world's largest lagoons. The three largest islands, Kwajalein, Roi, and Namur, had been turned into major Japanese military installations. Kwajalein resembles a pistol, with Roi and Namur on the northern end representing the cocking assembly, while Kwajalein is the grip of the weapon. Roi and Namur are small islets which are connected by a man-made causeway.[5] Both had been turned into an airfield, with Roi having three runways and facilities for basing 72 torpedo bombers and 100 fighters.[6] A Naval base located at the southern end of the lagoon off Kwajalein Island held a supply depot and was the advance naval headquarters of the Japanese Navy. On nearby Ebeye Island, two squadrons of scout seaplanes were stationed. Defending the atoll were over 8,000 troops.[7]

Eniwetok is the western most atoll of the Marshalls and lies some 300 miles from Kwajalein. It is a large round atoll resembling a donut, is comprised of 40 islets, and has the second largest lagoon in the archipelago. The Japanese had made military use of the three larger islands—Engebi, Parry, and Eniwetok. Engebi, to the north, had a 4,000-foot runway with anti-aircraft defenses, while Parry and Eniwetok were the sites of search radar stations, coast defense guns, and barracks.

Operations Shack on Apamama. Note squadron score board. *Courtesy of Oden Sheppard.*

Unlike Kwajalein, which took years of effort to fortify, the Japanese did not make use of Eniwetok until 1942 when construction of the Engebi airstrip began. Unlike its sister atoll, Kwajalein, the Japanese had made no attempt to defend Eniwetok until the Gilberts fell and had used it as a staging point for the Marianas and Carolines. However, there were 3,400 troops ready to defend the atoll.[8]

The job for Hoover's land-based planes preceding the invasion was to reduce Japanese air power in the Marshalls, particularly at the Japanese garrisons on Wotje, Maloelap, and Mili. American military strategists had no intention of landing forces on these three islands, but they held strong enough military forces to become a nuisance to the invasion force if they were not neutralized.[9] Mili is the nearest atoll to the Gilberts, and the Japanese had built two runways, barracks, and bomb and torpedo storage facilities. Taroa island at Maleolap Atoll had two runways over 3,000 feet long and numerous installations. Wotje, which VB-109 and other land-based squadrons would become quite familiar with, had two runways, a seaplane base, more than 50 buildings, and plenty of anti-aircraft gun emplacements. Jaluit, in the southern Marshalls, had a seaplane base with two squadrons of four-engine flying boats and one squadron of fighter seaplanes. Additionally, these islands had ample radio facilities, and some had search radar.[10] It was the job of VB-109 and her sister squadron, VB-108, to neutralize enemy garrisons stationed on the islands. For a period of seven weeks from 8 December to the end of January, Hoover's land-based planes assumed all air preparations for the Marshalls Campaign.

The primary mission of VB-108 and 109 was defined by Rear Admiral Hoover as, "Searching and patrolling assigned sectors and obtaining and transmitting information of the enemy, particularly ship movements." Secondarily, search planes were to "use any opportunity to attack enemy submarines or small vessels." Long range search and reconnaissance, in effect, was the primary burden of VB-109. Daily reconnaissance of enemy held bases, often at low level for photographic coverage, was soon added to the squadron's activities, and special missions and strikes often exceeded the routine patrols in number of planes employed and hours flown.

The squadron reached Apamama when minimum altitude or masthead height attack on enemy shipping and shore installations was becoming the tactic of choice in the Central Pacific. Three previous successful single-plane strikes at low level by Liberator pilots of VB-108 were based on the successful tactics of VB-106 and VB-104 in the South Pacific. VB-108 realized the unrivaled possibilities of this type of offensive tactic when Lieutenant Ackerman attacked Mille and Lieutenant Daley and Commander E. C. Renfro attacked Juluit in the Marshall Islands. Seeing the success of VB-108, Commander Miller had the squadron trained early in low level bombing and strafing tactics, and shortly began an uninterrupted succession of single-plane minimum altitude strikes against Japanese bases and shipping. Early results would prove so successful that permission was obtained in February, from Admiral Spruance, to attack all enemy land installations and ships in the Lesser

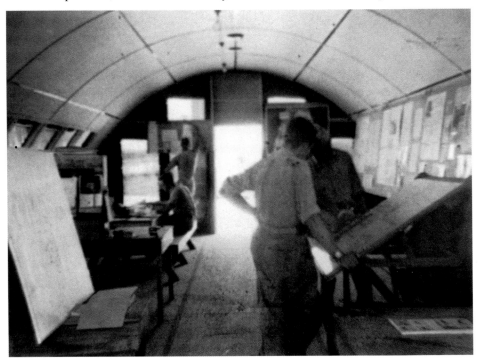

Inside the Operations Shack on Apamama. *Courtesy of Oden Sheppard.*

Marshalls which, in the judgement of the individual Patrol Plane Commander, were deemed worth the risk involved. Planes were permitted to go beyond and outside search sectors to strike enemy targets when such attacks did not minimize the effectiveness of the assigned patrol.

In masthead height attacks, the general pattern was a prolonged minimum altitude approach to the target, 20 to 50 feet off the water, to escape enemy radar detection, pulling up to 200 feet over the target. Bombing was done with precision at 200 feet altitude and at 200 miles per hour by the pilot pressing his bomb release mechanism, called a "pickle." Only on high altitude attacks, which were a rarity, did the bombardier, an enlisted crew member, initiate bomb runs. Instead, the pilot dropped by "seaman's eye." Some pilots of VB-109 followed the example of Lieutenant Hicks (Promoted to Lieutenant Commander during the squadron's tour). Hicks used a bomb sight consisting of a two-inch strip of masking tape located on the windshield that lined up with the "V" formed by the port pitot tube, which projected out from the nose of the fuselage. While the pilot made the bomb run, all ten machine gun positions trained on targets of opportunity. Complete surprise was nearly always achieved, and no serious casualties were suffered in any of the low level attacks.

Two routine searches per day were conducted from Apamama, were initially about 800 miles in length, and covered the Marshall Islands area from Mille and Maloelap to Kwajalein and Jaluit. With the invasion of the Marshalls, search sectors were extended to 1,000 miles in length to Eniwetok, requiring flights of 12 to 15 hours duration. Four were flown daily, each one scheduled to hit the end of their cross legs at or near sunset, which necessitated night flying and night landings in all instances. After Eniwetok was secure, these patrols were flown principally during daylight hours.

On the last day of 1943, the first combat patrols of the squadron were flown by two planes piloted by Lieutenant Harold E. Belew and Lieutenant (jg) John E. Stewart; both proved to be uneventful. However, on New Year's Day 1944, Lieutenant Commander John Bundy conducted the squadron's first successful strike against the Japanese.

3

Operations from Apamama

Conducting a routine search through the Marshall Islands and flying at an altitude of 700 feet through a rain shower, Lieutenant Commander John Bundy was six hours into his patrol when he sighted a two-masted, 2,000-ton freighter some 40 miles off of Mille Atoll on a northwest heading. Upon sighting the ship, Bundy dropped down to 200 feet and made a pass at the target as the bow, top, and starboard gunners began strafing the ship. Passing over the target on the first run, he released one 500 pound bomb, which sailed over the ship and exploded 50 feet off the starboard bow. As the plane finished its run, a 40mm gun on the stern of the ship began firing back at the attacking plane. Bundy swung his plane around and prepared for another attack. Coming in for his second run, Bundy's gunners quickly silenced the ship's gun crew, and there was no further firing from the enemy. As the plane flew across the ship, the pilot released another bomb, which again sailed over and exploded 30 feet beyond the target. Now that the enemy's gun had been silenced, Bundy decided to make a third run and finish off the ship. Banking the plane, he crossed over the ship and pressed the red button on his pickle to release the two remaining bombs, but they failed to release. Finding that his bombs would not release, Bundy left the area and headed back towards Apamama, leaving the ship smoking and listing some eight degrees to starboard, but still afloat.

Apamama was not out of the range of Japanese aircraft based in the Carolines and Marshalls and, the following day, Japanese bombers retaliated with a night air raid. Just after dusk, the sound of a lone Japanese bomber high above was heard approaching O'Hare Field. The wailing of the air raid siren began just as the enemy released his bombs on the field. Lieutenant George Mellard's plane, "Our Baby," parked on the field, was set afire by a daisy cutter bomb and destroyed. Three other planes were damaged by bomb fragments, and three enlisted squadron members standing guard next to their aircraft were wounded during the attack.[1] Because of the absence of adequate parking facilities, squadron planes were parked close to each other on the taxi strip. The damage could have been far worse, except for the actions of four members of the squadron who, regardless of enemy bombs and rupturing ammunition nearby, distinguished themselves by moving planes from the vicinity of the burning plane.[2]

Two days later, Commander Miller, Lieutenant Grayson, and Lieutenant (jg) John H. Herron, along with four planes of VB-108, were ordered to sow 28 Mark 47 mines from 150 feet altitude in the anchorage at Taroa, Maleolap Atoll. After sowing the mines, the planes strafed gun positions and radio and radar installations while setting a 2000-ton tanker afire before leaving the island. Upon making his approach to O'Hare Field after the mission, Lieutenant (jg) John E. Herron's plane struck a tree upon landing on the unlit runway, tearing off the outer wing panel on the port wing and damaging the number one engine and tail assembly. In the process he took out three Army P-40 fighters, and with them went most of the squadron's fighter protection; fortunately, no one was injured. Although the destruction of Herron's plane reduced the number of operational aircraft, as the weeks went by the squadron began suffering from a lack of spare parts and Herron's plane became the only source for replacements. After only one week in the war zone, VB-109 had lost four out of 15 planes and had three men wounded.

On the 9th, Commander Miller led two other planes of the squadron, flown by Lieutenant Commander Janeshek and Lieutenant Joseph H. Jobe, and four planes of VB-108 on a strike against Wotje at dusk. Coming in at 50 feet altitude, the seven planes swept over the island in a line spaced 500 to 600 feet apart. As the planes crossed over the island, gun positions, radio installations, and hangars were heavily strafed. However, a VB-108 plane took six hits from small caliber anti-aircraft fire on the starboard vertical stabilizer. Coming out over the water east of Meichen, the three planes of VB-109 heavily damaged a small patrol boat before it was finally sunk by strafing from Commander Miller's gunners. Before retiring, two Kawanishi H8K2 four-engine "Emily" flying boats parked on ramps were strafed and destroyed by Lieutenant Jobe and Lieutenant Commander Janeshek, while two other seaplanes were damaged by Commander Miller.

In order to obtain information on Japanese defenses on Kwajalein, Lieutenant Thomas Seabrook and Lieutenant William Bridgeman joined with two planes of VB-108 and two photographic planes of VD-3 on a high altitude mission over Kwajalein. The primary function of the VD-3 planes leading the sections was to obtain photographic coverage of the enemy airstrip under construction in order to determine the progress that had been made since the last coverage on 29 December 1943. The primary mission of the escorting planes was to offer protection from possible fighter interception and, secondly, to bomb Kwajalein. This was the first of several such missions, hated by the crews concerned. The necessity of flying the close formation required of a photographic run made it impossible to take evasive action against enemy anti-aircraft fire or against enemy fighters. Lieutenant Vernon E. Niebruegge of VB-108 was shot down by enemy fighters on a similar mission on 29 December 1943 while escorting VD-3 photographic planes. On the return leg of his mission, five enemy fighters consisting of two Misubishi A6M2 "Zekes" and three Kawasaki Ki-61 "Tonys" intercepted him and shot out his number three engine with 20mm gunfire. He fell out of formation and hit the water just southwest of the atoll—there were no survivors.

Now on this mission, after taking off from Apamama, the planes rendezvoused and flew in a tight V formation for mutual support. Arriving over Kwajalein, the aircraft received anti-aircraft fire from the southeast side of the island, which damaged the starboard wing and fuselage of the last VD-3 plane in the formation. Below, in the lagoon, lay 20 Japanese ships at anchor consisting of large freighters, two destroyers, and smaller merchant vessels. Just as the formation crossed over the southern part of the island on their bombing run, Lieutenant Bridgeman's number one and three engines lost power and the plane fell out of formation, almost colliding with a plane from VD-3 as it fell. After losing nearly 1,000 feet of altitude, Bridgeman managed to get the engines restarted, but it was too late to release his bombs. Over the target, Lieutenant Seabrooks released his bombs, but they

Towering brown smoke rises from a Japanese merchant ship attacked by Commander Miller at Kwajalein Atoll. *Courtesy of Thomas Delahoussyae.*

missed the island entirely and fell harmlessly into the water. Bombs released by VB-108 managed to hit the island, but damage assessment was impossible to determine, and damage, if any, was minimal. However, the primary mission of obtaining photographs of the atoll was achieved, and without damage to the aircraft the formation returned to Apamama.

Upon careful examination of the photographs VD-3 obtained, a strike in force was ordered and target assignments were made. Ten planes from VB-108, 109, and VD-3 would hit the shipping seen in Kwajalein Harbor.[3] All planes except VD-3, Lieutenant Ebright of VB-108, and Oden Sheppard of VB-109 were to cross the island from the south and select and attack the largest shipping targets. Upon reaching Kwajalein, Ebright and Sheppard were to drop back and provide cover for the formation. Upon reaching the island, Ebright would swing right over the island and drop two 500 pound bombs on a headquarters building east of a runway, and three more bombs on heavy gun positions at the eastern tip of the island. Sheppard was to cross over to the west with a boat basin as his primary target for two bombs and three others for a heavy gun position on the western tip. His alternate mission was to neutralize the runway and prevent enemy planes from taking off. All planes would then swing left and retire over the atoll above Enubuj and head home.

After taking off, VB-108 and VB-109 planes flew in a line formed on the leader Commander Renfro, while the two VD-3 planes formed on Renfro's left wing. The planes flew from Apamama to Makin and then to Kwajalein, passing midway between Mille and Jaluit and at an altitude ranging from 500 to 600 feet. Forty miles from the target, the formation dropped down to 50 feet to avoid radar detection, with Ebright and Sheppard dropping back 4 miles behind the formation. The bombers, in line, roared over the island near high noon with all guns blazing as they struck anchored shipping. Complete surprise was achieved, as Japanese personnel began running in every direction on the island while very little anti-aircraft fire was received. Striking the anchored shipping, Commander Renfro dropped 500 pound bombs on two 100-foot long merchant vessels and two more at a larger freighter. The first two bombs missed the smaller vessels, but the third one was a direct hit on the stern of the freighter. Crossing over Enubuj, he dropped his fifth bomb on a radio installation, which blew up. Renfro's attack awakened the defenses on the ships and the island as anti-aircraft fire began peppering the sky around the attacking planes. At the same time, Lieutenant Wengierski dropped a string of four bombs among the shipping. The first bomb hit a boat dock, and the second landed among small wooden coastal vessels. His third bomb was a direct hit amidships on a freighter, while his fourth bomb hit the stern of another ship anchored nearby.

Attacking a 6,000-ton freighter, Commander Miller dropped a string of five bombs towards the ship. The first two bombs fell short, ran like torpedoes, and detonated against the ship's hull. The third and fourth bombs were direct hits on the ship's deck, and the vessel began burning. The fifth bomb sailed over the intended target and hit another cargo vessel nearby. Finishing his bombing run, Miller's plane took several hits in the aft section from anti-aircraft fire.

Lieutenant Jackson Grayson spotted another medium size freighter off the northern part of the island, made a run on it and released a string of 500 pound bombs. The first two bombs fell short, while the third torpedoed through the water and exploded against the ship's hull. The fourth bomb hit the stern of the ship, and the fifth sailed over and hit the water. The ship was left burning and listing to starboard when Grayson's tail gunner saw the ship explode and sink.

Over the island, Lieutenant Elbright dropped two bombs in the headquarters area and two more on a gun position. His fifth bomb ricocheted off the gun installation and exploded in the water. As Ebright was hitting the headquarters area, Lieutenant Sheppard's plane crossed from the right of the formation and observed the airstrip with eight "Zekes," four parked on the runway and four on the taxiway, two of which were preparing for take-off. He immediately attacked from 300 feet altitude and dropped two bombs, which landed near the four fighters on the runway, while his gunners strafed those on the taxiway. Swinging over, he dropped his third bomb on a gun position seen firing southwest of the airstrip.

As each plane completed their strike, they left the island and headed back to base. Of the eight attacking planes, all but Lieutenant Daley's, whose bombs failed to release, had successfully completed their strike. In Kwajalein Harbor, the Ikuta Maru, a 3,000-ton cargo ship, was sunk, and at least six more merchantmen were severely damaged.[4]

Explosions hurl smoke and water around two Japanese merchant ships at Kwajalein. *Courtesy of Thomas Delahoussaye.*

4

Missing in Action

On the 13th, the squadron had their first combat loss when Lieutenant Coleman and his crew took off on a routine patrol and never returned. The plane he flew had been parked next to one of the aircraft damaged in the air raid on the 2nd. Whether their plane had been damaged that night without being noticed will never be known. No trace of them could be found, and the men and planes from VB-109 continued to look for the next three days without any luck—they simply vanished in the great expanse of the Pacific Ocean. Lost with Lieutenant Coleman were Lieutenant Amos Shriener, who had flown with the RAF, and Harry Donovan and Don Dujak, who had risked their lives saving squadron planes during the air raid. The loss of Lieutenant Coleman and his crew reduced the squadron's complement to eleven planes and sixteen flight crews.

While searching for Lieutenant Coleman on the 16th, Lieutenant Janeshek attacked a small 500-ton cargo vessel cruising at 7 knots forty miles southwest of Jaluit. After three bombing and strafing runs, the ship was left burning and settling dead in the water. On the same day, Commander Miller, while examining Likiep Atoll in the Carolines with hopes that some clue might be found concerning Coleman, spotted an anchored, single-stack cargo vessel bearing the white number "406" painted on each side of the bow. The ship was armed with two 20mm guns on platforms forward and aft, and it was camouflaged with palm leaves strewn about the superstructure. However, during the attack no return fire was offered from the ship. Miller made a run to port and dropped two 500 pound bombs, both of which went over the target. On his second run along the starboard quarter he released two more bombs. One was a direct hit on the superstructure. The ship blew up, leaving nothing more than floating debris, the largest being a 30-foot section of the bow.

Five planes of the squadron piloted by Commander Miller, Lieutenants Sheppard, Wheaton, Mellard, and Lieutenant (jg) Herron, with five planes of VB-108 escorted six photographic planes of VD-3 over Kusaie in the Eastern Carolines on the 17th. The primary mission of the VD-3 planes leading the sections was to obtain vertical photographic coverage of Kusaie Island, particularly of an airfield under construction. The escorting planes were to give added protection to the photographic planes in case of interception by enemy fighters, and all planes were to bomb Lele Harbor on the eastern side of the island. If there was shipping in the harbor, it would be the primary target, if not, the harbor installations on the south shore of Lele Harbor.

The planes joined together after leaving the base and climbed to 18,000 feet.[1] Visibility was unlimited when, five miles from the target, the formation broke up so that each section could make their bombing runs. However, shortly before reaching the target, Lieutenant Piper's and Webster's planes suffered mechanical failures and were forced to turn back.

In order to effect maximum surprise, all runs over the target started at Lele Harbor. As well as being the primary bombing target, Lele Harbor was considered the most strongly defended. After crossing the harbor, the second section broke off

Lieutenant Coleman and his crew failed to return from a patrol on 13 January 1944. *Courtesy of George Murphy.*

**Lele Harbor, Kusaie under attack by VB-108, VB-109, and VD-3 on 17 January 1944.
Note bomb splashes bottom center.** *Courtesy of the National Archives.*

Lele Harbor, Kusaie taken during an attack on 17 January 1944. *Courtesy of the National Archives.*

from the formation and made its photographic run over the most northeasterly part of the island. The first section then took the next sector westward, followed by the third section, the fourth section, and the sixth section. The fifth section took the most southeasterly sector including the airfields. No defensive anti-aircraft fire or interceptors were received as the planes made their runs.

The first photographic plane, piloted by Commander Stroh, had difficulty with its bomb release mechanism and was unable to release any bombs on the target area. Lieutenant Mullron, following Stroh, salvoed his bombs on a warehouse on the south side of Lele Island with unobserved results. The third plane, piloted by Lieutenant Martin, dropped all of his bombs across the harbor entrance and on the reef. Lieutenant Idleman dropped one 500 pound bomb and two 100 pound bombs on a radio station with unobserved results. Lieutenant Daley dropped a 500 pound bomb and five 100 pound bombs on a building near a seaplane base area on the southern side of Lele Harbor, again with unobserved results. Lieutenant Kiem dropped his bombs near a large wooden pier on the south side of Lele Harbor. Bombing runs made by the other planes achieved similar results. One plane dropped eight 100 pound bombs on the northwest end of the harbor, and all but one fell in the water. Two pilots had trouble opening their bomb bay doors, and the bombs fell into the water. Another pilot dropped 13 100 pound bombs for a direct hit on a native village on the western edge of Lele Harbor.

Repairing battle damage on a squadron plane. Note large flak hole in aileron. *Courtesy of Oden Sheppard.*

The accuracy of bombing runs made by VB-109 planes were more successful. Lieutenant Sheppard dropped 15 100 pound bombs in a built-up area on the southern shore of Lele Harbor, while Miller dropped 15 100 pound bombs in a building area on the south shore of Lele Harbor, and Lieutenant Herron dropped 15 100 pound bombs on the east side of the island between the harbor and the airfield. However, bombs dropped by Lieutenant Mellard and Wheaton fell harmlessly in the harbor. The medium altitude strike over Kusaie was over, and the planes headed home after conducting a somewhat disappointing bombing mission. From a strategic standpoint, the strike on Kusaie was a dismal failure, with the enemy suffering only minor damage. The strike was one of the few missions conducted from medium and high altitudes, and such raids, except for a hand full of similar strikes conducted in the months to come, would be conducted at minimum altitude.

While searching the Eastern Marshalls, Lieutenant Janeshek flew his plane through rain shower and saw a 4,000-ton ship, six miles ahead, 20 miles west of Maleolap cruising at a speed of 6 knots. She was accompanied by two small tug boats about 600 yards on either beam. The merchantman began circling to port as Janeshek made his first run in front of the ship. Below the plane, gunners aboard the ship were seen running to the guns on the ship's bow, only to become victims of Janeshek's belly gunner as he concentrated fire on these men. As the plane circled to the left and made its bombing run, four men were seen lying on the deck area near the bow gun, apparently victims of the belly gunner's fifty caliber fire. However, anti-aircraft fire from smaller guns along the sides of the ship was encountered as the run was made along the starboard beam and four 500 pound bombs were dropped. The first bomb hit directly forward of the superstructure, while the last three went over the ship. The explosion sent debris 200 feet into the air as the entire forward superstructure was blown off the ship. Flames and a cloud of thick black smoke enveloped the area where the bridge had been. A third strafing run was made with no return AA fire before the plane departed. Four days later, a radio message came in from an American submarine saying that a crippled enemy ship was being towed into Kwajalein and was being escorted by four gun boats. Assuming it to be the ship damaged by Lieutenant Janeshek, Commander Miller decided to send Lieutenant Hicks and Lieutenant Bridgeman after it.

Both aircraft flew along side of each other after climbing to an altitude of 4,000 feet before gradually dropping down nearer the water until they were skimming over the top of the waves. Less than an hour later, the Ogashima Maru, a 1,400-ton freighter, was spotted 30 miles southeast of Kwajalein being towed by a tug boat and three escorts. The ships spotted the aircraft, knew they were not friendly, and began firing a barrage of heavy AA fire. The towing and escorting tugs cast off their lines, and all five ships commenced circling while continuing to put up intense AA fire. The gun fire between the ships and the two aircraft became intense, and the air

A Japanese merchant ship off of Maleolap under attack by Lieutenant Janeshek on 19 January 1944. *Courtesy of the National Archives.*

was filled with black puffs of smoke from exploding anti-aircraft shells. As a result of the defensive fire, Hicks' plane took minor hits to the port wing.

While Hicks began his bombing run, Bridgeman's plane came low along side one of the gunboats not more than 100 feet beneath the plane. The gun crew from the stern of the ship started running down to the port-side to man their 40mm bow gun. The four Japanese had a look of total terror on their faces as they stared at the American plane flying along side of them. Robert Carey, the starboard waist gunner, opened fire, and one by one the four bodies of the gun crew fell into the ocean. After the death of the gun crew, the boat ceased firing, and the gunners began shooting at the boat's waterline, leaving it burning as Bridgeman circled around to protect Hicks during his bombing run.

Lieutenant Hicks, about a mile ahead of Bridgeman, took on another gunboat and began working over it quite well before making his bombing run on the starboard bow of the freighter. Hicks released three 500 pound bombs, which went over and exploded 50 feet beyond the ship. He circled around and made his next run from the aft section of the ship at 75 feet altitude before pulling up and over as he crossed the ship and released the remaining two 500 pound bombs. Both bombs skipped across the water and hit the starboard side of the ship. Now it was Bridgeman's turn to make a run on it.

Bridgeman came in from the stern to bow and dropped a string of five bombs 10-15 feet from the port side of the freighter. The explosions lifted the ship out of the water, exposing the starboard hull almost to the keel as she began listing to port. As the planes left, the Ogashima Maru keeled over and sank.

On the same day, while on anti-submarine duty near Eniwetok, Lieutenant Grayson spotted the 4,000-ton Japanese ship, possibly Special Submarine Chaser Number One, being towed by three gunboats. Carrying only two Mark 47 depth bombs, Lieutenant Grayson made a run on the ship as his gunners took on the three gunboats. The four ships put up heavy, accurate anti-aircraft fire, and the plane took several hits from 7.7mm machine gun rounds to the starboard wing and the aft portion of the fuselage. One round entered the fuselage, and one of his gunners, Bobby W. Fickling, received a minor splinter wound. Through the intense defensive fire, the pilot continued on his bombing run and released the depth bombs, and both fell 25 feet short of the target. The ship became enveloped in a thick cloud of black smoke and began listing heavily to port when Lieutenant Grayson ended the attack. Special Submarine Chaser Number One never made it to Eniwetok.

Lieutenant Joseph Jadin, for the last score of the month on the 27th, spotted three freighters cruising at a speed of ten knots 80 miles south of Eniwetok. Coming in for a strafing attack, which left two of the three ships in flames, the plane was considerably damaged by anti-aircraft fire, and his tail gunner, Joseph McKernan, received serious wounds to the back and head from fragments from a 12.7mm round. The bullet entered through the lower starboard side of the aft fuselage and then continued aft and up, entering the upper part of the tail turret before it wounded the gunner. After leaving the ships, Ensign Tischoff, the co-pilot, climbed back to the rear of the plane and administered first aid to the wounded gunner, who survived.

January had proved costly for the squadron. VB-109 had lost an entire crew to enemy action, and two other bombers had been destroyed, one during a night landing and the other through enemy bombing. Land-based planes had failed to gain air superiority over the Marshalls, and the Japanese still had 150 operational planes during the last week of the month. By February 1, though, these planes had been destroyed by American Carrier planes. On the 1st, the invasion of the Marshalls began with Marine landings on Kwajalein. In front of the Japanese garrison of 8,000 men were four American carrier groups, consisting of 12 carriers, eight battleships, and 54,000 men. Before the island would be taken, it would cost 370 American lives.

Preparing 50 caliber ammunition prior to a mission. Note the two 100 pound bombs and possibly a 250 pound bomb in background being ready for loading. *Courtesy of Oden Sheppard.*

5

Long Patrols

For the squadron, February was a very heavy operational month. During the operation, VB-109 flew some 200,000 miles of search and patrol, covering millions of square miles of water, and assured the Pacific Fleet in its Marshalls campaign that no major enemy shipping was within striking distance. The softening up of the Lesser Marshalls intensified with strikes on Jaluit, Rongelap, Wotje, and Mille, while shipping and installations at Kusaie were destroyed, and heavy damage was inflicted at Wake. Lieutenant Belew struck Jaluit and Lieutenant Hicks bombed Rongelap. On the 3rd, Lieutenant Janeshek obtained low photographic coverage of Engebi and Eniwetok Islands. Commander Miller bombed Wotje, Mille, Majuro, and Taroa, and Lieutenant Jadin bombed the Wotje airfield from 18,000 feet in a joint mission with one photographic plane of VD-3. On successive days from the 5th through the 13th, Lieutenant Sheppard strafed Wotje, while Lieutenant Mellard strafed the runway at Engebi. Lieutenant Jobe sank four small vessels at Jaluit, and Lieutenant Hicks strafed Ebon and Ujae. Lieutenant Commander John Bundy and Lieutenant Janeshek strafed Engebi, while Lieutenant Grayson bombed Rongelap. Lieutenant Sheppard strafed Parry Island at Eniwetok, while Lieutenant Mellard destroyed supplies and damaged a supply boat at Wotje. Lieutenant Oliver S. Glenn strafed Emidj; Lieutenant Jobe bombed Pingelap; Lieutenant Hicks strafed Lae, Wotho, Bikini, Ailinglapalap, and Jaluit; Lieutenant Commander Bundy strafed Mejit; Lieutenant Janeshek bombed and strafed Eniwetok, and Ujae and Commander Miller bombed and destroyed installations at Ujelang.

On the 13th, Lieutenant (jg) Herron and his crew, including a photographer from VD-3, borrowed Lieutenant Commander Bundy's plane and headed for Wotje for a routine search. He never returned. Searches for him were conducted for five days by all available planes without success. The day after Herron disappeared,

Radio Tokyo claimed the destruction of a B-24 over Wotje on the day in question, and even read the names of the crew. However, the names she read were Lieutenant Commander Bundy's crew, which had been written on the floor of the cockpit by a member of his crew. Herron's plane must have been hit close to shore and crashed on the beach or in shallow water. The ultimate fate of Herron and his crew will never be truly known, as their bodies were never recovered. If some of the crew had survived, they would have been killed shortly after their capture.

The squadron knew the Japanese gunners on Wotje were some of the best. The only thing in favor of the men from VB-109 on low level raids was the element of surprise. A PB4Y-1 flying at 200 feet or less and at 200 miles per hour was an easy target for a gunner, and if a plane was hit at that altitude, the crew wouldn't have enough time to bail-out. The effectiveness of enemy gunners on Wotje became quite apparent, and would almost cost the squadron another plane and its crew two days later.

On the 15th, Grayson was sent out to Wotje on a close photographic reconnaissance mission, accompanied by a photographer from VD-3. Grayson approached the eastern portion of the atoll from the south and crossed into the lagoon just south of the island. The approach was made at 100 feet, which was increased to 500 feet to enable the photographer to get his pictures. Above the lagoon, six of Admiral

Crew 14 failed to return from patrol 13 February 1944. *Courtesy of George Murphy.*

Rongelap Atoll, Marshall Islands. Wrecked Japanese Installation taken on 8 February 1944. Note line of bomb craters on left. *Courtesy of the National Archives.*

White plume of smoke and sand rises up from Wake Island during a raid on 29 February 1944 led by Commander Miller. *Courtesy of Thomas Delahoussyae.*

Spruance's Grumman TBF dive bombers were glide bombing the island. Lieutenant Grayson skirted the western edge of Wotje 1,500 feet above the beach, and his gunners started strafing the island, blowing up a large gasoline storage tank on the island's southwestern tip. Just as he was preparing for a steady photographic run and was just about opposite to the southern end of a runway, the enemy AA opened up. The fire was so intense and accurate that it seemed like the whole island was firing at him. Fire from a 12.7mm machine gun shot out the plane's hydraulic system and the number three engine, starting a fire. Grayson feathered the prop, and the wind extinguished the flames. The navigator, Ensign Harry Bigham, received a minor wound from a spent 12.7mm bullet, and fragments from a 20mm round inflicted minor wounds on two other crew members, Hugo L. Kluge and Bobby W. Fickling. Seeing that his plane was getting badly shot up and having three wounded crew members, Grayson flew directly to Roi. After lowering flaps and landing gear manually, Grayson made a successful landing on the partially completed strip. Upon inspection, 75 bullet holes were counted on his plane. The mission over Wotje was Grayson's third close call. Within two months, he was out of the squadron, and some of his men were transferred to other crews.

Grayson's mission was the climax of a costly five day operational period over Wotje in which a PB4Y-1 of VB-109 and a B-25 of the 398th Bomber Command were lost, while two PB4Y-1s were badly shot up, one from VB-108. The taking of

Lieutenant Hal Belew's Liberator "Climbaboard" was originally named "Pacific Vagabond" and later went to Lieutenant Bill Bridgeman. *Courtesy of Oden Sheppard.*

Three crew members stand in front of Crew 18's plane "Sugar Queen." *Courtesy of Oden Sheppard.*

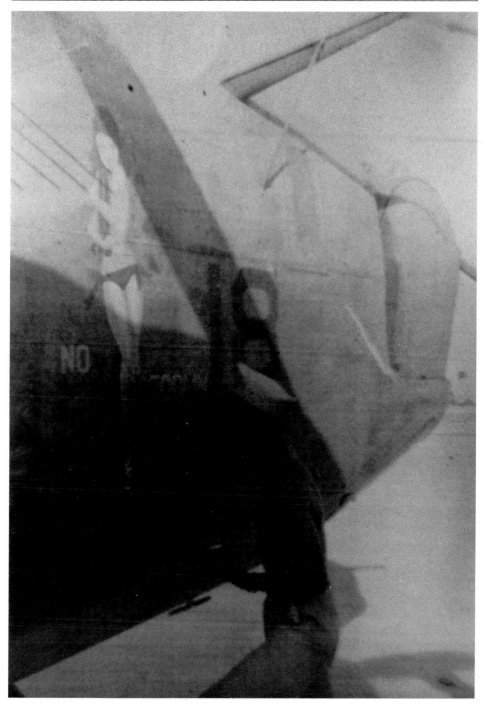

Applying the finishing touches on Lieutenant Clifton Davis' "No Foolin." *Courtesy of Oden Sheppard.*

low oblique photographs with a PB4Y-1 of enemy installations protected by strong concentrations of light and medium AA batteries was extremely hazardous. There was no opportunity for adequate evasive action if the photographer was given a reasonably steady platform to work from, and the enemy gunners could ask for no fatter target then a Liberator bomber coming in at 200 miles per hour and 200 feet altitude.

While Grayson was recovering from his close call over Wotje, Commander Miller and Lieutenant Seabrook joined Lieutenant John Muldrow and Lieutenant H.G. Crowgey of VB-108 to strike shore installations and shipping at Lele Harbor, Kusaie, at masthead height in the first of several such strikes. During the attack, Lieutenant Seabrook seriously damaged a 400-ton cargo vessel, but abrupt hills close ashore protected a larger ship from the low level attack. Lieutenant Seabrook and the two VB-108 planes dropped 18 500 pound bombs on a 200-ton patrol vessel at Fukiru Point, scoring five hits, but they failed to sink her. Miller had problems during three runs when his bomb release mechanism malfunctioned, and the bombs had to be dropped by emergency release. The bombs went over a barracks south of the harbor and landed among some trees.

On the 17th, Operation Catchpole, the invasion of Eniwetok Atoll, began. Enegbi fell the following day, followed by Eniwetok on the 23rd and Parry on the 24th. Flying on the 19th, squadron planes saw the American task force's battleships and cruisers firing on the island, while dive bombers came in and dropped their bomb

Lieutenant Joseph Jadin's "Helldorado." *Courtesy of Oden Sheppard.*

Lieutenant Oden Sheppard in front of his plane "Available Jones." *Courtesy of Oden Sheppard.*

Lieutenant Clifton Davis with "No Foolin." *Courtesy of Oden Sheppard.*

loads. It didn't take a detective to figure out that the Navy didn't need any help from VB-109.

On the 23rd Commander Miller and Lieutenant Sheppard returned to Kusaie at dawn with two planes of VB-108 at masthead height. A successful low level attack was difficult to make against shipping moored off the main island in a cove off the southern part of the Harbor. Hills rise abruptly, and the cove is sheltered, making low level runs virtually impossible. The whole harbor area is sandwiched between the mainland hills and Lele Island, which made masthead level approaches of any kind limited and very hazardous.

The four Liberators took off at 2AM in order to strike Kusaie at dawn, and proceeded to the target independently. The original plan called for Miller to lead his section into the Harbor over a pass between mountains from the western side of the island. However, when landfall was made, the mountain pass was enveloped by low hanging clouds, so plans were altered and all planes approached at low level from the north.

Miller entered Lele Harbor from the north between Kusiae and Lele, made a sharp turn to port, and proceeded through the harbor on an easterly heading. Light to medium anti-aircraft fire was received from several locations on Lele Island as the planes flew over the harbor. Miller spotted a 1,500-ton tanker at anchor off Fukiru Point and made a run on it as his gunners strafed the ship. The pilot dropped

Lieutenant Commander John Bundy's "Flying Circus." *Courtesy of Oden Sheppard.*

Lieutenant Commander William Janeshek's "Come Get It." *Courtesy of Oden Sheppard.*

a string of 500 pound bombs which straddled the ship. The ship listed heavily to port before sinking a few minutes later. During the bombing run, the plane took four hits from 7.7mm machine guns to the starboard wing, causing fuel to begin streaming across the wing.

As Miller left, a 100-ton escort vessel docked west of Yepan Point was spotted by Lieutenant Muldrow. Muldrow's plane closed for an attack and dropped five bombs, which missed the ship. He made a sharp turn to starboard and then, in a turn to port, flew over hills to the west of the harbor and made another attack on the escort. Coming in at a 45 degree glide from 200 feet, Muldrow released a bomb but missed again. After finishing his run on the escort, Muldrow's gunners strafed a gun position on Yepan Point at close range and silenced it. Not content on scoring misses on the escort, he went clockwise around Lele island, entering the harbor from the east, and made two runs, but both times the bombs would not release. He finally gave up and finished by making a strafing run on installations on the east coast.

Lieutenant Kile, flying behind Miller, attacked from the east and dropped one bomb on the escort, which missed. Returning for another run, he decided to target the freighter still afloat and dropped five bombs, scoring one direct hit amidships. A fire broke out, followed by a violent explosion, and the ship sank a few minutes later.

Lieutenant Sheppard finished the raid by dropping three bombs on installations on the east coast adjacent to a cultivated field before meeting up with the three other planes. Sheppard's plane took a hit from a 40mm shell, knocking out the number three engine and causing a fuel leak. The Liberators departed Kusaie leaving two ships sinking, one of them being the 2,600 Shunsan Maru, and two other merchantmen severely damaged.[1]

Sheppard turned for home on three engines and with no way of determining how much fuel remained. Commander Miller pulled up and flew alongside for several hours, surveying the damage before he had to return to Apamama for refueling. As Sheppard looked at the three Liberators disappearing ahead, the pilot requested that his navigator plot the best heading to Apamama, 750 miles away. There were no landmarks, no stars, just the compass, and a best estimate of wind drift for the navigator to get the plane back to base. Some five hours later, the shoreline of Apamama appeared in the distance. Any slight error in navigation would have forced Sheppard to ditch in the water because, as they were coming in on final approach, the plane ran out of fuel. The landing gear hit the beach hard, just beyond the water, and bounced along the runway before stopping short of the approach lights. The mission to Kusaie had taken some 11 hours to complete.

With the increased tempo of the Marshalls campaign toward the latter part of February, plans were laid to move the squadron forward. Commander Miller piloted the first four-engine plane to land on the newly completed airstrips at Majuro and Kwajalein on the 25th and 26th. Staging through the field at Kwajalein, Commander Miller, Lieutenant Hicks, and Lieutenant Jobe ended February's activities with a spectacular mission against Wake Island, which was subjected to the heaviest bombing strike of the war.[1]

Pursuant to an operational order, squadron planes, along with VB-108 and VD-3, were directed to conduct a daylight, low level bombing and strafing attack on Wake Atoll in conjunction with photographic coverage. After completing a night take-off and rendezvousing over O'Hare Field, Apamama, the formation flew to Kwajaelin Island to pick up two VD-3 planes. All eight planes then proceeded to Wake.

A low level approach from the east had been selected in order to take advantage of prevailing winds. Miller's section was to fly over Wake and Wilkes Island, flanked by a photo plane on the port wing taking pictures of the south portion of Wake Atoll. Muldrow's section was assigned a similar task along the northern part of Wake Island and Peale Island, with a single photo plane on the starboard wing to cover that portion of the Atoll.

The formation, excluding Lieutenant Webster, who was never able to join up after investigating what turned out to be a friendly submarine, reached a point 80 miles east of Wake before making its turn and then proceeded toward the target in a loose line abreast. Altitude was maintained at 50 feet before finally dropping down to 25 feet as they neared the atoll. When the atoll was finally sighted some ten miles out, the formation flew the last few miles in a southeasterly heading. As the planes closed in, a few rounds of light and medium anti-aircraft fire were encountered. When they were 2,500 feet out, the plane's gunners started strafing and continued until they had passed over the Atoll. The cumulative effect of this fire, coupled with what appeared to be complete surprise, resulted in relatively meager return fire throughout the attack. Many of the guns were still covered with canvas as their crews scurried to man them.

As the attacking planes pulled up to 200 feet to make their drops, Miller, in order to avoid cutting out his wingman, crossed Wake Island on a southeasterly heading. Along the southern edge of an airstrip were four fighters, one two engine bomber, and one torpedo bomber. As he crossed over the runway, he dropped a string of four 500 pound bombs along the northwestern side of the airstrip.

Lieutenant Hicks, to Miller's port, swung in back of him and proceeded along the southwestern part of Wake, dropping his bombs on installations. No shipping was found except two small craft in the lagoon and a large dredge near the seaplane base. Jobe, parallel to the course flown by Hicks, released 16 100 pound bombs among the parked planes south of the runway, on pillboxes and fuel tanks on the western end of Wake island, and on installations at the eastern and western portions of Wilkes Island. Six of the bombs landed on a barracks, resulting in a large explosion.

Muldrow and Piper came over Wake Island from the southeast, with Piper flying in fairly close formation on Muldrow's starboard wing. They turned right and flew in a course taking them over a heavily built up area on the northwestern tip of Wake and over Peale Island. While Muldrow dropped 500 pound bombs among the installations on the tip of Wake and one near the large dredge in the seaplane base, Piper dropped a string of 20 100 pound bombs along the northern part of Wake and along Peale Island.

While the pilots were initiating their bombing runs, the gunners strafed pillboxes, buildings, planes, and personnel with devastating effect. As the planes left the atoll, fires were burning throughout the atoll. Retirement was made to the southwest, and all attack planes landed at Roi to refuel before heading back to Apamama after a trip lasting 20 hours. This was not the last visit of VB-109 to Wake, and throughout the remaining months of their tour, squadron planes visited the former American possession to remind the Japanese garrison on the atoll that they had not been forgotten.

On the 3rd, Lieutenant Hicks and Lieutenant Jobe, with two planes of VB-108, struck Ponape in a low level dawn attack. The two squadrons were ordered to attack a freighter, destroyer, and two escort vessels reported in Ponape Harbor.[2] In the early afternoon, the planes joined up in night rendezvous and proceeded to Ponape at an altitude of 8,000 feet. After reducing altitude to 500 feet 100 miles from target, the formation flew the last 50 miles at 50 feet. However, Lieutenant Ackerman from VB-108 lost the formation during the night and never reached the target. As the flight passed Ponape some 20 miles to the East, the course was changed, bringing the formation due north of the harbor area. Lieutenant Hicks turned to port and proceeded on a southerly course into the target. He was followed by Lieutenant Daley and Lieutenant Jobe in column spread 2,500 feet apart.

When Hicks saw that the reported shipping was not present, he made a 180 degree turn in the harbor area and passed over the eastern coast of Langar Island. Intense but inaccurate anti-aircraft fire greeted the formation as they arrived. Coming in, Hicks' gunners strafed a multi-engine seaplane on the water. Passing the burning seaplane, Hicks proceeded to a large built-up area on Langar Island. Strafing and four 500 pound bombs caused considerable damage to a pier on the southern tip of the island, a seaplane ramp, a hangar, and a warehouse building on the southern end of the island. Lieutenant Daley, following behind Hicks into the harbor, spotted a 100-foot long coastal vessel under way and dropped four bombs. One near miss caused the ship to catch fire and to circle to port out of control. Lieutenant Daley followed Hicks out of the Harbor on a northerly heading, strafing the western slope of Langar Island heavily as he retired.

Jobe, following Daley, selected Langar Island as his target and dropped four bombs in a string across the center of the southern portion of the island. The coastal

Lieutenant Bill Bridgeman's first plane "Sky Cow" crashed on take-off from Eniwetok by Lieutenant Leo Kennedy. *Courtesy of Oden Sheppard.*

vessel damaged by Lieutenant Dailey in the harbor was finally sunk by Jobe's gunners. After joining up northeast of Ponape, the planes landed at Apamama after refueling at Kwajalein.

The raid on Ponape was the last large strike conducted from Apamama. Apamama had been a shake down for the squadron to test the limits of the flight personnel and the planes. They had now become proficient in low-level bombing and strafing tactics. Four days later, the anticipated movement was ordered, and squadron planes left in two sections to base permanently at Kwajalein.

By the end of their stay on Apamama, most of the squadron's planes had been decorated with a variety of artwork. Commander Miller's plane sported a chamber pot with wings and was named "Thunder Mug." Almost all of the planes were decorated with nude women: Lieutenant Wheaton's "Sugar Queen," Lieutenant Seabrook's "Mission Belle," Lieutenant Davis' "No Foolin," Lieutenant Mellard's "Our Baby" (which was destroyed on the ground on Apamama), Commander Janeshek's "Come Get It," Lieutenant Glenn's "Urge Me," Lieutenant Belew's (later Bridgeman's) "Climbaboard," and "Flying Circus." Two of the planes were painted and given names due to chronic mechanical problems. These were Lieutenant Jobe's "Consolidated's Mistake" and Lieutenant Bridgeman's "Sky Cow." Rounding out the nose art was Lieutenant Sheppard's "Available Jones," Lieutenant Jadin's "Helldorado," and Lieutenant Commander Hicks' "The Stork."

A grainy photograph of Lieutenant Thomas Seabrook's "Mission Belle." *Courtesy of Oden Sheppard.*

6

Operations from Kwajalein

On the heels of the squadron's arrival, Army B-24s of the 7th Army Air Force moved into Apamama and began to stage through Kwajalein on missions. The Navy's relationship with the Army Air Force was never cordial, and it continued to decline. The dislike for each other reached from the bottom of the enlisted ranks to the very top, with Admiral Hoover having a very tenuous relationship with General Hale, Commander of the Army Air Force. Hoover didn't care for the Army's performance in the Central Pacific, and made it quite clear that the Air Force bombed from too far up, 20,000-foot missions being the norm, against enemy-held islands that could be measured in yards and not miles. The Admiral wanted the AAF to move down to strike shipping targets, which General Hale considered a waste of time.[1] From the standpoint of many men in VB-109, the Army was only getting in their way and, as some individuals pointed out, bombing at 20,000 feet only killed a lot of fish and, therefore, the Army was aiding the enemy by feeding them. There was quite a bit of jealousy involved, as squadron personnel felt that the Army was getting all the glory and the medals, and the Navy was getting nothing. As the rivalry intensified, there was talk about shooting down 7th Air Force bombers that came into range of VB-109 aircraft. The feud was never resolved and, fifty plus years later, former squadron personnel sometimes begin a conversation about the Army with, "Those God damn idiots in the 7th Air Force..."

Kwajalein was chaotic when the squadron arrived, and the turmoil continued throughout the stay. The Sea Bees and Army Construction Units were doing a remarkable job in a short time, and work was continuous. The island was hot, with little wind, and it was very dusty. The black dirt, churned constantly by the hurrying construction machines, covered everything, and was quickly transformed into gumbo by the frequent rains. Apamama, in contrast, seemed a pleasant and relaxing spot in

51

Lieutenant Oden Sheppard in "Available Jones" closing in on a Japanese radio station on Oroluk Atoll in the Marshall Islands. *Courtesy of Oden Sheppard.*

The aftermath of the Liberator's ten machine guns trained on Oroluk. *Courtesy of Oden Sheppard.*

which to live. Dynamiting and blasting, and the incessant rumble of the trucks continued throughout the night at Kwajalein, which became very trying to the men. The smell from dead Japanese soldiers still lingered everywhere on the island, and big green flies grew fatter and more plentiful as they fed on the unburied dead. In one large hole alone the Army Engineers, using bull-dozers, buried some 5,000 of the enemy dead. As there were no recreational facilities of any sort, no swimming or spot in which to exercise, nerves became taut and squadron morale declined.

The squadron, both officers and men alike, lived and messed with the CASU unit, and a large camp had already been built with accommodations for permanent personnel and transients. There was a separate Officers Mess, and the food, drawn from the Army, was according to advance base standards, palatable if unvaried. Officers' tents had wooden decking and plywood half walls and slept six. Enlisted men slept eight to a tent, which had no decking at first, but squadron labor and ingenuity shortly added both decks and half walls. In fact, the squadron more or less built and maintained its own camp within the larger CASU camp. Steel springs and mattresses were an unexpected and welcome surprise, and some of the beds and most of the mattresses made their way with the squadron to Eniwetok, where the squadron had canvas cot accommodations.

Preparing to load bombs aboard a PB4Y-1 Liberator on Kwajalein, March 1944. *Courtesy of the National Archives.*

Squadron maintenance improved at Kwajalein, as the mechanics became increasingly familiar with the PB4Y-1, but a number of planes passed the 500 hour mark on their engines and required engine changes and general overhaul. On the recommendation of Commander Renfro, engine aircraft overhaul was undertaken at Apamama instead of at Kaneohe. However, Apamama was not equipped for overall field maintenance, lacking equipment, engines, and spares, and the time involved was considerable. The first two planes sent to Apamama required a month's operational absence to complete the work.

Between March and May, the squadron operated with an average of eleven planes and eleven to fourteen crews. Of these planes, it proved difficult to keep five in commission daily as fuel cell leaks and other mechanical problems multiplied. Returning with mechanical problems or on three engines became a common occurrence and, frequently, pilots took off two or three times in different planes before one would satisfactorily complete the mission. The reduction in the number of crews available resulted in each crew at Kwajalein flying an average of 100 hours during the month.

Kwajalein was controlled by the Army and technically the Army Air Command was the squadron's direct operational superior. As Commander Miller considerably outranked the Lieutenant Colonel in command, who was unfamiliar with Navy search planes and bombing operations, the squadron's extra-curricular strikes and missions were left largely to its own discretion. Routine searches changed from the lengthy patrols to the northwest from Apamama to westward searches varying from 600 to 850 miles through the Marshalls and eastern Carolines, stopping just short of the great enemy base at Truk.

Search planes were diverted to photograph and destroy military installations in the Lesser Carolines, and substantial damage was inflicted on the formidable enemy strongholds at Ponape and Kusaie, and several enemy outposts, including Pingelap, Oroluk, Pakin, and Ant, were neutralized. When the Marshalls were taken, the enemy strongholds of Wotje, Malaolap, Mili, and Jaluit were leapfrogged as the Pacific Fleet moved towards the Marianas, and would remain under enemy control until the final Japanese surrender.[2] These islands were not considered valuable enough to waste the time and personnel to take them. Left to "wither on the vine," they became practice targets for land-based Army and Navy planes based in the Marshalls. Minor atolls in the Marshalls were attacked periodically through March until they fell to small teams of Marines and soldiers. Mopping up of these atolls began immediately after the fall of Kwajalein and Eniwetok. On Ujae, a small force of Marines landed only to find that the six Japanese in charge of a weather station had committed suicide.[3] On Ailinglapalap, 46 Japanese from a grounded barge were hunted down by Marines, and 37 of them were killed and the rest taken prisoner.[4] On Uterik, 14 Japanese were killed, while on Ujelang, 18 Japanese were killed by members of the Army's 11th Infantry Regiment.[5] By the end of April, the Marshall

A PB4Y-1 Liberator preparing to take off on a strike. *Courtesy of the National Archives.*

Islands were under American control, except for strongly defended Wotje, Malaolap, Mili, and Jaluit.[6]

Throughout March, VB-109 continuously launched one plane strikes on the minor Japanese installations of Oroluk, Kusaie, Pingelap, Rongerik, Pakin, and Ant Islands. The day after the squadron arrived, Lieutenant Commander Bundy bombed a 1000-ton cargo vessel in Lele Harbor, Kusaie, which was subsequently found beached and gutted, and Lieutenant Janeshek damaged four and sank one small coastal vessel off Oroluk. On the 9th, Commander Miller bombed the dock area at Kusaie and radio installations at Pingelap. As the squadron moved closer to the Japanese stronghold of Truk, there were increasingly frequent encounters with enemy planes.

Lieutenant Mellard, on the 12th, had instructions to observe Ponape Harbor for enemy shipping. He approached the area from the east at 25 feet altitude in an attempt to stay below enemy radar. Three miles off the harbor entrance, he pulled up to 1200 feet to look into the harbor, only to find it empty of shipping, except the usual small harbor craft. At this point, E.R. Lally, the tail gunner, spotted two "Zeke" fighters about five miles behind the Liberator. Mellard pulled back into the clouds and climbed to 3,000 feet while turning on a northerly course. Ten minutes later the Zekes intercepted him approximately 30 minutes northwest of Ponape Harbor.

Lieutenant Mellard jettisoned his bombs before the fighters closed, and one of the planes followed them down to the water as though expecting them to be mem-

bers of the crew who had bailed out. Unfortunately, the delayed fuse settings prevented what might have otherwise been an interesting episode. After following the
bombs down, the fighter took up station out of gun range and darted in from time to
time without completing any pass or opening fire. On one such pass, at about 1,500
feet, C.M. Lee, the port waist gunner, fired a short burst from his machine gun and
hit the Zeke aft of the engine. At the same time, the tail gunner scored hits aft of the
fighter's cockpit. After ten minutes, the fighter broke off the engagement and headed
towards Ponape.

As Lieutenant Mellard's gunners were taking on the first Zeke, the second fighter
was flying along out of range some 300 feet below the bomber. After the first Zeke
left, the second fighter made three runs on the bomber. On the first and second runs,
the fighter came in low, but broke off before coming within effective range. As the
fighter started his last run, Mellard turned into the attack, which was pressed to
about 500 feet above the water, with the result that it ended up as a high side attack
from about 11 o'clock. The bow and top turrets scored hits as the Zeke got in one
burst without hitting the bomber. The fighter made a split S, followed by a sharp
pull up and, for a few seconds, seemed to hang in front of the Liberator at some 800
feet. He was then hit repeatedly by fire from the bow and top turrets. As tracer fire
hit the starboard wing about a third of the way inboard, black smoke began streaming from the wing as it rolled to the left and passed overhead into the sun. When last
seen, the plane was in a shallow glide, at about 1,000 feet altitude, smoking badly
from the starboard wing, and the pilot was apparently having difficulty in keeping
the wing up and the plane in level flight. After the Zeke departed, Lieutenant Mellard
continued his patrol without encountering further enemy activity.

On the 13th, Miller decided to strike Ponape and obtain low-level photographs
of the island, however, the squadron's commander had an unusual reason for going
there that day. VB-109 had become superstitious about the 13th of the month and,
to some of the men, their fears were justified. On 13 December, VB-108 had lost a
plane and crew; on 13 January, VB-109 had lost Lieutenant Coleman and his crew
and, on 13 February, the squadron had lost Lieutenant Herron and his crew. Miller
wanted to go out on the 13th and make a point that luck only plays a minor role, and
that skill is the key to a flight crew's survival. Therefore, Commander Miller decided to obtain low photographic coverage of the airfield area at Ponape.

Due to known enemy radar, which had effectively picked up low flying planes
of the squadron approaching Ponape Harbor from the north and east, Miller decided to approach from the southeast, keeping the mountains in the south central
part of the island between the plane and the airfield. From 40 miles out, he changed
course to the northwest, and Miller dropped the Liberator down until it was 25 feet
off the water. Upon reaching the south side of the island, Miller climbed to 300 feet
to clear the hills and then proceeded northwest across the central part of the island.
This strategy proved effective, and the enemy was caught completely by surprise.

Commander Miller dropped 3,000 pounds of bombs among barracks and a hangar area located south of the runway. Continuing on a northeasterly heading, Miller spotted a new 4,000-foot long runway under construction that looked to be three quarters completed. Numerous men were moving dirt by pick and shovel and hand-cars from the side of a hill to the west and filling in across the strip to the east. Miller had his cameraman take pictures of the new airfield and then headed away from Ponape. As the plane left, bursts of light and heavy anti-aircraft fire trailed behind them.

Strikes on minor atolls in the Carolines and Marshalls intensified throughout the rest of March. Lieutenant Bridgeman bombed installations at Pingelap and Kusaie on the 15th, followed by a raid on Pingelap and Langar Island, Ponape, three days later. On the 16th Lieutenant John Keeling discovered and bombed radio installations on Pakin. Lieutenant Janeshek struck Kusaie on the 17th. The next day, Miller attacked a Mitsubishi G4M2 twin-engine Betty bomber 50 miles east of Oroluk. Coming from behind, Miller closed within range of the Japanese bomber. The only gunner able to bear his guns was Andrew Halasz in the bow turret. The gunner, who was a member of Lieutenant Mellard's crew, began firing his bow guns, but, after a few bursts, the guns jammed. The gunner cleared the guns, only to have them jam again. After a 15 minute chase, the PB4Y broke off and headed home. Lieutenant

The squadron's main living area on Kwajalein. *Courtesy of Oden Sheppard.*

Wheaton bombed the radio station at Pingelap the next day, and Lieutenant Glenn hit Pingelap on the 19th. Lieutenant Keeling made the squadron's first submarine attack on the 20th. Commander Miller demolished the RDF station at Ant Island, bombed installations at Pakin, and destroyed a small cargo ship nearby on the 21st. Lieutenant Wheaton destroyed a small ship at Ponape the following day, and Lieutenant Glenn bombed a small ship at Ponape on the 23rd.

The squadron now knew the islands like the back of their hands. Each patrol plane commander had a pet island, and had become experts on its defenses. Strikes were hardly ever formerly ordered from higher authority. Instead, strikes were hatched during a poker game or over a cup of coffee. The patrol plane commander would outline a strike and ask Commander Miller for approval.[7]

Lele Harbor, Kusaie, was the target of several raids by squadron planes during the last week of March. On the 22nd, it was bombed and strafed by Lieutenant Seabrook; two days later by Lieutenant Keeling; four days later by Lieutenant Hicks and Lieutenant Commander Bundy. Lieutenant Janeshek ended the squadron's strikes on Kusaie on the 30th. Oroluk was bombed and strafed by Lieutenant Wheaton on the 25th. The following day, Lieutenant Hicks destroyed Pingelap installations, and Lieutenant Jobe destroyed one of the island's radio station buildings to close March's activities.

Now that the Marshalls had been taken by American forces, the Japanese Navy had to rely on submarines to supply their garrisons on bypassed islands. The increased presence of enemy submarine activity between March and June resulted in VB-109 taking on the additional duty of anti-submarine patrols.

Searching through the Eastern Carolines on the morning of the 31st, at an altitude of 2,500 feet, Lieutenant Bill Bridgeman was on anti-submarine patrol when his co-pilot, Ensign William Wiley, spotted a surfaced submarine crash-diving. Bridgeman dove the plane down, and the bow gunner, George Murphy, began firing his twin fifty caliber machine guns at the submarine from 1,800 feet, and tracers began bouncing off the base of the conning tower. He fired 250 rounds into it before it disappeared from his view. The submarine was now in range of other gunners. Warren Griffin in the tail turret, and Robert Carey, the port waist gunner, started firing at the conning tower that remained above the surface. They were still firing when Bridgeman released two Mark 47 depth bombs from 200 feet. Two large geysers of water shot up into the air almost simultaneously as the bombs detonated. At least one-third of the aft section of the submarine came high out of the water, and the conning tower was rocked to port. The sub went down rapidly at a 45 degree angle, with the gunners still firing when it disappeared from the surface. As the plane circled the area, a dark greenish oil slick 75 feet in diameter appeared and dissipated within 15 minutes. However, no debris or bubbles appeared on the water's surface, which may have indicated that the submarine had been destroyed. Bridgeman continued to circle the area for eight hours before another plane flown by Lieutenant Hicks came out to relieve them. After arriving back at base, the crew was credited with damaging the enemy submarine.[8]

Planes from VB-109 continued a cat and mouse game with submarine contacts for the next 48 hours. During the evening of the 31st, Lieutenant Hicks made a radar contact and dropped two depth bombs without any observable results and, on the following day, Lieutenant Commander Bundy, in a night radar attack, slightly damaged a submarine 20 miles from where Bridgeman had made his attack.

On 2 April Commander Miller approached Ponape for the purpose of taking pictures of the new air strip he had observed on the 14th. Adverse weather conditions prevented reaching the objective, so he continued on his search. Returning to Ponape a couple of hours later, the rain had let up enough to permit crossing the southern end of the new airfield, and photographs were obtained without any AA being encountered. Personnel as well as one truck on the airstrip were strafed in passing. Ten minutes later, a small 200-ton cargo vessel was seen 3 miles off the southwest shore of Ponape cruising at 10 knots. During the initial strafing run, the ship's crew launched a lifeboat, and Miller's gunners concentrated their fire on these men. Miller then dropped two 500 pound bombs on the target, and the ship was blown to pieces, leaving nothing but floating debris and bodies.

Proceeding to Pakin, another 200-ton vessel was sighted leaving Eikalap Island, one mile southwest of Nikalap Island. The ship had cargo piled on the deck,

One of the large Japanese coastal guns on Kwajalein which fired on attacking VB-109 planes on 11 January 1944. *Courtesy of Oden Sheppard.*

which burned like oil after being set afire by strafing. The ship turned into a reef and was beached. The ship was burning brightly from the holds and deck as Miller headed his plane for Kwajalein.

While reconnoitering Wake on the 1st, Lieutenant Wheaton sighted what appeared to be a submarine anchored in the lagoon some 400 yards off the east end of Wilkes Island. The following day, Kasperson flew west and, at 15 miles out, dropped down to 50 feet and crossed Wake Island along the east-west runway ten minutes after sunrise. The Japanese garrison was taken completely by surprise. A 200-ton freighter in the lagoon off Wilkes Island was spotted, and a run was made on its starboard beam. Kasperson dropped six 500 pound bombs, with one direct hit on the superstructure. A tremendous explosion tore the vessel apart, sending debris flying through the air, and the ship disappeared. After sinking the ship, installations on Wake Island were strafed as the plane crossed over the island. Strafing started one fire in a new construction site east of a water tower, while one small boat lying in the lagoon off the western end of Wilkes Island was strafed as the plane left the area.

Staging through Eniwetok on the 4th, Commander Miller was ordered to attack a reported enemy carrier and two destroyers in Nonwin Lagoon in the Hall Islands. Upon arriving at the reported position, he found no shipping and radioed back to base that he was proceeding to Truk.

A Japanese artillery piece soon after the Battle of Kwajalein. *Courtesy of Oden Sheppard.*

Before the Marshalls campaign began, Truk was considered by some military strategists as the Japanese Pearl Harbor or the Japanese Gibraltar. The atoll is located in the Caroline Islands and consists of 12 major islands rising to 1,500 feet above sea-level.[9] The islands can be approached by any of four passes through the coral reef, which encircles the atoll.[10] It possesses one of the best anchorages any place in the Pacific, and the Japanese knew the importance of it by building one of the world's best military fortifications. The Japanese had built strong fortifications on Moen, Dublon, Fefan, Uman, Eten, Param, Ulalu, Udat, and Tol. All military fortifications on these islands were heavily defended by coast artillery and anti-aircraft guns. Moen had a 3,300-foot bomber strip, a fighter strip, radar, a torpedo storage area, and a torpedo boat base. Dublon was the primary town in the atoll and contained docks, a seaplane base, submarine base, naval headquarters, oil and torpedo storage, ammunition magazines, and an aviation repair station. Fefan was the main supply center, with a pier, warehouses, ammunition dumps, and search radar. Other islands being utilized were Uman, which had search radar and a torpedo boat base. Eten had a 3,300-foot air strip and revetments for fighter aircraft. Param had a 3,900-foot airstrip. Ulalu had a radio direction finder. Tol had radar and a torpedo boat base.[11] Usually, the lagoon at any one time contained countless merchant ships and naval ships of all sizes and classes.

The Japanese expected that once the Marshalls were taken by the Americans, it seemed likely that Truk, with its military fortifications and anchorage, would be the next target. They planned on keeping it at all costs. However, the usefulness of Truk as a major staging point for the Imperial Japanese Navy came to a disastrous end between 17 and 18 February 1944.

Two American Carrier Forces under the command of Vice Admiral R.A. Spruance and Rear Admiral M.A. Mitscher converged on Truk and won a decisive victory over the Japanese, which effectively neutralized the offensive capability of Truk. During two days of air strikes, carrier-based planes sunk an estimated 137,000-tons of shipping in the lagoon. In addition, 24 merchant vessels, 2 light cruisers, 2 sub-tenders, and between 250-275 planes were either destroyed or damaged.[12] However, the air strikes did not totally destroy the atoll's defensive capability, and it still had formidable anti-aircraft positions and some 100 serviceable fighters.

Closing in on Truk under an overcast sky, Miller crossed the northern part of Truk Atoll just east of North Pass and proceeded directly to the main anchorage west of Moen at minimum altitude. He saw what appeared to be a small destroyer anchored a half mile south of the island, which he mentally noted as a possible target should nothing more promising develop. Continuing southward to a point north of Fefan and circling to port, he flew northward along the western side of Moen. The faint, diffused light of the moon through the overcast disclosed land at a distance of 5 miles, but he was unable to see the destroyer until she suddenly loomed three-quarters of a mile ahead on his port bow, lying approximately a mile off the center of Moen.

Still not content to accept this ship as the final target, he returned south again and investigated the area between Moen, Dublon, and Fefan. No shipping was found, and then anti-aircraft fire and searchlights started up from several locations. Miller abandoned the search and proceeded to attack the destroyer. After making one run to orient himself, he made his bombing run crossing the port quarter to the starboard bow of the ship. As he closed for the kill, the destroyer opened up with gunfire. Roaring through the face of this fire, Miller pickled off four 1,000 pound bombs. The bombs exploded, straddling both sides of the warship. There was no opportunity to further appraise the results of the attack as the plane was immediately caught in the glare of two searchlights from the airfield area on Moen.

For the next 30 seconds he maneuvered as best he could without diving into the water, trying to break out of their billowing circle and evade the blistering anti-aircraft fire from Moen Island. This was finally accomplished by a radical turn to starboard followed by a turn to port. Flying northwest, Miller departed the atoll and thus completed the first attack at Truk by a lone plane. The destroyer was claimed sunk by the squadron, but no records substantiate this claim. However, unknown to Commander Miller, the raid had more devastating results than he realized. At the

A depth charge attack conducted by Lieutenant Bridgeman on a Japanese submarine on 31 March. *Courtesy of the National Archives.*

time of the attack, Truk had five submarines at anchor in the lagoon. All were ordered to submerge, and one of them, the I-169, made an emergency descent to the bottom of the lagoon, but a ventilation tube did not close and flood damage in the control room prevented the boat from surfacing. A crew of 77 was trapped inside, and two days of rescue efforts failed to raise the boat. Many of the crew, safe behind closed compartments, survived the flooding, but perished when the sub's air supply ran out.[13]

The strike on Truk was the last mission conducted by VB-109 from Kwajalein. The following day, the squadron was ordered to base at Eniwetok and, on 5 April, squadron planes began landing at Stickell Field, Eniwetok.

7

Operations from Eniwetok

The base at Eniwetok was well established when the squadron arrived. Stickell Field was a 8,200-foot airstrip named after Commander John H. Stickell, who was mortally wounded on a strike at Jaluit on 12 December 1943.[1] The Bomber Camp, built and operated by VD-3 (later relieved by VD-4), supported the photographic squadron and Bombing Squadrons 108 and 109. It was located at the northeast end of the island, a mile from the line, and was pleasantly cool and free from dust. Quonset huts provided living quarters for the officers, 10 officers to a hut, and enlisted personnel were housed in floored tents with plywood and half-walls, six men to a tent. The bomber camp was a self-contained unit, officer country and the enlisted men's area being separated by offices and the messhall. Showers were provided and were periodically available. Fresh water was still in short supply, with photographic facilities being supplied first.

Recreational facilities were adequate, and morale rose as a direct result. Two baseball diamonds and volleyball courts were available, while shell-gathering and spear-fishing provided alternative recreational activities. Food became somewhat of a problem, as it was unvaried, largely field ration, and was indifferently prepared and grew poorer in quality as other atoll messes improved. Commander Forward Area intervened personally in late July, ending a five-week period during which no fruit, meat, or fresh vegetables were available.

Maintenance problems diminished during the latter part of the stay at Eniwetok. Engine changes and overhauls continued at Apamama with tantalizing slowness but, as the changes were affected, fewer planes returned early due to mechanical failure.

Enemy shipping targets constantly diminished, disappearing completely from search areas by mid-May. Planes ranged further and further out of their assigned sectors in an effort to ferret out worthwhile targets. Strikes on land installations in the Carolines increased, and the Mariana Islands were reached and attacked by the squadron. Strikes on the lesser Marshalls, which had been bypassed, were now in the process of being taken by small armed reconnaissance parties of the Marines and Army and, by the middle of May, VB-109 would halt further attacks on these islands.

April on Eniwetok was a month of long patrols, frequent skirmishes with the enemy, and steady pounding of minor enemy bases, punctuated by several brilliant long-plane sorties. Commander Miller bombed and strafed installations at the new Ponape airfield on the 9th, killing enemy personnel and destroying equipment. After bombing the airstrip, Miller left Ponape only to return an hour later to surprise the enemy repairing the damage. Two small freighters were also destroyed during the raid. Lieutenant Janeshek destroyed a sawmill, lumberyard, and small boat way at Ponape on the 11th. Pakin was bombed by Lieutenant Hicks on the 12th and by Lieutenant Jadin on the 13th. On the 14th, Lieutenant (jg) Kasperson sighted but could not engage a Misubishi Ki-21 "Nell," a Japanese two-engine bomber. Lieutenant Seabrook continued the destruction of Oroluk. Lieutenant Bridgeman and Lieutenant Belew bombed Pakin and Ant successfully on the 15th and 16th, burn-

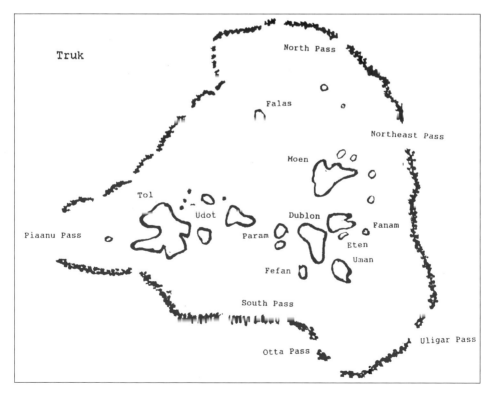

Truk Atoll in which Commander Miller struck for the first time in April 1944.

ing buildings, and Lieutenant Bridgeman started fires at Ulul with incendiary bombs on the 17th. On the same day, Lieutenant (jg) Kasperson found an enemy destroyer at the end of his sector, but encountered such a stiff barrage of anti-aircraft fire that Kasperson prudently decided against an attack.

The neutralizing of Truk continued between the 17th and 21st, with special mining missions in conjunction with VB-108 and VP-13, a Navy patrol squadron flying PB2Y Catalina flying boats. Lieutenant Jobe successfully sowed mines in Northeast-Pass, Truk Atoll, on the 18th, and on the 19th, Commander Miller and Lieutenant Hicks, Lieutenant Commander Bundy, Lieutenant Seabrook, and Lieutenant Clifton Davis sowed mines in South Pass, Truk Atoll. The same day Lieutenant Janeshek bombed coastal gun emplacements on the coast of Ponape, returning on the 22nd to destroy more. On the 19th, Lieutenant Mellard gave chase to a Betty bomber, but was unable to make a kill. The following day Lieutenant (jg) Kasperson bombed a ship beached on Minto Reef and, on the 21st, Lieutenant Seabrook attacked an enemy submarine north of Truk.

During the late afternoon of the 22nd, Miller, on a regular search through the Caroline Islands area north of Truk, reached Namonuito Atoll after having gone the full length of his sector. He dropped an incendiary bomb on a V-shaped building in the radio and weather station area on Ulul Island. On Igup Island (Norwin Atoll) a large storage building and a fifty-foot long boat drawn inland received a second incendiary bomb. Miller's next stop was at Ruo Island (Murilo Atoll), some 60 miles from Truk, where 5 small wooden coastal vessels were anchored in the lagoon.

Light and medium anti-aircraft fire was received at first from several of the ships as well as from the shore, but there was no damage to the plane. Bombing runs were made and 100 pound bombs were released without a direct hit, but a number of near misses contributed to the final destruction. For the next 15 minutes, Miller made 12 strafing and two bombing runs. The two ships were rocked by explosions, one emitting a large yellowish cloud of smoke. As the ship's crew tried in vain to put out the fires, they were caught in the fire from Miller's gunners and killed. The two ships, together with a third one, were either burned to the water line or gutted beyond repair. The remaining two were seriously crippled with large holes, oil streaming and spreading on the water and parts of the ships torn off and afloat. Members of Miller's crew hung two more 100 pound bombs to the bomb racks, and a visit was paid to Murilo Island.

Two coastal vessels, larger than the first five, were tied up alongside a small patrol vessel in the lagoon with Japanese flags waving in the breeze. Miller made a run on the ships, but the two bombs missed. The vessels got underway and started circling as strafing runs were made. They suddenly gave up this defensive strategy, and the patrol vessel and one coastal ran for the reef, where they beached themselves. Ten strafing runs inflicted extensive damage, which caused fires to spring

Japanese Cargo Ship grounded on Minto Reef taken in April 1944 *Courtesy of the National Archives.*

Commander Miller striking Murilo Island, Caroline Islands on 22 April 1944. *Courtesy of the National Archives.*

up as oil covered the water. Approximately 30 of the ship's crew leaped into the water, but few survived the devastating fifty caliber fire from Miller's gunners. The other coastal vessel never reached the reef, and she shuddered under several violent explosions, stopped dead in the water, and became engulfed in a mass of flames.

The only damage to the plane and crew occurred during the strafing attack. The port waist gun mounting post broke away during firing, and before the gunner could quit firing, he shot a three-inch hole into the fuselage below the port waist hatch. The gunner, B.R. "Whiskey" Jaskiewicz, fell back and struck an object behind him, causing a large contusion on his back. Having expended all his bombs and 3,500 rounds of ammunition, Miller returned to base, completing a flight of nearly 15 hours duration. Examination of photographs taken the following day at Ruo found two ships sunk near the beach and two farther out in the lagoon. At Murilo, the patrol vessel had drifted downwind across the lagoon to the opposite side of the reef, beached, and deserted.

On the 28th, Commander Miller discovered an airfield on Puluwat and, through intense AA fire which damaged the plane, destroyed buildings in a radio station area, as well as equipment along the runway. This attack marked the beginning of a personal six-week campaign by Commander Miller to reduce Puluwat defenses.

On the 29th, sneaking into Truk at 200 feet altitude at night, Commander Miller approached the atoll from the northeast and crossed the reef five miles south of Northeast Pass. Reaching a point eight miles northeast of Dublon, a large red flare

Lieutenant (jg) Elmer Kasperson's gunners strafing a Japanese cargo ship on 30 April 1944.
Courtesy of the National Archives.

arched into the sky and was visible for about 5 seconds, apparently an air-raid signal from a hill on the north side of Efan. Miller maintained his southwesterly heading as he entered the lagoon and proceeded directly to the Eten anchorage. The moon was still in its early phases, almost directly overhead, and a thin film of haze partially obscured its light, but the islands rising out of the lagoon were outlined at ten miles.

The outlines of Eten and Dublon took definite shape when Miller spotted two warships lying at anchor between these islands. Unable to turn in time, he continued on his course, skirting around the south end of Eten before swinging wide as he made a 180 degree turn to bring him back between Eten and Dublon. As he was executing a radical flipper turn it became difficult to gauge his height above the water. His co-pilot, Lieutenant (jg) N.L. Burton, watching the radio altimeter, saw the plane heading perilously close to the water and pulled up on the yoke in time to prevent the plane from crashing into the water. Miller regained control and, in a moment, the plane was righted and heading back on a northeasterly course.

The larger of the two warships again appeared dead ahead three-quarters of a mile away and was identified as a light cruiser. Miller closed the range, flew down the length of the ship from stern to bow, and dropped three 1,000-pound bombs. The three bombs hit the water 10 to 15 feet from the starboard side of the hull near the fantail. Explosions lifted the stern out of the water, and the ship was turned 90 degrees to starboard and began listing to port.[2] Miller turned towards Eten and flew down the enemy runway at 200 feet as his gunners opened up and blasted installations along the airstrip.

The attack on the cruiser woke the enemy, and anti-aircraft guns started firing up and, for the next two minutes, the fire was the most intense and accurate that Miller and his crew had ever experienced. The plane was caught in a cross fire from gun positions on Eten and Dublon. A steady hail of tracers streamed across the top of the plane from both directions, which inexplicably did not hit the plane. Miller's gunners returned fire, and the muzzle blast of the bow guns nearly blinded the pilot. The muzzle flashes from the plane's guns forced Miller to fly almost completely on instruments at low altitude through murderous cross fire.

Passing northwest between Dublon and Fefan, Miller's gunners strafed the western shore of Dublon while continuing to receive heavy accurate return fire. The seaplane base at Moen and a number of small naval auxiliaries anchored west of Moen were also strafed in passing. The Liberator then flew down the length of the Moen airfield, strafing heavily, but received no return fire. Miller then flew to the North Pass in search of further targets for the M-47 depth bomb he carried, but finding none, he turned around and made his exit from the lagoon over the Northeast Pass and returned to base.

On the last day of the month, Lieutenant (jg) Kasperson attacked and severely damaged a 500-ton freighter and a 600-ton escort ship north of Truk during a 30

Kasperson's gunners intense strafing causes the cargo ship to begin burning on 30 April 1944.
Courtesy of the National Archives.

Crossing over the 500-ton ship at 200 feet just before Kasperson releases a M47 depth bomb.
Courtesy of the National Archives.

minute engagement. Through intense and accurate AA fire which damaged the leading edge of the wing between number one and two engines and the port horizontal stabilizer, Kasperson made four strafing runs and dropped M47 depth bombs on the ships.

On 7 May, Lieutenant John D. Keeling, on a routine search through the northern Caroline Islands, had reached a point 85 miles north of Ulul at an altitude of 3,500 feet when his radioman in the port waist hatch sighted a plane silhouetted above the cloud layer at 5,000 feet, 15 miles ahead. The other plane apparently sighted the PB4Y at the same time and reversed course and started to climb.

Keeling turned to port, increased power, and in a slight climb, rapidly gained on the other plane, shortly identified as a four-engine Kawanishi H6K "Mavis" flying boat. The PB4Y jettisoned its two Mark 47 depth bombs as the distance closed. The Mavis started to dive, turning to port toward the cloud bank. Keeling, now two miles behind, dove to keep between the Mavis and Truk. The Mavis reached the cloud before Keeling's gunners could open fire, and both planes were continuously in and out of the clouds during the next 20 minutes in a hide-in-seek chase.

After the initial attempt of the Mavis to outclimb the PB4Y, the Japanese's evasive tactic became a continual turning and variation of altitude in an unsuccessful search for cloud cover sufficiently large enough to hide in. No attempt was made by the enemy pilot to get down on the water where the grey-green camouflage might have complicated the race. The flying boat began a turn before entering

Enveloped in a fountain of water, the ship is severely damaged by the bomb blast. *Courtesy of the National Archives.*

the cloud, enabling Lieutenant Keeling to turn with him despite the concealment of the cloud. The Mavis came into the clear a little above and to the starboard side of the PB4Y and headed for a rain squall.

The bow turret of the PB4Y fired a few bursts at extreme range and opened up again as soon as the planes came into the clear. Keeling broke out at 1,500 feet with the Mavis close above on the starboard bow. The Mavis turned to port, presenting its starboard beam side to the Liberator, and tracers from both top and bow turrets of the PB4Y began hitting between the number three and four engines and at the starboard wing roots.

A long burst from the starboard waist gun entered the fuselage at the red disc, and the tail gunner reached the trailing edge of the port wing, drawing smoke. As the Mavis banked, the tail gunner raked the top of the flying boat from the bow to the center of the wing. The enemy top rear, tail, and starboard side gunners opened up immediately, and one bullet hit the bow turret of Keeling's plane. Both planes went into a cloud again, and Keeling broke out 50 feet below and 500 yards directly behind the Mavis. The PB4Y bow turret knocked out the Japanese tail gun, and, as Keeling pulled off to starboard about 100 feet from the Japanese, both the bow and top turret shot through the wing to the number three engine, which began to smoke, followed by a stream of fire, apparently hitting the fuel tank. By now, all the enemy guns had been silenced, and the port waist gunner, who alternated at the starboard

Between patrols members of the squadron play volleyball on Eniwetok. *Courtesy of Oden Sheppard.*

gun while the other gunner acted as cameraman, turned his fire to the red disc on the fuselage.

Fragments of the Mavis's wing peeled off, and a sheet of flame from the fuel tank between number three and four engines came back and seared off the starboard rudder and a portion of the starboard horizontal stabilizer and elevator. The plane lost speed and began to sideslip down and under, and the PB4Y pulled up and over him in a turn to port, reversing the bank with the top turret still firing at the number three engine nacelle. The Mavis at 3,500 feet entered a dive to starboard out of control towards the water, and the Liberator's tail gunner raked the bow as it dropped off. The starboard wing of the Mavis folded back just before it struck the water and blew up. Keeling circled at an altitude of 1, 000 feet, but only an oil slick remained to mark the position were the enemy plane had crashed. After four months in the forward area, enthusiasm for going out on a strike began to wane. Being woken up from their sleep, rolling down towards the field in the dead of night towards their plane, they were now too tired to be apprehensive. With their heads bobbing on their chests, arms hanging loosely, they appeared to be most reluctant to go out again. They had become Miller's Reluctant Raiders, but they kept on going, again and again.

On the 14th, Commander Miller continued his trips to Truk and Puluwat. Having completed the coverage of his sector, he headed for Truk, approaching the atoll

Engine maintenance on a squadron plane. *Courtesy of Oden Sheppard.*

A Japanese Navy/Kawanishi I6K5 "Mavis" patrol seaplane afire while being shot down by a VB-109 plane flown by Lieutenant John D. Keeling on 7 May 1944. The flames from the wing fire have burned away much of the seaplane's tail surfaces. *Courtesy of the National Archives.*

at low altitude from the northeast and crossed the reef near North Pass. Miller scanned briefly for shipping reported at anchor north of Moen, but found the anchorage empty. He proceeded directly to the anchorage west of Dublon and north of Fefan. In the lagoon, 8 to 12 freighters from 1,000 to 5,000 tons were at anchor. The atoll's defenses were now alerted, and intense and accurate heavy and medium anti-aircraft fire was encountered from the ships, and from shore installations on Fefan and Moen. Selecting one 5,000-ton freighter as a target, the range was closed, and Miller continued through the increasing tempo and uncomfortable accuracy of their anti-aircraft fire. The bombing run was made across the ship's beam, and Miller released four 1000 pound bombs. The bombs went over, and the first explosion occurred 30 feet from the starboard side of the ship. Before an attempt could be made to determine the results of the attack, the plane took two hits in the number two engine from anti-aircraft fire.

Proceeding east of Fefan, on a south and southwesterly heading, Miller passed another 8-12 merchantmen anchored off Uman, but did not attack, and Miller left Truk bound for Puluwat. Eight miles from Puluwat at 100 feet altitude, a red flare shot up from the water in front of the plane. A quick glance showed three men in two yellow rubber life rafts southwest of Puluwat. One turn was made to sight them again and check the position before continuing to Puluwat.

Coming in over Puluwat field, sporadic bursts of heavy but accurate anti-aircraft fire were received from a gun position on the east point of Alet Island. Miller dropped five one hundred pound bombs, which hit directly in a housing and lighthouse area. Having expended his bomb-load, Miller returned to the sighted life rafts to pinpoint the position. To avoid attracting the attention of the Japanese, he did not remain in the area, but sent in a contact report and continued on patrol.

Commander Miller was now providing most of the enthusiasm for the squadron, and went out on some of the most dangerous missions. On the 16th, Commander Miller gave his crew a rest and took Lieutenant Bill Bridgeman and his crew along for one of the squadron's most successful masthead-height exploits at Truk.

It was five o'clock in the morning and not quite daylight yet, with a full moon clearly outlining the islands at 8 miles. Miller proceeded directly to the anchorage north of Fefan and west of Dublon, where he had seen ships at anchor two nights before. Searching the harbor, Miller soon found a 5,000-ton freighter dead ahead laying at anchor. Approaching from the stern of the ship, he dropped three 500 pound bombs. The bombs hit 10-15 feet from the starboard side of the hull, and the ship was rocked by explosions and began listing heavily to starboard. The explosions were the first indication the enemy had of the plane's presence. Miller turned south and then to the east, skirting Dublon, and then circled widely around Eten in an attempt to locate the ships he had seen two days before, but they had moved.

Flames from the wing fire have burned away much of the seaplane's tail surfaces before finally crashing into the water. *Courtesy of the National Archives.*

Returning between Fefan and Dublon through increasingly intense AA fire, Robert Carey, the port waist gunner, sighted a 10,000-ton tanker a half mile off Dublon. Miller acknowledged the gunner, and a moment later flew across the ship, dropping three 500 pound bombs.

The first bomb fell short 15 feet from the starboard side of hull, the second one hit directly on the deck, 40 feet from the stern, and the third fell long over the ship and hit the water. The explosions lit up the whole sky behind the plane as the ship became engulfed in flames. The exploding tanker finally stirred the enemy into action, as anti-aircraft fire from the ships and shore installations became accurate, and searchlights on Moen and Fefan closely followed the plane's course. Miller headed westerly across the lagoon and left Truk by Piaanu Pass with the course set for Puluwat.

Approaching Puluwat from the northeast just before dawn, Miller made a run down the airstrip at an altitude of 25 feet, surprising a party of Japanese on their way to work in a battered pickup truck. The bow gunner, George Murphy, started shooting at the truck, and both seemed to be on a head-on collision, except the plane was just barely higher than the truck. Bullets slammed into the truck with such force that the two front fenders went flying off in different directions, and the truck caught fire. Japanese troops were killed by the bow gunner when they jumped

A new Japanese airstrip on Puluwat discovered by Commander Miller on 9 June 1944. *Courtesy of Thomas Delahoussaye.*

off the truck and tried to find shelter from the attacking plane. Forty more troops along the edge of the runway were decimated as they tried to take cover behind some coconut trees. Twenty more men running out of a barracks also became victims of the Liberator's gunners.

Miller dropped one 500 pound bomb at the end of an airstrip for a direct hit on a revetment, destroying it completely. Miller then circled to starboard for a run on the radio station and lighthouse on the northwest corner of Alet Island. Several new gun positions were encountered, as bursts of heavy and medium anti-aircraft fire began appearing around the plane. Miller dropped two more 500 pound bombs for direct hits on the radio station on this run, but smoke and dust from the explosions obscured the results. The Liberator made a little climb, banked to the right, and came down the runway again from the same direction as the first pass. However, this time the enemy had their guns in operation and began firing.

Miller flew past the lighthouse again, but this time, an enemy gunner in the top of it opened fire with a 7.7mm machine gun. Returning fire, the tail turret knocked the enemy machine gunner right off the top of the structure, and he fell to the ground 135 feet below.

Closing the range for a second attack upon the radio station, a three inch anti-aircraft shell exploded directly above the plane. The plane gave a little lurch, and debris came flying past outside the waist section. Howard Bensing, the top turret gunner, was firing straight ahead over the cockpit when the shell exploded just above him. The blast forced the twin guns downward, and the mechanical stops on the turret that were designed to keep the guns from firing into the cockpit broke off. The concussion from the blast dazed the gunner, and he continued to fire off rounds into the cockpit before he finally released the trigger. The bullets demolished the greenhouse, and both pilots sustained wounds to their head, arms, and back from shrapnel, flying glass, and metal. The navigator was hurled from a position between the pilots back against the bomb-bay hatch, happily escaping the shrapnel.

Even though he was wounded, Miller continued the run, instinctively pressing the pickle, and four bombs struck directly on the weather and radio station, while two others landed over and on the beach. After leaving Puluwat, the pilots were given first aid by the plane captain, Ed Watts, and Commander Miller recovered enough to fly the plane and land at Eniwetok seven hours later.

8

Supporting the Marianas Invasion

June, with the invasion of the Marianas, was a busy month for the squadron, with special flights and additional searches expanding and augmenting an already heavy operational schedule. On the 6th and 7th, a continuous special search for Japanese naval shipping was flown west of Truk, and nightly searches were conducted west of Truk and in the surrounding areas of Puluwat and Pulap from the 12th to the 21st. Special six-plane fleet protection patrols to intercept possible enemy search planes from Truk, Marcus, Guam, and Saipan were flown from the 10th through the 13th, and similar four-plane patrols on the 17th and 18th. Except for two four hour periods, continuous special anti-submarine searches were conducted from the 17th through the 22nd.

After recovering from his wounds sustained on 16 May, Commander Miller conducted a masthead-height raid against Truk on 2 June. Approaching Truk just after dusk, a rising moon provided excellent visibility for a low-level attack against shipping targets. While still 15 minutes away from Truk, a searchlight appeared low on the water 15 miles ahead and made one quick sweep in the plane's direction.

Commander Miller held his low altitude and entered the lagoon over Northeast Island. As the plane swung wide two miles west of Moen on a southerly heading, a 7,000-ton freighter at anchor was sighted three miles ahead. Miller turned to port and headed towards it, dropping three 500 pound bombs towards the ship's starboard bow. The first bomb struck approximately 100 feet short of the intended target, the second fell 20 feet short and torpedoed on to strike the ship just below the water line, while the third was a direct hit amidships on the bridge. A great internal explosion occurred, lifting the ship out of the water and blowing the central bridge structure off and upward into the air. As the plane left, an intense red glare of towering flames had broken out amidships. As Miller's plane departed the burning ship, intense anti-aircraft fire followed the plane's course. Continuing through the atoll, his gunners strafed a parked plane at Eten airstrip while silencing two medium anti-aircraft positions, blew up an ammunition dump at Dublon, and set fire to buildings on Moen, Eten, and Dublon.

After completing the strafing run, Miller turned to starboard towards the seaplane base at Moen as medium and heavy anti-aircraft fire increased in intensity and accuracy throughout the remaining runs. At 300 feet, installations at a seaplane base on Dublon were heavily strafed. Continuing on a southeast heading, the bomber passed a dozen freighters anchored northwest of Dublon. Concentrated fire from the belly turret, starboard waist gunner, and bow turret started fires on five of the freighters. As the ships were being strafed, heavy and intense anti-aircraft to port disclosed the presence of a destroyer anchored between Moen and Dublon. The port waist gunner and tail turret gunner immediately answered the warship's fire, scoring direct hits and silencing some of the destroyer's guns before their fire was directed to new targets along the western shore of Dublon. When last observed, the fires on three of the five burning freighters seemed under control, but two others remained burning and engulfed in flames.

On the 3rd, with the long absence of enemy shipping in assigned search areas and by the constant presence of it in the lagoon at Truk, Lieutenant Commander

Lieutenant Commander William Janeshek intercepted a Nakajima B5N "Kate" torpedo bomber west of Truk on 6 June. Smoke is streaming from the engine nacelle after being hit by the Liberator's bow guns. *Courtesy of the National Archives.*

Hicks became convinced that the enemy was supplying Truk largely at night, south and west of current patrol limits.

The navigator, Ensign Dicky Wieland, sighted an enemy convoy of 11 ships consisting of a large freighter, two medium freighters, a destroyer, and seven escorts five miles off to port and on the same course as the plane. With the darkness and poor visibility, sight contact was lost, and Hicks circled, hoping to locate the convoy silhouetted against the moon.

Dropping from an altitude of 1,500 to 400 feet, Hicks circled and came directly over the convoy. The enemy gave no sign they were aware of the plane's presence. The course was reversed, and the plane circled to starboard wide around the convoy and dropped to 200 feet on a northerly direction before heading directly over the middle of the convoy. Hicks selected the large freighter as a target, and the range was closed.

One of the escort vessels on the near flank of the convoy opened fire when the plane had closed to 1,000 yards, and tracer fire was received from all the ships when the plane was 500 yards from the freighter. Immediately, the tail, belly, and waist gunners returned fire, having held their fire while the advantage of surprise existed. The tail gunner directed his fire at gun positions on one of the freighters, which ceased firing abruptly. The belly turret fired steadily at the target freighter,

The rear gunner of the Kate is already dead seconds prior to the plane hitting the water. *Courtesy of the National Archives.*

silencing some of the more accurate AA training fire on a destroyer to port of the convoy. The waist gunners fired at the escorts and the top turret joined them, starting flash fires on two of the ships.

As the plane passed over the nearest escort on the bombing run, the bow turret joined the belly turret's fire on the target freighter, shifting to a second freighter at the bomb drop and then to a far escort, knocking out two AA guns. The bombardier, after coaching the pilot on the bombing run by means of the low altitude sight, manned a 30 caliber machinegun through the bombardier's starboard window against an escort gunboat on the far side of the convoy.

Hicks made his bombing run across the ship's port beam. A 1,000 pound bomb was released and hit directly on the deck approximately 60 feet from the stern, and a 500 pound bomb went over, entering the water 15-20 feet off the starboard side of the hull. Bomb detonations were followed by a violent explosion aboard the freighter. The freighter was left on fire, dead in the water and listing heavily to starboard. Hicks' plane was caught in the deadly crossfire of the larger ships over the center of the convoy. Hale Fisher, the plane captain and starboard waist gunner, was hit by a

Heavy black smoke pouring from a merchant ship on 16 June 1944. *Courtesy of the National Archives.*

shell after it entered the fuselage beneath the cockpit and traveled the length of the plane, holing the bomb-bay door actuating cylinder, the bomb-bay tank, and two bulkheads before striking the gunner in the abdomen. Hicks, with the aid of his co-pilot, began radical evasive maneuvers as soon as bombs were away, skidding sharply and dropping down almost to the water.

When out of range, Hicks reversed course and climbed to an altitude of 7,000 feet. The navigator went aft when the waist gunner was wounded and remained with him for a large part of the return flight, giving first aid. With the loss of hydraulic pressure, Hicks found it impossible to close the bomb-bay doors. One of the doors was finally closed manually, but the other was impossible to close until return to base. Reaching Entiewtok, a safe landing was effected with manual lowering of flaps and wheels, and despite the loss of outboard brakes. Two days later, the entire squadron lined up outside the church on Eniwetok as the flag draped coffin bearing the remains of Hale Fisher passed by on the way to the cemetery.

On the following evening, the sun had just set as Lieutenant Wheaton set his plane on a course West of Puluwat, hoping to find enemy shipping targets along the Truk-Guam lane that Hicks had found the night before. When the plane was at an altitude of 1,500 feet, the starboard waist gunner sighted a convoy at a distance of 6 miles. Wheaton turned starboard and reduced his altitude to 800 feet with the intention of circling the convoy, and silhouetted them against the remaining daylight in the western sky for his bombing run.

The gun fire from all ships began as soon as the turn was initiated, with heavy anti-aircraft fire from a three-inch gun on a destroyer being consistently accurate. The enemy fire was an intense protective barrage as the plane passed to the rear of the ships on a southerly course. As the plane circled, three escort patrol vessels a half mile apart were sighted four miles behind the main convoy. Wheaton selected the escorts as his targets, and the plane passed at 500 feet altitude between the first two ships.

The starboard waist gunner opened fire on the leading escort as Wheaton turned to port, circling the second patrol vessel, and was soon followed by the other gunners. The two patrol boats answered with accurate 20mm tracer fire, but concentrated fire from the PB4Y stopped all defensive fire from both vessels and stopped the second ship dead in the water.

Wheaton turned to starboard and headed for the third escort as intense, accurate gun fire was being received from a freighter and destroyer in the main convoy. Climbing to 1,500 feet, Wheaton approached the escort on a northerly heading and, through intense and accurate fire, made a glide bombing run and released four 500 pound bombs in train at 500 feet altitude, recovering from the run at 200 feet. This was one of the very few attacks made by VB-109 pilots at an altitude above masthead.

The first three bombs fell short, with the third striking the water 20 feet from the port hull. However, the fourth bomb dropped directly on the deck amidships. The explosion picked the ship up, twisted it 45 degrees to starboard, and, as the starboard waist gunner described it, "laid it on its side," as flames amidships rose twice the height of the ship. Before the plane had completed its pull-out and had begun to turn to port, the ship had sunk. With the help of his co-pilot, Wheaton pulled out of his dive and climbed to 6,000 feet as anti-aircraft fire followed the plane as it departed.

During the late afternoon of the 6th, Lieutenant Janeshek, on routine search through the Northern Caroline Islands, having partially completed the outward leg of his search sector, altered course toward the area West of Truk where enemy shipping had been encountered by Hicks and Wheaton. Cruising at 1,400 feet, he reached a point in sight of Truk when Joseph Yates, the bow gunner, sighted a Nakajima B5N "Kate" torpedo bomber slightly off the starboard three miles away at 1,000 feet headed straight for Truk. Janeshek increased power, headed toward the enemy plane, and closed on it rapidly. While still two miles away, the enemy plane apparently sighted the PB4Y and nosed over. Janeshek nosed over as well, and the PB4Y's bow turret opened fire at 1,200 feet at the Kate.

The first burst hit the Kate's engine and the fuselage by the starboard wing root. Flames appeared on the cowl flaps on the Kate's port side and began streaming up and over the cockpit. The second burst at 800 feet went under the Kate harmlessly, but the third burst at 500 feet hit the Kate's tail as the bow turret gunner held the Kate directly in his fire. The port waist gunner, Jack Biggers, picked the Kate up under the wing at 300 feet range and riddled the rear-cockpit, and then the engine as the Liberator banked slightly to port. The rear cockpit gunner of the Kate pushed his canopy back and was standing up preparing to bail out as the Kate came into the sight of the PB4Y port waist gun. Jack Biggers, the port waist gunner, fired a short burst, and observed the enemy gunner to suddenly sit down again.

Janeshek started a 180 degree turn to starboard and, as soon as he had passed the Kate, Joseph Rodgers, the tail turret gunner, opened fire at 600 feet and followed the smoking Kate almost to the water. He was joined in the final stage by Robin Allen, the starboard waist gunner. About 500 feet from the water, the Kate jettisoned two depth bombs, fell off on the port wing, and then hit the water without bouncing and exploded.

As the PB4Y completed its turn to starboard, the water subsided, and the starboard wing of the Kate appeared before it slowly sank, the red disc of the Rising Sun gradually being swallowed up by the oily and wreckage-strewn waves. The entire action had taken less than five minutes. The Liberator circled the position, 15 miles from the reef of Truk Atoll with Tol Island plainly visible, observing the wreckage, before returning to complete the coverage of his assigned search sector.

During the night of the 6th, Lieutenant Mellard, on a search for shipping through the northern Caroline Islands and in the lanes west of Truk, was at an altitude of 1,000 feet when his radioman made a radar contact at 14 miles. Through poor visibility, Lieutenant Mellard made a 30 degree turn to starboard. Five miles away a convoy of ships silhouetted against the moon was sighted at a speed of 12 knots. Mellard circled briefly, diving to 300 feet, picked a large freighter as a target, and began a bombing approach. However, with deteriorating visibility, the target was shortly lost, and Mellard turned to starboard. A few minutes later, a freighter was sighted just as the plane flew across the length of the ship. The bow turret opened fire on the freighter at 1,500 feet, and his tracers hit the ship. The top and belly turrets joined in, and their converging fire started a blaze forward of the superstructure which burned throughout the attack. As the bomber passed to starboard of the freighter, the bow and tail turrets with the starboard waist gunner shifted their fire to an escort on the starboard side of the formation, with the belly turret and port waist gun directing their fire at a possible destroyer off to port and to the rear of the freighter.

Mellard turned to port in front of the freighter, banking sharply, and came down to 200 feet for a run on the destroyer. A bombing run was made from the starboard bow to port quarter across the warship, and two 500 pound bombs struck the water ten feet from the starboard side of hull and near enough together to form a single

Intense machine gun fire envelops a hapless merchant ship on 16 June 1944.*Courtesy of the National Archives.*

bomb splash before they exploded. The ship's stern rose out of the water and was kicked around 45 degrees to port. Thick black smoke poured from the stern, but there were no visible flames. When last observed, the ship was down by the stern with a heavy starboard list and was stopped dead in the water.

The bombing run carried the plane close to an escort vessel, which fired a little 20mm tracer fire in the plane's direction—the only AA fire noted during the entire run. Pulling out after the run, Mellard flew up moon for about 10 miles, debating further possibilities. Aware of the destruction possible to achieve with machine gun fire and persuaded by the lack of anti-aircraft fire, he decided to return and try to finish off the cripple.

Mellard returned on the port side of the convoy, turning to port when abreast of the burning freighter, and crossed the beam of the formation with all guns strafing. The crippled destroyer had dropped behind the formation and out of lethal range of the plane's concentrated gunfire, but now the enemy was thoroughly alert. The convoy, with the exception of the destroyer, began firing simultaneously and sending up a barrage of light and medium AA. Remarkably, the plane was not hit. Deciding to end the attack, Mellard turned to port and set course for base.

Commander Miller's personal war with Puluwat came to an end on the 9th. On a search through Northern Carolines, he left his search sector in the Hall Islands and proceeded to a point 20 miles west of Truk to investigate the enemy shipping lanes. Sighting no shipping targets, Miller approached Puluwat from the east and attacked the concentration of gun emplacements on Alet Island, which had given him difficulty on previous raids.

A low level approach ranging from 50 to 200 feet for 30 miles was made towards Puluwat, and complete surprise was achieved. An initial run was made across the northern part of Puluwat Island and down the length of the eastern point Alet Island directly over the target gun positions. Miller salvoed ten 100 pound bombs on the gun positions. The first two bombs fell short, exploding on the beach. However, the succeeding eight hit directly in a string across the concentrated gun positions, shattering the emplacements and wrecking the guns.

The bow turret opened fire at 1,500 feet, followed by the top turret and both waist gunners. The gun positions were the primary strafing targets, with the top turret and starboard waist shifting fire to a group of six tents and shelters adjacent to the gun emplacements and along the beach. The fire of the tail and belly turrets on the same targets after the bomb-drop added to the devastation.

Skirting the shore at the western end of the runway, Miller circled to port and flew wide around the island group for a bombing run on the remaining installations in the lighthouse area on the northwest side of Alet. Heading towards the lighthouse, heavy and medium anti-aircraft fire was received from positions along the southwestern shore until the plane passed to the east around Puluwat Island. Bombing runs against targets in the lighthouse area were made from the north and south with recovery in a circle to starboard. On the first run, three 500 pound bombs were dropped over the lighthouse area of northwest Alet. The second drop was a direct hit on a generator building adjacent to the lighthouse. The third run was made on the radio station, and the bomb detonations destroyed the station and blew the roof off the last remaining building in the area. Anti-aircraft fire by heavy three-inch guns on the southern shore of Alet became very intense on the third run.

While attacking the lighthouse area, the plane was damaged from small caliber rounds to the starboard side of the fuselage, vertical stabilizer, tail, belly, starboard wing, and the lower starboard waist hatch, barely missing the waist gunners. Only a badly damaged lighthouse remained standing. Miller returned to his search sector by way of Ulul before returning to base.

Four days later, Lieutenant Mellard, on fleet protection patrol, in conjunction with Lieutenant Harvey H. Hop of VB-108, was flying along a north-south line some 400 miles east of Saipan when Hop reported a Betty at 9,000 feet. Mellard immediately altered course to parallel that of the Betty and climbed to 11,000 feet to obtain an altitude advantage. The enemy bomber was soon sighted by the pilot 1,500 feet above and eight miles ahead of the Liberator. Mellard increased power and climbed to 14,500 feet in pursuit. Twelve minutes later he brought the PB4Y in position to attack, and nosed over and closed the range. A cross-over from the Betty's

Lieutenant Clifford Nettleton, Oden Sheppard's co-pilot, during a flight. *Courtesy of Oden Sheppard.*

starboard side was planned, keeping the belly turret retracted until ready for the attack.

Thomas C. Lee, the bow turret gunner, opened fire at a range of 1,500 feet. The initial burst was extremely accurate, with incendiaries splashing over the starboard wing root and fuselage of the enemy plane. Robert L. Dumais, in the top turret, fired a short burst, scoring hits along the fuselage and in the cockpit area. There was no return fire from the Japanese plane, and when the range was closed to 1,000 feet, the Betty broke away in a vertical power dive, smoke pouring from the starboard wing just outboard of the engine nacelle. The Betty continued its dive straight into the water, suggesting the pilot may have been killed. The plane hit the water with a great splash and exploded, leaving only a dirty brown slick in the water. Fourteen minutes later, Mellard encountered an American Carrier Task Force, the existence of which it was his mission to keep from enemy search planes.

Mid-June brought a final succession of submarine attacks north of the Carolines. On the 17th, Lieutenant Bill Bridgeman had been airborne for two hours on anti-submarine patrol duty when George Murphy, in the bow turret, spotted an enemy sub cruising on the surface. It was the RO-117, a 525-ton submarine with a crew of 75. Bridgeman acknowledged him, started playing four-engine dive bomber, and began diving towards the ocean. The sub must have seen the aircraft coming towards it and immediately began to crash dive. Bridgeman's run on the submarine was almost identical to the previous one on 31 March. The boat was almost submerged, with the conning tower still out of the water when Bridgeman released the Mark 47 depth bombs.

Both charges hit close to the submerging boat, and immediately, a large oil slick appeared after the explosions. They circled the area for many hours before another plane from the squadron relieved them, but the submarine never surfaced. After landing the crew were not given credit for sinking it. After the de-briefing, Bridgeman told the crew if they ever came across another sub, he intended to run like hell in the opposite direction. Only after the war was the RO-117 confirmed sunk by VB-109.

For the next three days, squadron aircraft continued to make contacts with enemy submarines, with Lieutenant Stewart making one on the following day, but he was unable to deliver an attack. Lieutenant Sheppard continued the chase on the 20th, and Lieutenant Belew delivered an attack on the 21st without any observable results.

On the 17th, in answer to Admiral Hoover's request for aerial photographs, Lieutenant Commander Janeshek flew low over Saipan defenses and, two days later, Lieutenant Jobe covered Tinian Island. Liuetenant Wheaton obtained low oblique photographs of enemy installations on Saipan on the 28th, and landed the first heavy bomber at Aslito (Isley) airfield, proving the fighter strip was feasible for Liberator operations.

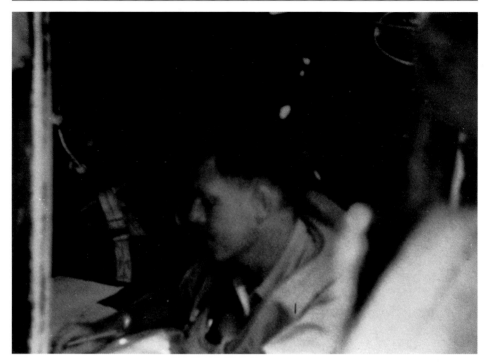

A navigator had to be precise in his calculations over water. A minor error could cost a crew their lives during a flight. *Courtesy of Oden Sheppard.*

During the month of July no enemy contact of any type was made in routine search areas, and only by moving an advance echelon to Saipan did important skirmishes with the enemy become possible. Flying from Eniwetok, Commander Miller bombed and strafed Ushi Point airfield at Tinian and heavily strafed Marpi Point airfield at Saipan in a low-level photographic sortie on 1 July, returning four days later to bomb and strafe Marpi Point field and silencing three-inch gun emplacements that naval vessels were finding difficulty in reaching.

On 8 July, VB-108, with whom the squadron had operated since entering the combat zone, ceased operations and began to retire to Hawaii. All flights from Eniwetok were assumed by the squadron until VB-116 arrived at Eniwetok and began operations on the 12th. With the arrival of VB-116, Commander Miller and Lieutenant Jobe, as an advance echelon of the squadron, moved temporarily to Isley Field, Saipan.

9

Operations from Saipan

With the invasion of the Marianas on June 14, code-named Operation Forager, most of the squadron's operations were restricted to flying twelve to fifteen hour patrols and providing air cover for the task force. The Marianas consist of 15 islands which stretch 425 miles.[1] The four largest (Saipan, Tinian, Rota, and Guam) were the targets for invasion. With Saipan taken, B-29 Superfortresses would have a base close enough to bomb the Japanese mainland.[2] In front of the invasion force were 32,000 Japanese defenders and, for the first time, American forces would confront Japanese civilians.

Before Saipan was declared secured on July 9, there would be 16,500 American casualties, including 3,400 killed. During the invasion, the patrols became pretty monotonous, and most of the men, including Commander Miller, were getting impatient to see some action. Finally, in early July, Commander Miller appealed to Commander "Bucky" Lee, operations officer to Rear Admiral Hoover, to detach some of the squadron's aircraft to Saipan and, on 12 July, the request was granted.[3]

The following day, Commander Miller and Lieutenant Joseph Jobe flew their aircraft to Aslito Airdrome, later renamed Isley Field, Saipan. Fighting was still going on at the far north end of the island where the Marines were flushing out·the last remnants of the Japanese garrison. The water below some cliffs was tinted a crimson red from the blood of hundreds of civilian men, women, and children who had committed suicide by blowing themselves up with grenades, or by jumping off the cliffs rather than being captured by the Americans. True to the code of Japanese troops, the civilians on Saipan believed that being captured was the ultimate form of humiliation, and took death before dishonor.

As the planes from VB-109 began staging from Saipan, Army Air Force P-47 fighters took off and flew towards Tinian just a few miles away, dropping their bombs and making strafing runs on the island as a precursor for the invasion. The fighters swooped in over the island and delivered their loads, only to fly back to Isley Field to rearm, take-off, and resume their deadly business of war. Army engineers were working night and day turning the northeast-northwest cross-strip into the first of Isley's B-29 strips, and only the east-west fighter strip was in use. To its 3,200 feet of bomb-pocked macadam had been added 500 feet of Marston matting, sufficient for local operations of the TBFs, P-47s, P-51s, and hospital planes which cluttered the parking areas. The PB4Y-1s of VB-109 were operationally welcomed despite the crowded conditions.

Tents were pitched in a muddy sugar-cane field behind the remains of a concrete Japanese operations building. The constant bombardment of Tinian and return fire disturbed the nights, but Saipan fighting had moved to the north. Signs of battle were very fresh, and sight-seeing or "Japanese-hunting" became the constant recreation when the crews were grounded.

While waiting two restless days on call for anticipated shipping strikes, Commander Miller planned and finally received permission to strike the Bonins and Iwo Jima. On the 14th, Iwo Jima was raided for the first time by land-based aircraft just after sunset.

A devastated airfield on Tinian taken on 1 July from Commander Miller's plane. *Courtesy of Thomas Delahoussaye.*

A member of VB-109 inspecting a Japanese plane on Saipan. *Courtesy of Oden Sheppard.*

Taking off from Isley Field in the late afternoon, the PB4Ys headed northward and passed to the west of the northern Mariannas at an altitude of 1,000 feet. At a point 50 miles northeast of Iwo Jima, the final approach was made at 25 to 50 feet off the water, and the PB4Ys pulled over the hills at the northeast end of Iwo Jima, just after sunset.

Enemy radar apparently failed to pick up the low-flying planes, and complete surprise was effected as they approached the four by two mile square, pear-shaped island. No enemy aircraft were airborne as the Liberators came down the length of the airfields. When the island was reached, the two planes were abreast about 800 feet apart, Jobe on Miller's port. Fire was opened immediately by all machine guns of both planes, and answered immediately by enemy guns around Noto Jima and Furun Yama.

Anti-aircraft fire of all types was shortly encountered, and the barrage rapidly became more intense and withering than anything experienced in the Marshalls or Carolines. The low altitude of the planes and the surprise achieved, however, carried them through the murderous blanket of fire with only slight damage to Miller's plane. Initial strafing targets for the PB4Ys were anti-aircraft gun positions on the hills and near the fields, but fire was rapidly shifted to airfield installations, barracks, and enemy planes. Of 30 to 40 operational aircraft sighted and strafed in revetments and on the taxiway consisting of Zekes, Bettys and Tonys. One Betty

Commander Miller following a strike on Iwo Jima on 14 July. *Courtesy of Thomas Delahoussaye.*

was blown up, and another, along with two Zekes, was set afire by the combined gunfire of the machine guns. Numerous planes were damaged and probably destroyed. Parked in lines and crowded in revetments, they presented excellent targets.

At 150 feet altitude, Miller came down the west side of both airstrips and turned to starboard over the taxiway and parking areas to head for a destroyer about a mile offshore, which added to the fierce tempo of the anti-aircraft fire. As Miller began his bombing run on the destroyer at 200 feet, his gunners set ablaze a medium-size freighter to port and a coastal vessel on the starboard side; the fires were still visible and raging when the planes left the area. Several coastal vessels lying off Hiraiwa Saki were heavily strafed and smoking, and some gunfire on a destroyer escort to starboard was silenced. Miller's run was made from the starboard quarter to the port bow of the destroyer, and four 500-pound bombs were dropped.

The first two bombs fell short, but the third struck the ship at the water line and the fourth hit directly on the fantail. The bomb detonations kicked the ship 45 degrees to starboard, and explosions followed with debris flying through the air. With bombs away, Miller began to jink and turned to port to join up again with Jobe, as persistent anti-aircraft fire from the damaged destroyer followed the plane's course.

The seaplane Base on Chichi Jima taken by a plane from the U.S.S. Yorktown on 8 July 1944.
Courtesy of the National Archives.

As Miller was attacking the destroyer, Jobe had cleared the initial hills of the island at 50 feet, passed down the eastern edge of the upper strip, over the taxi and parking areas, and along the southern edge of the lower field. Barracks and buildings were strafed, starting several fires, and planes were damaged along the strips, taxiway, and in revetments, causing a number of planes to burn briskly. Three planes in the revetments, apparently carrier based with their wings folded, parked close alongside two other planes took continuous hits from Jobe's gunners.

Turning northwest at the southern end of the lower field and passing a boat yard, Jobe began a run on a 2,000 to 4,000-ton freighter about a mile offshore. A dozen or more small coastal vessels were moored close inshore to starboard of the plane's track, and two small oilers to port. Both of the oilers were set afire by heavy and repeated strafing, as were five of the coastal vessels, and all of the vessels in the group were left smoking, although no actual flames were visible.

Spotting a larger 6,000-ton freighter about a mile beyond his target ship, Jobe broke his run on the smaller merchant ship and headed for the large freighter. A large fire from his gunner's strafing had already broken aft of the freighter, and a destroyer escort further to port was strafed in passing. Jobe's plane crossed the large merchant ship from starboard quarter to port bow with concentrated fire, with all guns scoring continuous hits.

The ship was rocked by an internal explosion almost immediately after the plane had passed over, followed by a large fire and several smaller explosions occurring at short intervals thereafter. Jobe turned south and joined up with Miller, and the two planes headed for Ninami Iwo Jima and Saipan. On Iwo Jima, five large distinct fires were burning, and, as the two planes left the island behind, three large explosions from oil and ammunition dumps were observed in the vicinity of the airfields. Successful night landings were made at Saipan shortly after midnight, concluding a highly successful sneak attack.

The number of operational aircraft present, the amount of shipping clustered offshore of Iwo Jima, together with the vicious curtain of protective anti-aircraft fire thrown up from the ships and all parts of the island, announced the enemy's determination to maintain, protect, and build up this outer stronghold, only 625 miles from the Japanese home island of Honshu. Therefore, preparations were made for another strike on the Bonin and Volcano Islands, with Miller ordering Lieutenant Commander Janeshek and Lieutenant Bridgeman with their crews to Saipan.

While waiting for the arrival of Janeshek and Bridgeman to arrive at Saipan, Commander Miller flew Marine Battalion Commanders and Intelligence Officers of the Tinian landing force over the selected invasion beaches at minimum altitude for over an hour while they gained accurate intelligence of their objectives. With the arrival of two additional planes and crews, another strike on the Bonins was ordered.

During the pre-flight briefing held in the early evening of 18 July, Commander Miller told the three crews that the mission would be a raid on the Bonin Islands. The Bonins are comprised of four major islands named Ototo Jima, Ani Jima, Chichi Jima, and Haha Jima. These are barren, rocky volcanic islands lying approximately 120 miles north of Iwo Jima and approximately 800 miles from Saipan.[4] The Japanese had fortified three of the larger islands: Haha Jima, Chichi Jima, and Ani Jima.

Chichi Jima, located only 500 miles from Japan, is approximately four miles long and hook-shaped, with the hook enclosing Futami Ko Harbor.[5] The planes would hit Chichi Jima at dawn in a staggered formation, with Miller's plane "Thunder Mug" going in first, followed by Lieutenant Jobe in "Consolidated's Mistake," and with Bill Bridgeman in "Climbaboard" coming in last. After attacking Chichi Jima the three planes would head south and fly across twenty miles of open water and hit Haha Jima.

On this mission, each plane would carry 2,200 gallons of fuel and three 1,000 pound general purpose bombs. Under normal circumstances, taking off with this type of load wouldn't present a problem, however, Isley Airfield was a fighter strip (only 3,800 feet long), and at the end of it was a shear cliff that dropped down to the ocean. After the briefing was over, the crews climbed into their aircraft and prepared for departure. As each plane took off, at the end of the runway it dropped below the cliff before climbing back into the air. Anybody standing on the ground watching the take-offs would see the plane disappear before reappearing.

Commander Miller led the formation in an extended right echelon, with Lieutenant Jobe approximately 400 feet away and slightly behind the commander's plane, while Bridgeman's plane took up the rear some 600 feet away. The planes headed northwest at altitudes ranging from 800 to 1,000 feet. Approximately 125 miles Southeast of Iwo Jima, the aircraft descended to 200 feet. Approaching Chichi Jima,

"Climbaboard" preparing to take-off from Eniwetok. *Courtesy of Oden Sheppard.*

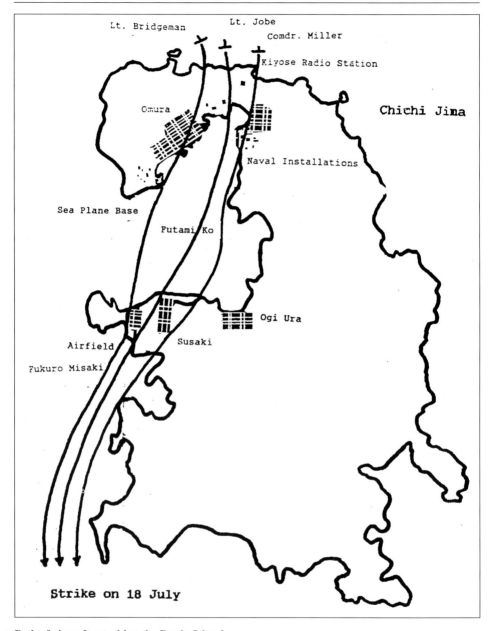

Path of aircraft attacking the Bonin Islands.

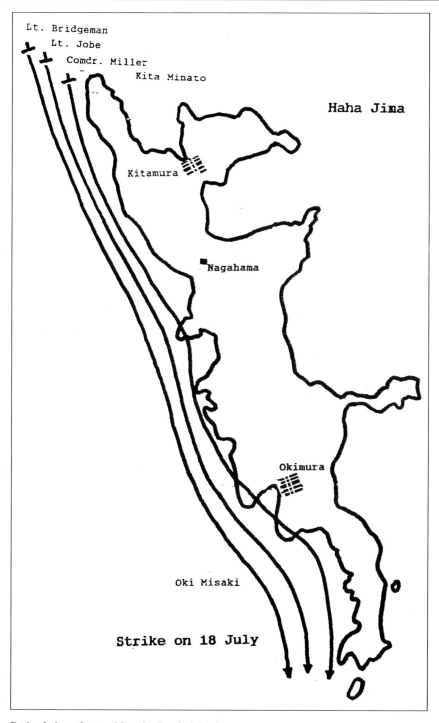

Path of aircraft attacking the Bonin Islands.

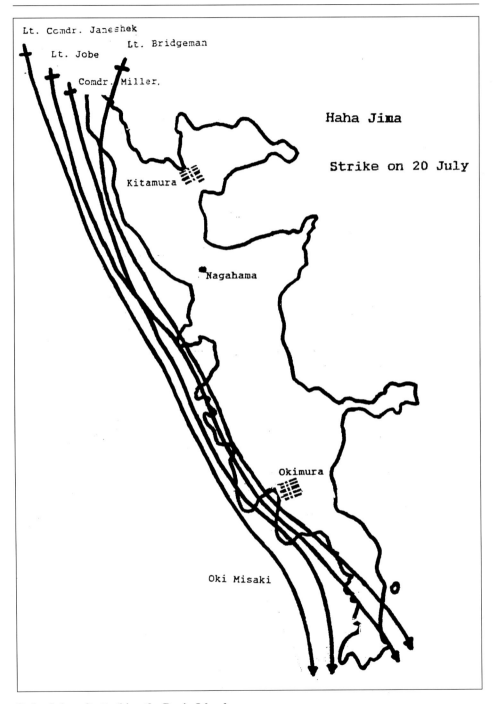

Path of aircraft attacking the Bonin Islands.

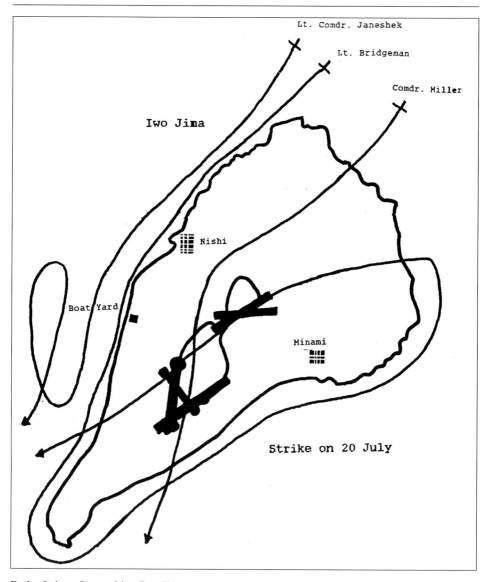

Path of aircraft attacking Iwo Jima.

the aircraft descended to 50 feet to avoid radar detection; then slipped through a channel between Ani Jima and Chichi Jima before climbing again to clear the hills on the southern end of the island. Just as they cleared the hills on the northern edge of the island by some 75 feet, shooting erupted.

Japanese machine gunners on a hill above the aircraft began firing down at the intruding aircraft. Suddenly, enemy gunners on the ground below joined in and also began firing. Within seconds, thick anti-aircraft fire erupted all around the planes. Rounds from 12.7mm anti-aircraft guns began straddling Bridgeman's plane, and the sound of flak could be heard hitting the aircraft. Immediately, every gun on board Bridgeman's plane opened up in an attempt to silence the guns on the ground. Up in the bow turret, George Murphy returned fire and immediately knocked out a big 90mm gun emplacement. In a matter of seconds, the rest of the gunners on board managed to silence quite a few more of the gun positions before the aircraft cleared the hills and headed towards the seaplane base at Omura.

Now flying at an altitude of 150 feet, they reached the seaplane base and found it full of aircraft. Below the attacking Liberators were "Pete," "Rufe," and "Emily" seaplanes tied to their moorings, with Japanese personnel frantically trying to get them airborne.[6] Every machine gun on board the three Liberators opened up in unison at the seaplanes as enemy anti-aircraft guns continued to put up a protective curtain of fire. In front of Miller, a solitary Rufe seaplane managed to get into the air for a few seconds before his gunners open fire, and the Japanese plane crashed into the side of a hill.

Coming into range of the seaplanes, Bridgeman's starboard waist gunner picked out a Pete that came into view, aimed at the gas tanks, and squeezed the trigger of the machine gun. After only firing a few rounds, the plane exploded, carrying its ground crew with it. Similar results were achieved with two more aircraft. After damaging or destroying 11 aircraft, Bridgeman's gunners began training their fire on shore installations and fuel storage areas, leaving several buildings burning in their wake. The planes then headed out over the harbor and bore down on anchored merchant shipping.

Gunners took aim on the small wooden coastal vessels and opened fire, sinking seven and setting afire many more. Heading southward, the three Liberators reached Susaki airfield, where the targets were so plentiful that it was hard for the gunners to decide which one to shoot at first. Parked planes, hangars, barracks, and other buildings were heavily strafed in passing. In front of Bridgeman, Lieutenant Jobe released a 1,000 pound bomb at a hangar and blew it up. The enemy gunners were still firing in vain as the three planes flew out of the harbor.

The three planes passed Kukuro Misaki and set course for Haha Jima. At 200 miles per hour it wasn't long before the Liberators came roaring single file along the western edge of the island, headed towards Okimura harbor. The enemy on Haha Jima must have been alerted by their comrades on Chichi Jima, as thick anti-aircraft fire greeted the planes as they headed towards the enemy shipping. While Commander Miller's and Lieutenant Jobe's gunners were busy pummeling approximately sixteen coastal vessels, Bridgeman spotted a 4,000-ton cargo ship in the harbor and pointed "Climbaboard" towards it as he began his bomb run.

The ship's gunners must have known they were the intended target, because they began to fire wildly back at the plane that was rapidly approaching. Tracers from enemy machine guns came whizzing past, and black puffs from anti-aircraft guns filled the sky around the plane. Closing in on the ship, Bridgeman released three 1,000 pound bombs. Japanese sailors standing on the deck looked at the plane passing overhead with their mouths wide open, staring in disbelief. The first bomb fell short, while the second and third bombs entered the water approximately 10 to 25 feet off the ship's stern. A moment later, Bridgeman was taken by surprise when the bombs detonated on impact without waiting for the four second delay. The ship, apparently carrying ammunition, seemed to disintegrate in an explosion of fire and smoke. Pieces of steel from the ship came sailing past the waist position, with some hitting the plane. It seemed like the whole world had blown up, as the explosion hurled the aircraft up some 1,000 feet. Out of control, "Climbaboard" started down towards the water. Bridgeman gained control just as the plane came down, skimming across the propellers not more than a foot above the ocean. The pilot leveled the PB4Y out, regained altitude, and headed back towards Saipan. The raid seemed

Twisted and bent, "Sky Cow" after crashing on take off from Eniwetok. *Courtesy of Robert Carey.*

to have taken hours, but the entire engagement over both islands had lasted only 20 minutes. Approximately 12 hours after taking off, the planes arrived back on Siapan with 30 gallons of gas left in their tanks.

Another strike was ordered the following day for Bonins and Iwo Jima, before the Japanese caught on to what was happening and strengthened their defense. In addition to the three crews which participated in the raid the day before, Lieutenant Jansehek would go along. On this mission, each plane would carry four 1,000 pound bombs in its belly and 2,400 gallons of gas. The mission was timed so that the aircraft would take-off shortly after noon and arrive at Chichi Jima at dusk. Then, as with the previous mission, they would hit Haha Jima. After attacking Haha Jima, the planes would finish by hitting Iwo Jima.

A little before noon on the 20th, the crews boarded their planes and began to taxi out for the mission. This time, all of the Army personnel working nearby stopped what they were doing and watched as the four Navy Liberators passed by. They were well aware of the loads each of the planes were carrying, and probably couldn't believe the crazy sailors were about to attempt such a mission. The four air crews on board the aircraft waved to the men lining the runway as the planes taxied by.

The four aircraft flew abreast of each other, except this time coming in from the northeast through a narrow corridor between Ani Jima and Chichi Jima. The first

Bill Bridgeman shows his glee after receiving a New J model Liberator. Note: His crew never flew the plane and it was transferred to VB-116. *Courtesy of Oden Sheppard.*

Japanese to spot them was a machine gunner on top of a hill right in front of Bridgeman's plane and at about the same elevation. Immediately, the enemy gunner started firing, and tracers passed by a foot-and-a-half over the tail turret. The tail gunner gave a short burst from the twin .50s, and the enemy gunner quit firing.

At the seaplane base at Omura, just as on the previous raid, enemy seaplanes were tied to their moorings with Japanese personnel trying to get them airborne. Coming over the seaplane base, an enemy 40mm antiaircraft gun zeroed in on Jobe's plane. Louis Paulukonis, in the bow turret, took a direct hit, and a big section of the turret was blown away. Jobe was sure that his gunner had been killed. Another shell hit the number three engine, then another hit the wing near the landing gear, and another one hit near the belly turret, wounding the gunner, Robert Sims. Jobe now had two wounded men on board and was flying a severely damaged aircraft. None of the men on the other three planes knew how bad off Jobe's plane was as they headed towards Haha Jima.

It was pitch dark as the four planes arrived over Haha Jima, and the anti-aircraft fire was thick and accurate as the Liberators swept over the shore bombing and strafing coastal vessels in the harbor. Suddenly, Jobe's plane got hit again as a shell tore through the flap on the starboard wing, and "Consolidated's Mistake" dropped out of formation. Jobe radioed Miller on his condition, apologized for having to drop out of formation, and said he was unable to continue to Iwo Jima. He jettisoned his shattered belly turret, climbed slowly to 8,500 feet, and headed the plane towards Saipan. The crews from the remaining three aircraft wished him the best of luck and prayed that he would make it back the 700 miles to Saipan in his crippled plane. Miller, with the remaining two air crews, set course for Iwo Jima.

On the way to Iwo Jima, the three Liberators ran into a band of thunderstorms and became separated; each plane was now on its own as they continued on to the target. Commander Miller reached Iwo Jima about ten minutes before Bridgeman, while Janeshek was still somewhere behind him. At that time, Bridgeman was unaware that Miller had already attacked the island and had worked it over pretty good, leaving the Japanese in an ugly mood.

It was dark and quiet when Lieutenant Bridgeman in "Climbaboard" came cruising into the harbor. Looking down and to the right of the tail turret, the gunner saw an enemy destroyer. The ship didn't fire, and neither did anyone on board the aircraft. Too late to drop his bombs, Bridgeman turned the plane around and headed back for the destroyer. The belly turret shouted over the intercom about a ship to starboard. Bridgeman banked the plane a little to the right, realized that they were now over the island, and ordered nobody to shoot.

"Climbaboard" flew over an enemy gun position, and they could clearly see the flames coming out of the engine exhaust under the wings. This made a beacon for them, and instantly three machine guns opened up on the plane. Rounds began hitting near the waist position and port wing. Without waiting for orders, the tail gunner began firing towards the gun emplacements. The tracers arched downward, and within a few seconds, the three gun positions ceased firing. When the first three machine guns opened up, every gun with varying calibers began firing towards the sky, but most of them were shooting wildly. Coming over an airfield, Bridgeman released the 1,000 pound bombs on the runway before heading over the water, encountering a barrage of thick anti-aircraft fire as he headed towards Saipan.

Bridgeman arrived at Saipan before the other two planes and, after parking, the crew climbed out and waited in the rain under the plane's wing for Jobe. Less than an hour later, Jobe nursed the damaged bomber in on the final approach, keeping the shot up wing a little higher than the other. When the plane touched down one of the main tires blew out, but somehow Jobe managed to keep control of the aircraft. Jobe cleared the runway, and soon Miller landed "Thundermug."

Two days later, Lieutenant Commander Janeshek and Lieutenant Bill Bridgeman returned to Eniwetok, temporarily retiring the advance echelon at Saipan. On the 21st, Commander Miller returned to Eniwetok with Lieutenant Jobe and his crew as passengers. Back at Eniwetok, Lieutenant Leo Kennedy crashed on take-off, and "Sky Cow," a plane with a Disney style cow painted on the fuselage, was destroyed, but none of the crew was injured.

10

Last Missions

By the end of July, allied air activity in the Central Pacific was largely confined to mopping up operations in the Marianas, nuisance raids on the Bonins, and regular neutralizing blows at Truk. Commander Miller paid Truk two farewell visits on the 27th and 29th. On the 27th, a 1,500-ton freighter was seriously damaged in a night masthead height attack, and a dozen Japanese LCTs huddled together in a boat pool were damaged by direct hits with three 1,000 pound bombs. Installations at Dublon, the airfield and seaplane base at Moen, Falo, and Mor Islands were also heavily strafed.

Returning at dawn on the 29th, on a mistaken report of enemy naval vessels present at Truk, Miller and Commander Donald G. Gumz, Commander of VB-116, took off from Stickell Field and reached their objective as they covered the lagoon at 50 to 200 feet altitude for 30 minutes. Entering the lagoon, the only shipping present were three small craft in the Dublon-Eten area of Truk, which were damaged by strafing.

After completing the bomb run, the planes were intercepted by a Nakajima Ki-43 "Oscar" and four Zekes southwest of Uligar Pass. For the next 30 minutes, the Oscar and one of the Zekes pursued the bombers and periodically closed for an attack. On the last run made by the Oscar, Lawrence B. Johnson, Miller's top turret gunner, and Henry F. Saligar AOM1c, Gumz's top turret gunner, scored hits on the fighter's belly. While the two top turret gunners were busy fighting off the Oscar, the Zeke made a frontal assault on the bombers, but took hits to its fuselage from Bernard R. Jaskiewicz, Miller's bow turret gunner. Making another run on the Liberators, the fighter took additional hits from Gilbert E. Downing, Gumz's tail turret gunner, and Robert Gariel, Miller's tail turret gunner. The fighters broke off their attack, and the two Liberators proceeded to Ponape.

Reaching their next objective, each Liberator dropped two 1,000 pound bombs on a military headquarters building and radio station at Ponape Town and installations on Langar Island. During the run, Miller's plane took accurate medium and heavy anti-aircraft fire, knocking out the hydraulic system, radio antenna, and interphone. With all bombs dropped and seeing that his plane had been damaged, Miller and Gumz left Ponape and headed back to base. Landing at Eniwetok, Miller found that the brakes would not work, and the plane ran off the end of the runway and into the water, smashing the nosegear and tearing off the bow turret. "Thundermug" was a complete loss, and it was towed by a bulldozer and dumped in the boneyard.

On the 29th Lieutenant Seabrook, followed a day later by Lieutenant Commander Hicks, re-established the advance echelon at Saipan by basing temporarily at the newly completed East Field. They were joined on 1 August by Lieutenant Commander Bundy and on the 3rd by Lieutenant Kasperson. East Field provided a 5,000-foot runway, and operations were easier despite a difficult approach over a mountain. Officers and men were still quartered in muddy tents in the cane field, but the food was good, and a floored Japanese hen-house served as squadron office and provided some additional protection from the frequent rain showers.

The squadron had been in commission a year on 2 August, and the event was celebrated at both Eniwetok and Saipan. At Eniwetok, VB-116 assumed all flights for the 3rd, allowing the squadron a night and day of relaxation. Enlisted personnel had an afternoon party at an adjacent island in the atoll, and Commander Forward Area was a guest of the officers for dinner. At Saipan, a Japanese pig, caught and barbecued by squadron personnel, was the feature of an informal celebration in the hen-house office.

The first week of August closed the squadron's active operations at Saipan. Orders were issued that Iwo Jima and Chichi Jima be struck on the 5th by Liberators of the 7th Army Air Force based at Saipan. The night strike, coming between two days of carrier strikes on the 4th and 5th, would deny the enemy uninterrupted hours to repair damaged air facilities and bring in new planes. When it became apparent, however, that Army Liberators would not be operating from Saipan until after 4 August, the Navy Liberators of VB-109, based on Saipan, assumed the mission. On the evening of the 4th, four PB4Ys of VB-109 took off singly from East Field, Saipan, in adverse weather conditions to heckle Iwo Jima and Chichi Jima. The plan called Lieutenant Commanders Hicks and Bundy to strike Iwo Jima, while Seabrook and Kasperson were to hit Chichi Jima.

Hicks took off for Iwo Jima and flew west of the Northern Marianas to a point 80 miles Northeast of Iwo Jima. Approaching the island, altitude was reduced from 1,500 to 500 feet, but the target was completely obscured. Rain squalls were numerous in the area, and the island was covered by thick cumulus clouds from the ground up to 20,000 feet. With almost zero visibility, Hicks could not distinguish the island on the initial pass, and six successive sweeps were made at 150 feet altitude before the shoreline was dimly glimpsed. Climbing to 6,000 feet, Hicks made a bombing run from the northeast to the southwest and dropped 23 100 pound bombs blindly over the center of the island. Continuing his passes at varying altitudes and from various directions, Hicks dropped ten bombs from 1,000 feet in the center of the island between the two airfields, with the island faintly visible through a temporary break in the clouds. No anti-aircraft fire was received, and Hicks left the area and returned to base.

Bundy took off for Iwo Jima an hour after Hicks and reached the target before Hicks. Iwo Jima was hidden in a rain squall on his initial approach, however, and he returned to orbit Minami Iwo Jima at 300 feet until the squall had passed. Flying back to Iwo Jima, approaches were made at altitudes from 500 to 2,000 feet without sighting the target.

A radar approach was made from the northwest at 50 to 100 feet altitude, and the island was crossed just north of the upper strip, the plane passing south of Osaka Yama and Moto Yama town. Thirty bombs were dropped in train from 50 feet, the first bomb being released just after the beach was crossed. No enemy fire was received until the bombs began to explode. The plane's gunners returned the awakening enemy fire, training on the revealed gun positions, but the encounter was brief due to the plane's speed.

Only moderate medium and light AA was received, but the blind protective fire of the enemy's 40mm guns scored hits on the plane's port vertical stabilizer, and the accessory section of the number two engine was struck by a round, which exploded inside, severing oil lines. A 20mm round went through the skin next to the feed box at the port waist hatch, exploding inside and starting a fire from oxygen bottles and ruptured ammunition. Bundy climbed to 1,300 feet, feathering number two engine, lightened the plane, and returned on three engines, landing at Isley Filed 10 hours later.

Lieutenant Seabrook took off 30 minutes after Commander Hicks for Chichi Jima, flying an almost direct course. The weather became increasingly poor as the plane neared the target, and Chichi Jima was hidden in a rain squall on the initial approach. Turning south to Haha Jima to check his position, Seabrook flew down Haha Jima, dropping 12 bombs from 7,000 feet with the island faintly visible. Returning to the east of Chichi Jima, Seabrooks' approach was made from the northeast at 9,000 feet over Omura town and Susaki air strip. Half the island was covered by heavy clouds, but the shore line and a small fire on a hill north of Omura were visible. Returning from the southwest at 6,000 feet, Seabrook dropped a salvo of 16 bombs on Omura town. No further bombs were dropped, but Seabrook continued to cross the island at varying altitudes and circled the area for an hour without any anti-aircraft fire being received.

Kasperson was the first plane to take-off, and he planned to reach Chichi Jima an hour before Seabrook. Hicks, taking off 20 minutes later, passed close to Kasperson about half way to the target. Kasperson's gunners were then test-firing their guns, and Hicks, thinking it was an enemy plane, began a run on the plane, breaking it when friendly identity was established. It was the last time anyone saw Kasperson's plane again.

An hour past his expected arrival at East Field, and when radio communication had not been established with the plane, Task Force 59 organized a very comprehensive search. Within two hours, a Dumbo plane of VH-1 was flying up Kasperson's assumed course, two regular PBM search planes had been diverted in their regular sweep to the northwest of Saipan, Carrier Task Group 58 had been informed and their planes requested to keep lookout, and ComSubPac had been notified to advise the lifeguard submarines. The destroyer U.S.S. *Prichett* was alerted and began to zig-zag on a northerly course from Saipan.

On the 6th, Hicks and Seabrook searched north and west of Chichi Jima and Iwo Jima, while the two special Dumbos and the U.S.S. *Prichett* continued the search between Saipan and the Kazan Islands. The following day, special searches of the Dumbo planes and the destroyer were reluctantly canceled, while regular PBM searches carried on. On the 8th, a final effort was made by Commander Gumz and Lieutenant Cervone of VB-116, who searched a triangular area west of Chichi and Iwo Jima without success. What happened to Lieutenant Kasperson's plane

"Thunder Mug" after running off the runway at Eniwetok after its hydraulics were shot out by flak during a raid on Puluwat. *Courtesy of Thomas Delahoussaye.*

remains a mystery. Possibly, the small fire spotted on a hill on Chichi Jima by Lieutenant Seabrook was the resting place of the lost Liberator—the victim of enemy fire. As with the two other squadron planes lost in previous months, what happened to Kasperson and his crew remains a mystery. Missions flown by VB-109 and her sister squadrons were quite different than the 1,000 plane missions flown over Europe. Flying alone over the ocean and enemy held territory, there were no eye witnesses when a Navy Liberator went down. The squadron lost three planes and their crews without ever knowing what happened to them, and, over half a century later, squadron veterans still wonder what happened to their friends.

On the morning of the 6th, six planes from VB-109 conducted an ambitious photographic and bombing strike on Truk in conjunction with eight PB4Y-1Ps of VD-4, two F7As and one F7B of the 86th Combat Mapping Squadron, six PB4Ys of VB-109, and seven PB4Ys of VB-116. Each VB-109 plane would carry 30 100 pound bombs, while VB-116 carried three 500 pound bombs and VD-4 carried ten 100 pound bombs. The mission was coordinated with an Army bombing strike by the Eleventh Bombing Group, with the strike scheduled to begin take off an hour before the Photo strike. Weather for the mission was doubtful, so it was determined to await the report of a VB-116 search plane on the weather enroute to Truk, causing a delay of an hour.

The first plane in the formation departed Eniwetok at eight-thirty in the morning and proceeded straight ahead for 15 minutes at 1,000 feet, then reversed course back towards the field.[1] Take-off was accomplished under difficult conditions, as a severe rain squall interrupted the interval of take-off between planes several times. The planes climbed to a cruising altitude of 8,000 feet and proceeded toward the target.

The weather from Eniwetok to Minto Reef was largely flown on instruments and it formation flying became difficult. The Army bombing strike was called off, and they returned to Eniwetok because of bad weather. At Minto Reef the weather became clear, and a climb to 20,500 feet was begun.

Approaching Truk, the planes began a gradual dive from 20,500 to 19,500 feet for the photo runs. Scattered clouds over the target didn't prevent obtaining good vertical coverage of all the main areas except Dublon by VD-4 as the photographic run commenced. The formation began dropping their bombs on targets falling on the flight lines of the photo runs. VD-4 scored 60 hits on the islands of Moen, Dublon, Eten, Param, Tol, and Ulalu. Barracks and an air strip on Param Island, shore installations on Dublon town and Eten airfield, and Dock installations on Tol Island were bombed and left on fire by VB-109. Dublon Town, barracks on Moen, buildings on the northwest tip of Tol Island and Tol Canal were hit by VB-116. As the formation completed its bombing run, it came under fighter attack.

Lieutenant Clark was attacked by one fighter between Fefan Island and South Pass within the atoll. Two fighters were observed flying on the port wing slightly above him out of gun range. One fighter slightly ahead and above flipped over on his back, made a frontal pass, then passed under to the starboard side. Harold E. Mittendorf in the belly turret fired 200 rounds at the plane and scored hits on the fuselage and wing. The fighter then went into a dive, but pulled out, apparently under control before going into a cloud. Lieutenant O'Brien was attacked by two fighters dropping three phosphorous bombs. One fighter made a run above at the bomber, and the bombs were released in a glide at 500 feet above and burst near the tail of the Liberator.

The section of six planes led by Lieutenant Mather bore the brunt of the fighter attack. The section approached the lagoon at Northeast Island and proceeded on flight lines over Param Island and the northwest tip of Dublon Island, where it was jumped by a dozen fighters. One fighter made a run on Mather with phosphorous bombs, then pulled up on the starboard side and retired. A second fighter attacked from 1,000 feet above Mather's plane, where he did a half roll, a split recovery, and dropped a bomb in a glide run.

Northwest of Tol Island one fighter made a high overhead run out of the sun from 7 o'clock, scoring three 20mm hits on Mather's plane. The fighter out of the sun was not observed by the gunners until it was too late for defensive action. One shell hit the horizontal stabilizer on the starboard side, while another hit the port wing just aft of the number two engine and forward of the leading edge of the flaps, tearing a large hole in the wing. A third shell entered the engine through the cowl flap opening and exploded in the air duct to the oil cooler, blowing shrapnel through the inboard side of the engine and piercing the fuselage in the radio compartment in six places, as well as the forward bomb bay, severing the throttle control cable to the engine.

Immediately upon being hit, the pilot feathered the engine and, without a supply of oxygen at 20,000 feet, the plane captain, Kenneth Gaddis, began the transfer of fuel, which prevented a fire. One fighter closed on the tail, and one from below, but both broke away before coming in to close range. Even after the Liberators left Truk, one persistent fighter followed this section for 55 minutes before finally giving up.

The second division was attacked by six fighters consisting of Zekes and Hamps. Lieutenant Tuttle's gunners scored hits on one fighter. One fighter started an attack from at the same level as the bomber, closed to 1500 feet, and then turned to starboard. His gunners reported hits on this fighter, which made a snap roll, then went into a dive straight down before being lost in cloud.

Two Zekes intercepted VB-116 and VB-109 planes just outside Truk Reef. One Zeke made a run on Lieutenant Graves' plane, reaching a position immediately beneath the bomb bay doors at which point the enemy fighter skidded to port. The port waist gunner, W.T. Logam, opened fire, scoring hits on the fuselage forward of the wings. Black smoke began pouring from the cowling, followed by flame. The enemy fighter went into a spin before it disappeared into a cloud. Lieutenant Anderson's plane was attacked by a Zeke, and his port waist gunner fired 75-100 rounds into the engine and wing roots. Black smoke began pouring out of the cowling and the starboard wing root, and the fighter went into a steep dive, disappearing in the clouds below. The remaining fighters lost their taste for battle and left the bombers, which all returned to Saipan.

The Saipan echelon was withdrawn on the 10th and returned to Eniwetok as VB-116 took over. Back on Eniwetok, the squadron continued with harassing strikes on bypassed islands, with Lieutenant Jobe bombing Ponape on the 8th and Ensign Mainfeldt following on the 10th, which resulted in the destruction of installations at a new airfield. Lieutenant Sheppard on the 10th and Lieutenant Commander Janeshek on the 14th made a night reconnaissance of Truk and bombed Ponape at low altitude. Ponape was a further target for Lieutenant Davis on the 12th and Lieutenant Keeling two days later. Wake was a target for Lieutenant Mellard at night on the 10th, Lieutenant Bridgeman at low altitude at night on the 12th, Lieutenant Warren during the day, and Lieutenant Glenn at night on the 14th.

Even as plans were being confirmed to move the squadron to base permanently on Tinian, three planes of VB-102 arrived at Eniwetok to relieve the squadron. On the 16th, Lieutenant Davis flew the last combat patrol of the squadron, and on the 18th, VB-102 formally relieved VB-109.

Between 14 and 18 August, the squadron returned from Eniwetok to Naval Air Station Kaneohe in three plane increments. With "Well Done's" from Commander

"Thunder Mug" after being moved to the boneyard on Eniwetok. *Courtesy of Oden Sheppard.*

Forward Area, Commander Air Force, Pacific Fleet, and Commander-in-Chief, U.S. Pacific Fleet, seven and a half months of operations in the combat zone came to an end, with many of the men wondering who stood up better, they or the aircraft. War-weary and battered, the stress of eight months of combat was reflected on both man and machine. Faded uniforms, bleached by the Pacific sun, the slim bodies of the men from months of an inadequate diet and the stress of combat were the outward physical signs of battle scarred veterans. Green irregular patches on the skin where damage from anti-aircraft fire had been repaired and the faded olive drab paint on the aircraft were the markings of machines that had been through hell.

Upon the squadron's arrival in Hawaii, the squadron was welcomed at Kaneohe by Rear Admiral John D. Price, USN, Commander Fleet Air Wing Two, and invited to rest and relax for five days before returning to the United States. The officers enjoyed the comforts of a private estate, and the enlisted crew members took full advantage of the facilities at the Royal Hawaiian Hotel at Waikiki. After eight months of combat, a considerable number of the enlisted men wanted to do what most Navy men dream of doing upon reaching port. However, the civilian population and the Navy Shore Patrol had a different perspective on how Navy personnel should act once in port, and a number of the squadron personnel had to be personally bailed out of jail by Commander Miller.

Considerably refreshed after their stay in Hawaii, the squadron departed for San Diego on 23 August and completed the movement by 12 September. Some of the squadron returned by ship aboard the S.S. *Sea Marlin*, but the majority returned by squadron aircraft. On 1 September the squadron became non-operational and inactive by orders from Commander Fleet Air, West Coast. Upon arriving in San Diego, personnel were screened rapidly, leave was granted, and new orders were issued. With all squadron personnel on leave pending re-forming, Lt (jg) Leland Russell, USNR, was appointed as temporary commander.

The squadron aircraft were transferred to Headquarters Squadron, Fleet Air Wing Fourteen, as rapidly as they entered the country. Too war-weary and battle scarred to see further combat, most of the Liberators were sent to training squadrons and, after the war, sold as scrap and melted down.

11

Reformation of VB-109 as VPB-109

In October, the squadron was redesignated as Patrol Bombing Squadron 109 according to a new Navy regulation and was reformed at Camp Kearney, California. This tour would be quite different than the last, since the squadron would not be flying ex-Army B-24 Liberators, but instead would have the new Consolidated Vultee PB4Y-2 Privateer, an aircraft specifically designed for the Navy's need for a long-range patrol plane.

On 6 December Lieutenant Commander Hicks, former Executive Officer of VB-109, assumed command of the squadron, with Lieutenant Commander Bundy as Executive Officer. Due to the lack of aircraft and experienced flight crews, it was determined not to form permanent flight crews until the deficiencies were corrected. Former crews of VB-109, however, were left intact insofar as their experience allowed.

While waiting for the squadron to reach full strength, all personnel attended a two week gunnery refresher course and a one week radio refresher course at North Island Naval Air Station. Additionally, each flight crew attended a sixteen hour course given by the Advanced Base Air Training Unit over the fuel system, ignition, structure, radio, and operational functions of the PB4Y-2 Privateer.

By the end of December, the first three PB4Y-2s were transferred to the squadron from Fleet Air Wing 14. Although constant shifting of crews took place in an effort to use experienced personnel to the best advantage, the air training program progressed fairly rapidly. Flights were scheduled to enable each crew to become an integral and coordinated working unit as rapidly as possible, with flights consisting of high and low level bombing, strafing, and sleeve gunnery runs. For the last two months of training, at least one fleet problem per week was conducted consisting of simulated attacks on carriers, battleships, cruisers, and destroyer squadrons. Exercises in fighter tactics were conducted in conjunction with Navy and Marine air groups and squadrons stationed in the San Diego area. In conjunction with this training phase, captured Japanese Zekes were used to train flight crews in evasive action against enemy fighters. Each crew completed the Anti-Submarine Warfare Training Program, consisting of one week of ground lectures and twelve hours of bombing, simulated attacks on a live submarine, flare attacks, and live depth-charge drops.

It was not until the final weeks of training that sufficient personnel were available in the squadron to bring the authorized complement to full strength. VPB-109, among the last of the PB4Y-2 squadrons to be formed, suffered greatly from the drain on trained crews. Five complete crews, three with inexperienced co-pilots, were sent to the squadron solely to check out as Patrol Plane Commanders before being assigned to other combat units in the Pacific. Additionally, operational aircraft were not made available to the squadron in sufficient numbers, nor were combat planes obtained in sufficient time to allow proper acceptance or run-in time before departing to Hawaii.

Through January 1945, while less than one half of the combat planes had been assigned, more than seventy percent of the training program had already been completed. Toward the end of the month, all training flights were suspended while planes were made ready for simulated flights to Hawaii. Once these flights were completed, the planes were prepped for their flight, and Commander Hicks gave the men a few days shore-leave before departure.

Profile of a PB4Y-2 Privateer belonging to the squadron possibly taken on Okinawa. *Courtesy of Roy Balke.*

On 30 January, the ground echelon of the squadron left for Pearl Harbor aboard the carrier U.S.S. *Fanshaw Bay* (CVE-70), and on 11 February, planes began the movement from Camp Kearney to Kaneohe, Hawaii. The planes left in increments of three on alternate days and, with the exception of one new plane delayed for a staff inspection trip, the entire squadron movement was completed by 16 February. A tentative readiness date of 1 April had been set for the squadron's departure for the war zone, and, from a training and operational viewpoint, the squadron was ready.

Even before all of the squadron had arrived, training in Hawaii began with glide, night, and radar bombing runs on small island targets. Miniature bombs were dropped on a buoy target in radar bombing, and five radar flights were made on the islands. Crews were checked out in the use of Radar Counter Measure equipment, as all squadron planes were equipped with the gear, which gave early warning of enemy war vessels.

Early in March the squadron learned officially that it had been designated as one of three (the other two being VPB-123 and VPB-124) Privateer squadrons to be equipped with the radar-controlled bomb SWOD Mk-9 (Special Weapons Ordnance Device), designated as the "Bat," which described its homing mechanism.[1]

A late development of the discarded "Pelican" missile program, which was terminated in the Fall of 1944, the Bat was a plywood glider shell, enclosing a one thousand pound general purpose bomb. One was to be suspended under each wing outboard of the engines, both units being centrally controlled within the plane until

The SWOD MK-9 "Bat" air to ground guided missile on a cart. *Courtesy of the National Archives.*

individual radars in the aircraft were locked on given targets for directional homing.[2]

On 17 March, Lieutenant Commander Otho E. McCrackin, USNR, reported for temporary duty from the Bureau of Ordnance, bringing the complete details and the operational possibilities of the Bat program. He was followed shortly by Lieutenants Francis A. Wilhelm, USNR, Hamilton H. Mann, USNR, Carlton F. Shaffer, USNR, and four civilian technicians, Field Engineers Willard O. J. Conrad, Louis H. Powell, Franklin C. McCoy, and Perry R. Stout. On 2 April, twenty-two trained enlisted personnel arrived at Kaneohe with the first of the Bat equipment.

Scheduled to arrive at Pearl Harbor before 1 April, the weapon's assembles and equipment actually reached Kaneohe three days later, and Hedron undertook the installations under the direction of the "Bat men." The Bat men worked night and day and pushed Hedron to maintain the pace, and, by 7 April, three of the squadron planes were equipped with the system.

The flight personnel who would be operating the system were briefly indoctrinated, and practice drops were made against a spar target for representatives of Commander Air Force, Pacific Fleet, and Commander Fleet Air Wing Two. The drops were not impressive against the target, but indicated the weapon might be of some use against shipping.

Having delayed departure for the forward area ten days to permit installation of the Bats and elementary training in its use, Lieutenant Commander Hicks and the first three planes of the squadron left Kaneohe on 10 April for Palawan, Philippine Islands, transporting, in addition to all squadron gear and personnel, the only supply of Bats and the Bat men.

12

Palawan, Philippines

On 14 April, the first three squadron planes piloted by Lieutenant Commander Hicks, Lieutenant Donald Chay, and Lieutenant Leo Kennedy, each carrying Bats under their wings, reported for duty to the Commander Seventh Fleet on the island of Samar in the Philippines. On arrival, Commander Hicks was informed that Westbrook Field at Puerto Princessa, Palawan, was not ready to receive the squadron. Planes were delayed for five days before moving to Palawan and beginning operations under Fleet Air Wing Ten.

Palawan is the fifth largest island in the Philippine archipelago, lying between the China and Sulu Seas, and extends 270 miles northeast to southwest, reaching a maximum width of 24 miles. General McArthur wanted Palawan as a base to extend airpower to the South China Sea and the Dutch East Indies. On 28 February 1945, the 41st Division's 186th Regimental Combat Team went ashore, and on April 22 the island was secured.[1]

Arriving at their designation, VPB-109 found there were no accommodations, and squadron personnel had to clear their own campsites and pitch their own tents before reloading the planes for operations the following day. The camp was located on a coconut palm plantation on the beach and was sufficiently removed from the airstrip to eliminate some of the confusion and turmoil of construction. Enlisted men slept nine to a tent, and officers five to seven. There was no flooring available and no electric lights, but showers had been erected, a necessity in the heat and dirt of the Philippines. For recreation, there was the adjacent beach for swimming and the inevitable lure of shell-gathering, but personnel were too busy with maintaining a heavy operational schedule to indulge greatly in recreational activities.

Westbrook Field's 5,000-foot runway, part Marston mat, part unrolled coral, was extremely narrow, not more than 100 feet wide, and did not stand up under the constant traffic of Army B-24s, B-25s and P-38s. With only one entrance to the taxi lane from the strip, all landings were made down wind to alleviate taxiing back the full length of the strip. The field was closed from sunset to sunrise, and late-returning planes landed only with special permission and after considerable delay. Fully loaded with a Bat under each wing, a Privateer could just stagger off the runway.

Search sectors from Palawan varied from 850 to 1,000 miles in length, covering the west coast of the Celebes, eastern and western Borneo, the coast of Malay from Singapore to the Gulf of Siam, and south to Indo-China. Commander Hicks soon found out that a duel chain of command of Army and Navy superiors often gave conflicting orders which would, on several occasions, result in hopeless bewilderment.

On the 23rd, Commander Hicks and Lieutenant Kennedy conducted the squadron's first strike. With each plane carrying a Bat under their wings, they headed for Japanese shipping anchored in Balikpapan Harbor on the southeast coast of Borneo, 700 miles from Palawan. Fifteen miles from the harbor, a large transport, a 4,000-ton freighter, and five smaller merchant vessels in the 300 to 850-ton range were sighted. From six miles out and at 10,000 feet, both pilots launched a Bat.

Attack on a small coastal vessel along Malayan Coast. *Courtesy of the National Archives.*

Both weapons traveled erratically and fell short of their intended targets. Due to the weight of the weapon system, the Privateers could not carry a conventional bomb load. Not wishing to try strafing attacks on the shipping, the Privateers headed back to Palawan.

For the next two days, Japanese radio and radar stations along the Borneo and Malay coasts provided the most popular bombing targets for squadron planes. As Commander Hicks and Lieutenant Kennedy were attacking Balikpapan Harbor, Lieutenant (jg) Oscar Braddock destroyed radio stations at Tambelan Island and South Natoena Island. On the 25th, Lieutenant Thomas Challis damaged both a radio and a radio-radar station on Tambelan Island, while Lieutenant Joseph Jadin damaged a radio station at Cape Paroepoe. Lieutenant Floyd Hewitt hit a radar station on Baican Island the following day, and Lieutenant Robert Vadnais destroyed a look-out station at Djemadja Island. On the 27th, Lieutenant Commander Bundy damaged lookout towers at Mapoeti Island, and Lieutenant John Keeling, ferreting Balikpapan, damaged a radar tower at Kabaladoea.

Lieutenant Jobe, flying 850 miles down the west coast of Borneo, at Brunei Bay, planned to attack a 5,000-ton transport beached off Labuan Island at the mouth of the bay and used by the Japanese as a flak ship. Using cloud cover at 800 feet in

Japanese ship being attacked by plane from FAW-1 off Korea April 1945. *Courtesy of the National Archives.*

his approach, he dived low over a protective peninsula on Labuan Island and made a bombing run on the flak ship.

Coming in at 150 feet altitude across the ship's starboard beam, the plane received light anti-aircraft fire from a 7.7mm machine gun and took two small bullet holes to an engine cowling. Crossing over the ship, he dropped one 250 pound bomb and three 100 pound bombs. The flak ship disappeared under a cloud of smoke and flying debris as the bombs exploded close to the ship's hull.

Continuing the search at 1,000 feet, the co-pilot spotted a radar station consisting of two buildings at Mukah on the southwestern Borneo coast. The Privateer descended to 200 feet and made one strafing attack on the installations. Both buildings were left smoking after the Privateer's gunners fired 600 rounds into them.

Two hours later, Lieutenant Jobe sighted a 100-ton freighter off of Temadjoe Island. His gunners left it smoking and dead in the water after strafing it with 3,800 rounds of ammunition. Four crew members abandoned ship by jumping into the water, only to become the targets of the Privateer's gunners. The men were quickly killed by a short burst from the plane's starboard gun turret.

Fifty minutes after leaving the damaged freighter, the navigator spotted a small 30-ton cargo boat off of Pandjang from the astro-dome. The boat was moving slowly as the Privateer circled from 400 feet. Aiming at the boat's water line, Lieutenant Jobe's gunners sank the vessel within minutes.

Not content on leaving a damaged freighter, Lieutenant Jobe returned to it and circled eight times as his gunners strafed it with 400 rounds of ammunition. Running short on fuel and ammunition, he finally broke off the engagement without sinking the ship.

On the 28th, in the early afternoon, Commander Hicks and Lieutenant Chay, each plane carrying two Bats, made another shipping strike at Balikpapan Harbor, picking out a large transport at anchor in the harbor. A Bat was released nine miles from the target from an altitude of 10,500 feet.

Hick's Bat traveled true, but struck a 800-ton freighter tied up to a dock at the Pandanseri oil refinery a mile short of the transport. The missile hit the smaller ship and blew it to pieces, and with it part of the dock. He tried to release the second missile, but it malfunctioned electronically and it was not released.

Lieutenant Chay targeted the same transport and released his Bat. The weapon locked onto a small 100-ton picket boat at anchor for a direct hit, and the ship was sunk. Releasing his second Bat at the same altitude from seven miles away, it made a 45 degree turn and followed a larger radar blip of Pandanseri oil refinery at Balikpapan and scored a direct hit on a large oil storage tank, three miles short of his intended target.

Lieutenant Clifton Davis, while searching the northeastern Malay coast in the early afternoon, was at 1,500 feet when his co-pilot spotted an 80-foot tug boat three miles away at a speed of eight knots. Lieutenant Davis reduced his altitude to

100 feet and circled wide in a power glide. During the first of three strafing runs, the tug was set afire before sinking rapidly by the stern, and personnel abandoning ship were strafed in the water, leaving no survivors. Continuing his patrol along the coast to the north at 70 feet, the starboard turret gunner sighted a 100-ton picket boat camouflaged with vegetation with its deck loaded with fuel drums.

After two strafing runs, Lieutenant Davis initiated a bombing run and dropped three 100 pound bombs along the length of the ship. All bombs missed, but the ship was left afire and moving erratically from the strafing attacks.

Lieutenant Kennedy, also on patrol along the Malay coast, sighted a small motor barge off Setju. On the only run, Kennedy dropped two 100 pound bombs, with one hitting the target amidships. The motorbarge split in two and sank within 20 seconds. Ten minutes later, three 40-foot sailboats were spotted and were strafed in passing, leaving one afire.

On the 29th, Lieutenant Howard Turner reconnoitered the west coast of Borneo. Six hours into the search, a 70-ton steel deck coastal vessel was spotted. Crossing over the boat from starboard to port, Lieutenant Turner released a bomb that went over and missed the target by 50 feet. The launch was thoroughly strafed and began to burn at the stern. The attack was broken off when one of his waist turret gunners

A Privateer from VPB-109 attacking two coastal vessels along the Malayan Coast. *Courtesy of the National Archives.*

sighted a 100-ton freighter three miles away. From an altitude of 500 feet, Turner's gunners began strafing it, and the ship caught fire, which rapidly spread and grew more intense. The freighter stopped dead in the water and had been abandoned by its personnel after the first run. The ship was strafed four more times and began burning furiously before finally sinking.

After only a week at Palawan, it was obvious that no worthwhile shipping was located in the routine search areas to warrant Bat attacks. Having been sunk or driven into areas beyond the range of squadron aircraft, the only possible targets for such attacks were against landlocked ships, which presented problems because of the weapon's target selectivity. Bat tactics were not successful because of the weapon's difficulty in detecting the exact target from long range, or when there

Lieutenant Floyd Hewitt and Crew 13's, "Sleepy-Time Gal." *Courtesy of Roy Balke.*

were multiple radar targets at the same range. The device would automatically shift its homing to the best target at the set range. It was also apparent that the only shipping left were the small, mostly wooden hulled coastal vessels (70 to 100 tons) which hugged the Malay and Borneo coasts. Borneo, which had supplied Japan's military with 40 percent of its oil, was rapidly being cut off by allied air and naval forces, and, on 1 May, the invasion of Borneo began with landings by the Australian 7th and 9th Infantry Divisions at Tarakan Island on the northeastern coast.[2]

By the beginning of May, the squadron had settled down in their home on Palawan, with some personnel having enough time for taking up the recreational hobby of painting nose art on their planes, with some emblazoned with nude or semi-nude women. By the time they left Palawan for Okinawa, most of the planes were decorated. Lieutenant Wilkinson's plane seemed to stand out the most with the name "Punkie" with a large nude blond covering the fuselage from cockpit to the nose wheel, while Lieutenant Challis' plane "Green Cherries" sported a tall statuesque brunette. Lieutenant Jobe decided to name his plane "Consolidated Mistake II" in respect of his old Liberator, which had served him so well in the Central

Lieutenant Howard Turner's Crew 2 had the lovely "Shanghai Lil." *Courtesy of Roy Balke.*

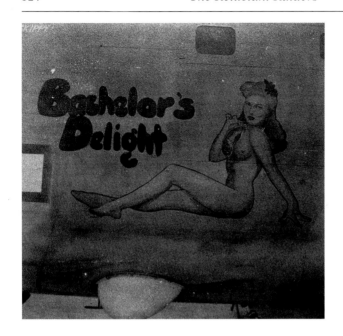

"Bachelor's Delight" went down with Lieutenant John Keeling and his crew during the last week of the war. *Courtesy of Roy Balke.*

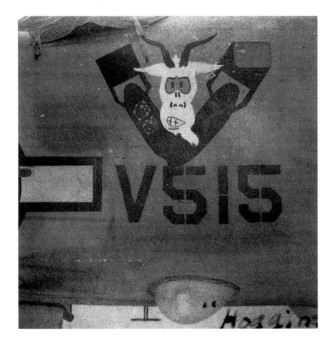

"Hogan's Goat" belonged to Lieutenant G.D. Fairbanks and Crew 7. *Courtesy of Roy Balke.*

Commander George Hicks' "Lambaster." *Courtesy of Roy Balke.*

Lieutenant William Warren and Crew 12's, "Blind Bomber." *Courtesy of Roy Balke.*

Pacific. Other Privateers in the squadron were Commander Hicks' "Lambaster," Lieutenant Turner's "Shanghai Lil," Lieutenant Jadin's "Miss Lotta Tail," Lieutenant Keeling's "Bachelor's Delight," Lieutenant Fairbank's "Hogan's Goat," and Lieutenant Warren's "Blind Bomber."

Between the recreational activities of painting nose art, the squadron continued with their searches. Lieutenant Davis, searching along the Makassar Strait in the western Celebes on 1 May, was at the end of his sector when he sighted a 60-foot motor launch. As he initiated a run at 500 feet, light and medium AA from the shore and from islands in the harbor caught him in a cross fire and hit the plane on the vertical and horizontal stabilizers. Breaking off the run on the launch, he flew close along the islands in the harbor to silence the enemy gun positions. Three gun positions at Madara Bay and in the town area were heavily strafed and silenced.

Circling inland, a second run on the launch was begun from over the hills behind the town. At 150 feet altitude, he crossed over the boat and dropped three 100 and one 250 pound bombs. All four bombs missed, with the last one hitting the water 25 feet beyond the boat. The launch began to sink rapidly by the stern and was well down when last observed. Still coming under anti-aircraft fire, he made two runs over the town and island area, which resulted in more gun positions being silenced and one supply building in a group of four set afire. Continuing north up the coast at 5,000 feet, five 100-ton freighters were sighted at anchor.

Part of Lieutenant Joseph Jadin's Crew 5 in front of "Miss Lotta Tail." L-R. Isadore Smith, Cecil Lee, Ned Jones, Emory Peterman, Ray Grover, and Roy Balke. *Courtesy of Roy Balke.*

Diving down to 50 feet, Lieutenant Davis' gunners began strafing the ships. One freighter burned to the water line and sank. Another was set afire, raced for the shore, beached itself, and was abandoned by its personnel, while three others were slightly damaged. Short on fuel and ammunition, Davis was forced to break off the attack and returned to Palawan.

On the same day, Lieutenant Braddock, following the Kapacas River in Western Borneo in a southeasterly direction, spotted a small 70-foot wooden lugger. The boat was canvas-covered with vegetation, painted white, and heading up stream. Braddock circled as his gunners strafed before making a bombing run. The craft tried to take evasive action by heading to the river bank just as a 100 pound bomb was released. A direct hit amidships caused the lugger to immediately blow up and sink, leaving a number of bodies floating on the river. Braddock left the area and headed for the river mouth.

At the river's mouth, a 100-ton picket boat and a 300-ton fuel barge were spotted tied up to the bank. At 50 feet altitude, Braddock conducted three strafing and bombing runs. Both craft were heavily strafed and set afire, and the picket boat took a direct hit from a 250 pound bomb. Both burned completely to the waterline before sinking. Flying on a southeasterly heading, a slow moving 300-ton ship was found off the coast. After releasing a 250 pound bomb which failed to explode, the ship was strafed and left burning and sinking.

In the early afternoon, Lieutenant (jg) George Serbin, covering the eastern Malayan coast from Merchang to Kota Bharu, sighted seven freighters at anchor

The most elaborate nose art in the squadron was Lieutenant Hugh Wilkinsons and Crew 15's, "Punkie." *Courtesy of Roy Balke.*

off Redang Island and some other shipping beyond shortly identified as one destroyer and one escort. Selecting a freighter as a target, Lieutenant Serbin at 500
feet was about to initiate a bombing run when his port waist gunner sighted a twin-
engine Mitsubishi Ki-46 "Dinah" six miles away at 1,200 feet. Serbin abandoned
the bombing run in favor of attacking the Dinah, which had now closed to three
miles away and was on a collision course with the Privateer. As he was turning
towards the Dinah, he sighted a Jake seven miles away over Redang Island.

Serbin pulled up to port, turning inside the Dinah. As the planes met head on,
Serbin's bow turret gunner opened fire at 150 feet and hit the Dinah's port engine
nacelle, drawing smoke. As the planes passed each other, the Privateer's number
one top turret gunner opened fire with his MK18 sight set at 40 feet and scored hits
on the Dinah's nose and starboard engine nacelle, which began to smoke, while the
number two top turret gunner raked the entire length of the Dinah's fuselage. As the
Dinah went past his position, the port waist turret gunner concentrated on the Dinah's
port engine as the tail turret gunner raked the plane's cockpit. The Dinah's bomb-
bay doors opened and a 500 pound bomb was jettisoned just as the Dinah dove
straight into the sea and exploded.

Having completed a 360 degree turn following the Dinah's destruction, Lieutenant Serbin turned toward the Jake that was moving in to look at the remains of
the Dinah. The Privateer was at 500 feet, the Jake at 350 feet, and, as the PB4Y-2
began the chase, the Jake jinked once or twice and then ran, firing out of range with
its 20mm cannon.

The Privateer rapidly overhauled the Jake, and the bow turret gunner fired one
burst out of range, and then held his fire until the Jake was but 300 feet away. He
opened up, hitting the wing roots and both sides of the fuselage. Lieutenant Serbin
chopped the throttles back as he caught up and passed over the Jake, which was
already afire. As the PB4Y-2 passed, the Jake pulled up, and the number one top
turret guns raked its port fuselage as the number two top turret guns scored hits
along the fuselage, and floats and the starboard waist gunner concentrated on the
cockpit and engine fuselage. Stalling out, the Jake plunged straight into the sea in a
vertical dive. As the plane hit the water, the parachute of the rear gunner streamed,
but was pulled under with the wreckage. Both encounters with the Japanese planes
had taken less than seven minutes. Short on fuel, Lieutenant Serbin left the area
despite the presence of shipping he had spotted earlier off of Redang Island.

Lieutenant Moyer had a busy day on the 3rd in northeastern Borneo when he
destroyed a pier at Kudat Bay, sank a river steamer on the Mahakam River, destroyed a sawmill at Tanahorogot near Balikpapan, and then bombed and strafed a
railroad train, destroying the engine and three oil-tank cars.

Lieutenant Chay had searched 900 miles down the Celebes coast before returning up the east coast of Borneo and to Makassar Harbor. In the harbor, he found two

100-ton freighters, a 300 to 800-ton freighter, a 4,000-ton transport, and a destroyer escort camouflaged and tied up at a pier.

Selecting one of the small freighters as a target, Chay made three runs over the ship at 100 feet. While his gunners laid down suppressing fire on the ship's gun crew during the runs, silencing one 20mm gun, Chay dropped two 100 pound napalm and one general purpose bombs. The second napalm was a direct hit, and the ship was left afire. Upon completion of the second attack and while withdrawing from the target the plane took hits from anti-aircraft fire. One 20 mm round hit the starboard wing and flap, which exploded inside the wing. Another hit the nose wheel compartment and exploded inside.

The absence of worthwhile targets caused some pilots to extend their search sectors. Lieutenant Vadnais extended his search along the west coast of Borneo to investigate Pangdangikar and Pontianak Harbors, an extension that proved to be a gunners' field day when he found a series of shipyards and newly completed coastal freighters at Pontianak, Borneo. Following a marked ship channel from Pontianak Bay and leading up the Kapoeas-Kegil River, the pilot sighted two coastals in a stream at anchor a half mile away on his starboard and a mile below the town. He immediately initiated a run on the ships at 50 feet altitude and dropped one AN 47-A2 depth bomb. The bomb missed, but, after completing two more runs on the ships, one of them burned to the waterline, and personnel abandoning the ships

Lieutenant (jg) George Serbin's bow turret gunner shoots down a "Jake" Note flames coming from engine nacelle. *Courtesy of the National Archives.*

were decimated by his gunners' strafing. Circling to starboard upon completion of the run, and passing over a shipyard and lumberyard on the north bank of the river, he sighted more shipping upstream.

The Privateer headed upstream 20 feet off the water, strafing a two-masted 60-foot schooner and setting it ablaze. As it passed, shipyards were observed along the north bank, with numerous shipping around the intersection of the river and a canal. Two coastals at anchor near the intersection were attacked and left afire from heavy strafing. Continuing upstream past two shipyards on the north bank and seven coastals anchored further upstream, Lieutenant Vadnais made figure eight runs over the area for the next half hour. A shipyard just west of the intersection and containing 4 ways, each with a coastal, was set afire by bombing and strafing and was completely destroyed. Six power launches tied up at the yard blazed from strafing and burned to the water line and sank. Further upstream, one large shipyard upstream from the intersection was heavily and repeatedly strafed during five runs, and an ensuing fire consumed a quarter of the yard and installations before the plane left the area.

The plane returned to the river and canal intersection to attack three coastals anchored in the stream. During five strafing runs, his gunners started fires which gutted and sank all three ships. Shortages of fuel and ammunition forced Lieuten-

Lieutenant Vadnais finds a boatyard along the Kapoeas-Kegil River in Borneo and destroys it. *Courtesy of the National Archives.*

ant Vadnais to break off the attack despite leaving an estimated 25 coastals and two more shipyards untouched.

The 5th proved to be a costly day for the squadron when Lieutenant Commander Bundy started for Pontianak, delaying to strike at Jesselton Field along the coast enroute. After making a strafing run on an airfield near Papar, Borneo, Bundy followed railroad tracks at 200 feet and flew over a bridge that had AA guns guarding it. The guns opened up, and the plane was hit, and critically wounded Bundy. The co-pilot, Ensign Leslie F. Hunt, and Lieutenant Ted Steele, the squadron's Intelligence Officer, were superficially wounded. Hunt immediately took control and headed for home. Because the hydraulics had been shot out, the plane captain, Alvin O'Brien, activated the plane's emergency system by rigging a parachute to help stop the plane as it landed back at Palawan. On a separate mission, Lieutenant Turner, preparing to attack shipping at Parepare Bay in the Celebes, also encountered accurate AA, which killed his plane captain, Joe W. Kasperlik.

Lieutenant Jobe ended the strikes at Pontianak, Borneo, with the successful destruction of four coastals cruising close together. Jobe made three strafing and bombing runs. On his first run at 100 feet, he dropped a one hundred pound general purpose bomb and a 100 pound incendiary, but both fell short. On the second and third runs, Jobe scored two direct hits by incendiary bombs. All craft caught fire and burned to the water line. Another coastal was spotted and, during the strafing run, the vessel caught fire and exploded almost immediately. Another one, apparently beached, but camouflaged, was sighted from 800 feet, and one strafing run was made, inflicting slight damage. Crossing over land, a 4,500-foot grass airstrip was spotted with a Dinah parked at the north center of airfield. Coming in from east to west the Dinah was strafed, and repeated hits set it brilliantly afire.

Jobe finished his strike by attacking enemy shipping at Pontianak shipyard. Approaching the shipyard, six 100-ton coastals were sighted in various stages of outfitting. Bombing at 100 feet, two 100 pounders were dropped 20 feet short of one vessel, setting it afire. Three other coastals were heavily and repeatedly strafed and also burned. The following day, the squadron was relived by VPB-106 and ordered to Okinawa.

From the outset it had been obvious that no worthwhile shipping targets were to be found short of Singapore, and the weight of the Bats prevented such strikes. It was, therefore, expected that the squadron would shortly be moved into more productive areas to test the Bat's effectiveness. Small shipping and radar stations had improved the squadron's low-level bombing tactics. In only 15 days of operations from Palawan, the squadron had sunk or damaged 98 ships. The Philippine days had been an operational shake-down, and the squadron looked to Okinawa and its proximity to the Japanese homeland for more worthwhile targets.

13

Okinawa

The first three planes of the squadron reached Yontan Field, Okinawa, on 10 May and reported to Rear Admiral John D. Price, Commander Fleet Air Wing One for duty in the Fifth Fleet. Already based on the island was VPB-118, a sister squadron of VPB-109.

Okinawa, only 350 miles southwest of Tokyo, was invaded the month before under the code-name Operation Iceberg on 1 April, and the island would not be declared secured until 3 July. It became the bloodiest land battle of the Pacific War with some 110,000 Japanese killed and another 10,755 taken prisoner during the 83 day struggle for the island. The invasion would cost the United States Navy 34 vessels and craft and 368 damaged, with the loss of 4,900 sailors killed, while the Army would lose 7,613.

Although conditions were far more primitive than at Palawan, there was far less confusion and turmoil. The runways, already five thousand feet in length, were being rapidly extended. With a good field and a simplified chain of command, which understood search plane capabilities and possibilities, operations were simplified from the beginning.

PB4Y-2 maintenance facilities were available for servicing only a squadron echelon instead of the two squadrons based at Okinawa. VPB-118 had preceded VPB-109, but were forced to retire to Tinian when 109 arrived for service and repair. Living facilities were equally strained, and the squadron flew in its own tents, cots, and equipment from Tinian.

Foxholes were a necessity at Yontan. Nightly at sunset came the first alert, followed frequently by actual enemy air raids. The Japanese were largely accurate in their bombing, even from altitude, and bombs invariably struck the airfield. Loss of sleep occasioned by the foxhole life and the loss of evening hours for work or personal relaxation were major irritations for the squadron. Operationally, the nightly alerts forced all patrol flights into daylight hours because the planes could not be serviced, gassed, or taken off during an alert. Similarly, all flights returned before dark to avoid mix-ups with the numerous bogeys and the 5th Fleet's propensity to fire at anything with wings after dark.

Patrols were short but full, consisting of two to six plane patrols to ferret the southern and eastern coasts of Korea, the west coast of Kyushu, Shimono and Kamino Shima, Goto Retto, and Saishu To of Japan. Such flights were largely anti-shipping, and special anti-shipping strikes were permitted wherever the hunting seemed best. Encounters with enemy planes became more frequent as the squadron skirted the Japanese mainland. Strikes began on the 12th with a two plane search along the west coast of Kyushu up into the Tsushima Strait.

Lieutenant Chay and Lieutenant W.N. Loyld of VPB-118 were off Shimono Shima when the planes came across a 3,000-ton freighter. Turning in to attack, Chay's gunners began strafing the ship as Lloyd began a bombing run. Chay's gunners concentrated their fire on a 20mm gun on the bow and a 40mm gun on the stern. Coming in at 100 feet from stern to bow, Lloyd dropped two 500 pounders which fell short near the stern. The whole aft section of the ship lifted out of the water, sending up debris and oily water as the ship went dead in the water.

While Chay made a curving strafing run along the ship, Lloyd made another run on the ship, this time from port to starboard. Anti-aircraft fire became intense, with a 40 mm firing a steady stream at the attacking plane. As Lloyd approached, the plane took several hits to the wings and fuselage. Under the intensifying fire, Lloyd's second run resulted in two near misses with two 500 pounders. The ship got underway and began moving slowly in a circle, as if the steering gear had been damaged. Once more Lloyd and Chay coordinated a run. The ship's gunners con-

"Miss Lotta Tail" preparing for take-off. *Courtesy of Roy Balke.*

centrated on the bombing plane, and their fire became more intense and accurate. Lloyd continued on his run even though the plane was being bracketed by the defensive fire, with the plane taking hits to the bow, wings, fuselage, and waist turrets. Lloyd dropped four 100 pounders in a string from stern to bow, and the ship disappeared as a cascade of water came crashing down on the decks. The Privateer's number two engine failed as he pulled out of the bombing run, but the pilot feathered the prop and turned for home on three engines, with Chay flying close to him.

Minutes after leaving the freighter, the Privateers were intercepted by three enemy fighters. The fighters proved to be unaggressive, as the patrol plane's gunners' fire drove them away after firing a few short bursts. After 45 minutes the fighters broke off and left. Lloyd landed at Yonton, and upon inspecting his ship, counted 80 holes in his plane caused by the freighter's gunfire.

On the 13th, Commander Hicks assumed command of Yontan Search and Bombardment Group, relieving Lieutenant Commander Arthur Farwell of VPB-118. The same day, Commander Hicks joined with Lieutenant Commander E.G. Binning of VPB-118 on a search northward from Yonton to the Southern coast of Korea.

Off the Korean coast, four large merchant ships were sighted. While Binning conducted bombing and strafing runs on three smaller ships, Hicks made a Bat

View showing service crew on the tail section of a Privateer taken on Okinawa. *Courtesy of the National Archives.*

attack against a 2,000-ton freighter. The first missile was launched from eight miles out and at 4,000 feet altitude. The missile traveled true, but hit the water 20 feet ahead of the ship's bow. The bow was raised out of the water by the explosion, but it failed to sink her. Hicks began strafing the vessel and was shortly joined by the other plane. Steam began pouring out around the superstructure, followed by fire and smoke, and the ship was left burning briskly and dead in the water as the two planes headed home.

The Bat men struggled with overwhelming difficulties. The Bats had been flown through two typhoons with subsequent warping and deterioration. They had been assembled and disassembled numerous times, stacked in the hot sun and dust of the Philippines, and left unprotected in the mud and mold of Okinawa. No test equipment was available, and it is a tribute to the perseverance and untiring energy of the men that the weapon managed even negative results.

The Japanese hit Yonton Field during the nights of the 10th and 12th, but failed to damage squadron equipment. However, on a raid on the 14th a squadron plane was damaged and considerably shook up squadron personnel working on the field. Accurate bombing during one of five raids on the night of the 18th destroyed one squadron plane and badly damaged four others.

On the 16th, Commander Hicks took off from Yonton Field with a mixed armament of one Bat and three 100 pound bombs on anti-shipping patrol in the Yellow Sea off of Southwestern Korea, and Commander Hicks sighted a destroyer moving at 20 knots. The Bat locked onto the warship and was released at 4,000 feet from a range of three miles. The missile passed over and beyond the target and hit the water 500 yards beyond the ship's stern. Knowing the potential hazard of attacking a destroyer on the high seas, Hicks sought out other game and soon found a 100-ton oiler. Gunfire from the Privateer killed the ship's deck gunners. The pilot had not made a low level drop in several weeks and made a bombing run at 100 feet, dropping one bomb largely for practice and planning the ship's destruction by strafing. The bomb struck the ship at the water line 30 feet from the stern, and the ship went down rapidly. The successful attack on the oiler was the squadron's first confirmed kill from Okinawa. The 16th also brought rain, and by the end of May, Okinawa would recieve some 21 inches of precipitation. The water mixed with the soil and made a thick, muddy "goo," which clung onto both men and machine and made life miserable on the island.[1]

On the 17th, Lieutenant Warren and Lieutenant G.D. Fairbanks were searching an island group off southeastern Korea when they sighted a 100-ton oceangoing tug. Light, intense, accurate AA was received from the tug and from nearby shore batteries. The planes circled it twice, silencing the boat's AA fire before Lieutenant Warren made a bombing run at 300 feet. Crossing the tug amidships from starboard to port he dropped two 500 pound bombs. One of the bombs was a dud, but the other hit the water 40 feet from the tug's stern and detonated. The explosion knocked the boat 90 degrees to starboard, and it began to settle stern first. With the tug afire forward of the stack, a large fire in the after hatch, and the ship obviously sinking, the planes continued on patrol.

On the homeward leg of their sector three hours later, the planes were jumped by 10 Nakajima Ki-44 "Tojo" fighters and Mitsubishi J2M "Jack" fighters. A running battle continued for the next half hour. The fighters were spotted by Fairbank's port waist turret gunner as the Privateers were at 1,200 feet. The fighters were composed of three, four-plane sections flying at 6,000 feet. The Privateers nosed over and reduced altitude to 400 feet, and throughout the action remained between 400 and 700 feet, constantly altering altitude slightly and making gentle turns towards the fighters.

Fairbanks flew close to Warren's starboard wing and remained in position throughout the action. Almost immediately the fighters began attacking by dropping phosphorous bombs. In all, 10 phosphorous bombs were dropped, three being duds, but the other seven were fairly accuratel, with streamers striking the wing

Japanese dead lay on the muddy ground of Okinawa after of a suicide attack on 24 May 1945. *Courtesy of Roy Balke.*

surfaces of the search planes with each burst. The fighters then broke up into individual runs, pulling up in front of the Privateers within 3,000 feet before making runs and then breaking to the rear.

Aggressive runs were made by single fighters, but were readily discouraged by a few bursts from the gunners. Then, fighters attacking in concert broke off under the search planes, which were at 600 feet, and both Privateers were damaged. Five bow runs by fighters were counted, with two fighters participating on each run.

Lieutenant Fairbank's plane took hits in the fuselage fore and aft of the number one top turret when a 20mm shell burst inside the plane, wounding the gunner and knocking the turret out of commission. Faulty installation of the side plate slides sheared off two ammunition belts and put his number two top turret out of commission early in the battle. After 15 minutes, the ejectors on the starboard waist turret broke, further diminishing the plane's fire power. Radio communication was destroyed, and the throttle control to the number two engine was destroyed, necessitating feathering the engine. Within minutes, Fairbanks had three wounded crew members.[2]

The two Privateers managed to fight back with Lieutenant Warren's bow, number one top turret, and the tail turret gunners scoring hits at 1,000 feet range on one Jack. The fighter took hits in the engine, fuselage, starboard wing, and wing root, and the plane crashed in flames. A second Jack was hit simultaneously by the bow and the number one top turrets of both patrol planes. Lieutenant Warren's gunners struck at the engine, belly, and starboard wing root as the Jack broke off below, and Lieutenant Fairbanks' gunners hit the port wing root and fuselage. Smoking, it crashed into the sea afire. After 30 minutes, the fighters broke off the attack and left individually and in pairs. Five minutes after the last enemy plane cleared the area, two PBM search planes of Fleet Air Wing One arrived at the scene, and the Mariners stayed with the Privateers until certain that Lieutenant Fairbanks could make it back to base safely.

On the 18th, Lieutenant Hewitt and Lieutenant Serbin sighted a 2,000-ton attack transport 3 hours into their mission off of southern Korea. Following the two plane tactics used successfully against shipping in this area by pilots of VPB-118 VPB-109, both planes circled the target several times, with maximum machine gun fire directed at deck gun positions before a bombing run was initiated. One plane continued the heavy strafing until the second had begun a bombing run, ceasing fire as the bombing plane came in.

At 100 feet, Lieutenant Hewitt made a bombing run and released two bombs. One fell 80 feet short, one was a direct hit amidship, while the third was considerably over. Circling, Hewitt came in, but his bombs hung up. Trying again, the Privateer flew down the ship from stern to bow, dropping a string of five bombs. One was a direct hit on the deck 25 feet from the stern, while another was a near miss 25 feet off the starboard side.

While Hewitt circled the ship providing suppressing fire, Lieutenant Serbin initiated his bomb run and dropped two 250 pound bombs. Both bombs straddled the ship, with the first falling 50 feet short and the second 50 feet over. Serbin swung the Privateer around and made a second bombing run and released a 500 pound bomb, which hit the water 50 feet beyond the target. The ship was stopped dead in the water with a sharp starboard list and was blazing furiously aft and amidships by Hewitt's direct hit. The freighter was settling by the stern as the two Privateers left.

Lieutenant Turner and Lieutenant Braddock, on the same day, were patrolling along the Southeastern Korean coast investigating fruitlessly the many small harbors and anchorages of the islands off the coast. Rounding the coast, they entered a harbor and spotted a 1,000-ton Oiler at anchor and other smaller shipping. The ship began sending up meager AA fire as the planes began their attack. Circling the oiler, the ship's fire was silenced by repeated strafing by both planes. The strafing caused the oiler to catch fire on its forward deck near the superstructure. Both planes then took turns making bombing runs on the burning ship.

Lieutenant Turner, coming in at 150 feet, dropped four 250 pound bombs which fell short. The bomb detonations caused a cascade of water to envelop the ship, apparently causing little damage. However, Lieutenant Braddock had better luck on his run. Crossing over the length of the oiler, stern to bow, at 150 feet, Braddock dropped two 500 pound bombs. The first fell 20 feet short near the stern, and the second entered water 15 feet off the bow, detonating 25 feet beyond. The ship was tossed violently by the explosions and began to settle down by the bow, listing 12 degrees to port. Leaving the oiler sinking, the two Privateers headed towards the other merchant shipping in the harbor.

Moderate fire from heavy AA batteries on shore and light AA from ships became increasingly accurate as the planes began their attacks. Lieutenant Turner selected a small coastal freighter as a target, but the bombs hung up in their racks. Unable to bomb the ship, Lieutenant Turner's gunners selected three coastals and began strafing.

As Turner's crew was raking the coastals with 50 caliber machine gun fire, Braddock made a run on another freighter at anchor in the outer harbor. Lieutenant Braddock circled the target so his gunners could suppress the light AA fire coming from the ship. Crossing the freighter from bow to stern at 150 feet, Turner pickled off four 250 pounders. The first fell short, but the second was a direct hit on the forward deck and the third a direct hit on the stern, blowing it off. The freighter, in flames with a large hole torn in its deck and starboard bow, sank rapidly.

As Turner began a second bombing run on a small coastal, his co-pilot sighted larger shipping in the distance in an inner harbor, the attack was broken off, and both planes turned to investigate. The investigation was short, for seven destroyer escorts, three large merchant ships in the 3,500 to 7,500-ton range, a larger ship of

7,000 tons, and several other ships of medium size were at anchor and began to put up a heavy curtain of AA fire. As the planes turned to port, out of range, Lieutenant Turner's number one top turret gunner sighted two enemy fighters and alerted both search planes.

The patrol planes were at 300 feet and immediately dropped down to the deck 30 feet off the water, turning south away from the harbor. The enemy fighters, identified as a Zeke and a Tojo, passed ahead and turned in for head-on runs. The search planes took no essential evasive action, as the fighters broke off all runs. After five minutes the fighters retired, and the search planes extended their formation. Ten minutes later, a single Tojo appeared and made a head-on run. The run was directed at Lieutenant Turner's plane in the lead, but came in between the two planes. Turner's gunners scored hits on the engine, cockpit, and along the starboard fuselage, while Lieutenant Braddock's bow and number one top turret gunners struck the engine, fuselage, and port wing root. The Tojo, smoking and losing altitude, disappeared to the north. Neither search plane was hit during the attack, and they returned to base.

Japanese dead lay on the muddy ground of Okinawa after of a suicide attack on 24 May 1945. *Courtesy of Roy Balke.*

On the 19th, Lieutenant Jobe was three hours into the flight and flying at 300 feet in near zero visibility due to fog along the Southern Korean coast when he sighted a small freighter heavily loaded with cargo and cruising at seven knots. The pilot made one bombing and strafing run at 100 feet, dropping one 500 pounder for a direct hit on the bow. The entire freighter was blown out of the water before settling back with the heavy sea completely covering it.

Five minutes later, a 2,300-ton Oiler was attacked at anchor between Saishu To and Gyoto, Korea. Dropping from 700 feet to 100 feet, Jobe released four bombs, which straddled the ship, while several small fires were started by the pilot's gunners. However, the extremely poor weather prevented them from assessing damage.[3]

On the 20th, Lieutenant Keeling and Lieutenant Kennedy, in addition to their regular search sectors along the Korean Strait, were to act as decoys for a flight of 8 Army P-47s and a PB4Y-2 led by Commander Hicks to wait expected enemy fighter interception.

Off Korea, the pilots spotted an enemy convoy consisting of four destroyers, one destroyer escort, and two small coastal freighters at anchor. From 300 feet, each plane made a strafing run at two small coastal freighters. While his gunners directed their fire on the ship's gun crews, Kennedy, on his bombing run, dropped three 250 pound bombs which fell short. Personnel on the gun deck were killed by intense strafing and their guns silenced. Repeated strafing runs by both planes left both ships dead in the water, with one smoking heavily.

While both ships were being destroyed, the attack was watched by three Zekes for 30 minutes, but they never intervened, the fighters staying at 2,000 feet while the Privateers at 200 feet finished their business. Lieutenant Keeling selected a 2,000-ton freighter going 12 knots as his next target and made four runs on it. Meager inaccurate AA was received, but by the third run, all guns on the ship had been silenced. On his first run, Keeling scored a direct hit, blowing off the ship's bow with a 500 pound bomb. Subsequent runs resulted in near misses, with one bomb exploding under the stern. On the fourth run, a 500 pound bomb hit amidships, ricocheted from the deck, and flew about 150 feet in the air before exploding, and a 250 pounder was a direct hit astern of the bridge, starting a large fire. The ship was left riddled, aflame, and sinking with its stern awash.

For two successive days, patrol PB4Ys of the squadron had been attacked by enemy fighters on the return leg of their search sectors, and two search PBM Mariners of Fleet Air Wing One had been shot down by Japanese fighters in the same area a day earlier. Enemy radar along Kyushu and on the islands just off the coast were tracking search planes continuously as they moved north past Kyushu. This had given the enemy sufficient information of search plane's courses and times to vector out intercepting fighters on the return leg. To provide variety for the enemy interceptors, it was planned that two regular patrol planes would fly routine patrol as scheduled at habitual latitudes and with no great time variation, consciously remaining on enemy radar screens.

Commander Hicks led the eight Army P-47s south to Kyushu in an effort to decoy and intercept enemy fighters. Commander Hicks rendezvoused a half hour after take-off over Ie Shima with fighters from the 318th Fighter Group. After reaching a point 50 miles due west of the returning patrol planes, they entered the area of probable enemy interception. However, no enemy air activity materialized, and the mission turned to destroying targets of opportunity.

Commander Hicks sighted a 150-ton picket boat, and the search plane and P-47s circled it twice to port, strafing and silencing the boat's AA fire. Diving from 1,000 feet to 300 feet on the initial strafing run, the deck gunners were killed and their 20mm gun spun crazily around like a pinwheel. The patrol boat, ablaze after Hicks' first run, exploded and sank. The pilots of the P-47s were pleased the day was not without incident, and apparently enjoyed the variation in their routine. With permission from Commander Hicks, they flew over to attack Tonis Field at Gotto Retto, strafing and discharging their rockets, destroying a hangar and setting fire to an oil dump before returning to the PB4Y for the return trip back to base.

By mid-1945 the Japanese were reduced to shipping supplies and personnel by small coastal vessels weighing less than 100 tons. Working together singly or in small convoys, these vessels sailed back and forth along the Korean, Chinese, and Japanese coasts.

In an action that took only three minutes, Lieutenant Warren and Lieutenant Turner, on the 22nd, attacked a 100-ton freighter late in their patrol along southern

Two privateers flown by Lieutenants Keeling and Challis attack a large transport off Korea on 25 May. *Courtesy of the National Archives.*

Korea. Coming in from stern to bow, Turner dropped a bomb which turned out to be a dud. However, on his next run he scored a direct hit at the water line. The ship, afire from strafing, exploded, keeled over to starboard, and sank, leaving survivors in the water.

The following day, Lieutenant Vadnais and Lieutenant Hugh Wilkinson attacked a 100-ton freighter three hours into their patrol on the high seas in the Korean Strait. On five successive runs the ship was strafed heavily from 400 feet, leaving it smoking and dead in the water. Three hours later, on the return leg of patrol, the ship was sighted drifting. One strafing run preceded a single bomb run. The ship took a direct hit from a bomb, and the ship sank immediately.

The same day Lieutenant Fairbanks and Lieutenant Braddock spent a profitable noon-hour against the enemy when they spotted two trawlers in the islands off Korea that were strafed in passing, starting a small fire near the bridge on one and drawing smoke from the second. An hour later, a 100-ton freighter was attacked with Braddock, making three bombing runs on it. The ship took one direct hit and two near misses during the first two runs. On the third run Braddock scored a direct hit amidships, but the 500 pound bomb ricocheted straight up from the ship and detonated at 200 feet altitude, causing the plane to be severely boosted upward by the explosion. The ship, afire stern and aft, went under 10 minutes after the attack.

Forty minutes later, another freighter was strafed heavily and repeatedly by both planes and bombed by Fairbanks. Attacking at 200 feet, Fairbanks managed to obtain near misses, with the closest bomb exploding 15 feet from the ship. The ship, dead in the water and listing, and afire aft, exploded and disintegrated.

On the 24th, a large amount of shipping was sighted by Jobe and Lieutenant Serbin in the Korean Strait. Both planes carried only one Bat each plus a bomb load, for the continued trouble with the Bats allowed good targets to escape which might have otherwise been attacked and destroyed by low altitude bombing runs. Three small coastal freighters in line sailing at eight knots were targeted, and the first ship in line was attacked by Lieutenant Jobe. One of the two bombs dropped entered the water 15 feet short, passed under the ship, and exploded on the port side. Jobe then turned his attention to the second ship. Releasing a 500 pound bomb, it fell short amidships and detonated beneath the hull. The ship was literally blown to pieces by the explosion, leaving only scattered debris on the water. Returning to strafe the first ship, Lieutenant Jobe made another three strafing runs, and the ship was left sinking.

Attacking the third ship, Lieutenant Serbin made a bombing run from bow to stern and dropped three bombs, which fell within 20 feet of the target. Explosions stopped it dead in the water before going down by the bow. Four heavy strafing runs by Serbin and one by Jobe completed the ship's destruction. A larger 800-ton freighter sailing at ten knots was the next victim of Lieutenant Jobe. In several strafing runs to port at altitudes ranging from 100 to 400 feet, the ship was set afire, causing a large internal explosion which blew the stern off, and it rapidly sank stern first.

Less than two hours after sinking the four freighters, a 7,000-ton troop transport was spotted. Lieutenant Serbin launched his Bat from 10 miles out and at an altitude of 4,000 feet. The missile traveled nose high and dove vertically into sea three miles short of target. Lieutenant Jobe sighted the ship visually on very rough seas and released his Bat from eight miles out at an altitude of 5,000 feet. The missile functioned normally until it neared the transport, when it struck the water a quarter mile short.

Lieutenant Chay and Lieutenant Hewitt, 30 minutes into their search, were off the southern coast of Korea seeking enemy shipping when an enemy destroyer was sighted which immediately opened fire at the planes. The planes started to gain altitude from the search altitude of 200 feet to 10,000 feet to prepare for an attack when Lieutenant Chay sighted three Rufe fighters coming up. The Privateers immediately joined up to present their gun power for whatever aggressiveness the enemy cared to show. While at 4,000 feet the enemy planes bracketed the planes with one coming to port at 5,000 feet, one to starboard at 4,000 feet, and the remaining astern at 2,000 feet, outside the range of the bombers' gunners.

Evidently awaiting more fighters, the Rufes continued to follow the bombers. Suddenly, a Nick, Zeke, and Tony came into sight to present their attacks. A Rufe came in on a head on run on Lieutenant Chay's plane, attempting to pull off to the starboard. Chay's bow gunner scored several hits that caused the Rufe to pull up, which presented a perfect target for the forward top turret. The top turret gunner opened up, and the fighter began a steep wobbly glide before crashing into the water.

The fighters used an altitude advantage of 1,000 feet, but simple evasive action of changing course and altitude rendered the attack ineffective. The Tony made a head on run on Lieutenant Hewitt's plane, pulling away to the starboard and slightly under. His bow turret and forward top turret scored hits that caused the fighter to start on a downward journey to the water. The Zeke attempted a side run on Lieutenant Chay who was covering Hewitt's wing and attempted to pull away to port. The starboard waist and tail guns of Lieutenant Chay's plane opened up, scoring hits that caused the Zeke to leave a trail of black smoke as it disappeared out of sight. With the Zeke trailing smoke, the fight was broken off just as the number two engine of Lieutenant Chay's plane started a gas leak and two of his turrets became inoperative.

Under a full moon and clear sky, the night of the 24th was full of Japanese air activity directed against Yontan Field, climaxed by the successful crash-landing of a Sally with its load of "Giretsu" (a special airborne attack unit) on the airstrip. Six Sallys carrying suicide squads attempted to land. Five were shot down by anti-aircraft fire, but one landed wheels up on the airfield, and 15 Japanese from the plane scrambled out. Before they were all killed, they succeeded in destroying seven planes (including two of the squadron's), damaging 25 more, burned a 70,000 gallon fuel dump, and made two runways inoperable until the next morning.[4] John O. Oates, standing as plane guard on the field, was seriously wounded when caught in the cross fire between the Japanese and the defending Marines. One of the planes shot down in flames crashed just short of squadron enlisted personnel tents, and two men, George R. McKeeby and Rodger W. Clemons, were injured while seeking foxhole protection.

Lieutenant Keeling and Lieutenant Challis managed to take off the following morning to attack a 3,000 transport off of Korea. Heavily and repeatedly strafed by both planes during eight runs, Keeling crossed over the transport at 100 feet and dropped three bombs, scoring direct hits on the superstructure with a 250 pound bomb, and blowing off the bow with a 500 pounder. Lieutenant Challis, following, dropped three bombs and scored one hit, causing the ship to list severely. Lieutenant Keeling on his second run, at 60 feet, dropped a string of three bombs, which straddled the target closely. Out of bombs and low on fuel, the planes left the area with the ship smoking and afire, but still afloat.

The squadron's score rose sharply on the 27th as the result of two separate attacks by four squadron planes. Lieutenant Jadin and Lieutenant Moyer on routine search and reconnaissance along the Southern Korean coast were told to pay par-

A large Japanese merchant ship under attack by Lieutenants Vadnais and Vidal off Korea on 29 May. *Courtesy of the National Archives.*

ticular attention to Japanese shipping along reported shipping lanes. A 2,300-ton stack-aft freighter was sighted, and both planes commenced strafing attacks. Meager AA fire was received from 20mm and 7.7mm guns, but they were soon silenced by the Privateers' gunners. Both planes then started bombing runs. One 250 pound bomb hit below the superstructure, causing major damage. On the second and third runs the ship took a hit on the stern from a 500 pound bomb, causing the ship to emit a heavy flow of oil. The ship was left afire, and the Privateers returned home. On the return leg, Lieutenant Moyer headed to Gaja Shima and spotted an operating radio and radar station. Encountering meager anti-aircraft fire, both installations were hit by strafing, and two 250 pound bombs for direct hits, causing a fire and an explosion.

Commander Hicks and Lieutenant Kennedy, on a special strike to destroy shipping along the coast of Korea between China and the Inland Sea, headed for the southeast tip of Korea and began systematically ferreting the maze and myriad of islands off the coast. Both Privateers carried a bomb load and a Bat suspended beneath their wings. A 100-ton freighter, moving slowly at four knots, was strafed by both planes, causing the ship to beach itself. Five minutes later, a 120-ton, large, four-masted schooner was sighted at anchor. Hicks went in at 100 feet and released two bombs. Both dropped just short of the schooner and detonated with a mining effect beneath the keel. The whole stern was blown off, and the target sank by the stern. Less than 10 minutes later, two 100-ton freighters were discovered at anchor.

Commander Hicks, at 100 feet, dropped one 500 pound bomb, and the ship literally disintegrated in the explosion, leaving only floating debris. Lieutenant Kennedy, attacking the other ship, released three bombs. One fell short, but two hit the deck near the stack, and the ship was blown out of the water. Seven minutes later, two 150-ton freighters were discovered at anchor in a small harbor. Commander Hicks' sank the first with one 500 pound bomb, which broke the ship into two parts. The two sections keeled over and sank. Attacking the other freighter, Lieutenant Kennedy's gunners began strafing, and suddenly the ship exploded internally near the stern. It blazed brightly, then turned over to port and sank. As the planes skimmed over the land, two small freighters were discovered at anchor in an adjacent small harbor. Again, Lieutenant Kennedy's gunners set one rapidly afire, which sank after having several small internal explosions. The second ship, strafed heavily, begun to burn brightly as the planes withdrew.

Almost an hour passed before another freighter moving slowly was spotted and was strafed by Lieutenant Kennedy in passing, drawing some smoke. Minutes later, they encountered a large 3,000-ton stack-aft freighter. Commander Hicks went in first and dropped a bomb which fell fifty feet short and caused no apparent damage. At 100 feet, Lieutenant Kennedy dropped one 500 pounder for a direct hit above water line near the stern. The explosion blew the stern off, causing the ship to rapidly heal over to port and sink.[5]

On their homeward path, two large single stack destroyer escorts of 2,300 tons were sighted by radar from 20 miles on the high seas cruising at 15 knots, and identified visually at 15 miles from 2,000 feet. Range was closed to six miles as the planes began their Bat attack, as both warships started sending up heavy to moderate, inaccurate AA. The planes made a 180 degree turn, with Lieutenant Kennedy climbing to 8,500 feet. Commander Hicks, at 6,000 feet, followed two miles behind. The AA, which was intense and increasingly accurate as the planes neared, ceased as Lieutenant Kennedy began his run. Three miles from the target, the missile was released from 6,000 feet. This time, the weapon traveled true, hitting the warship directly on the bow above the water line, blowing off the bow back to the 1st turret.

Both planes circled at 5,000 feet to assess the damage before AA fire from the undamaged warship was received, forcing withdrawal. As soon as the Bat detonated, the undamaged escort, originally a mile away, proceeded to a position 100 yards from her sinking sister ship. She then turned broadside and started throwing heavy to moderate accurate AA. The planes headed for base, leaving behind them 11 ships sunk or damaged.[5]

On the 29th, Lieutenant Vadnais and Lieutenant (jg) Albert Vidal, on an antishipping campaign against Japanese shipping off the southeastern Korean coast, attacked a 2,300-ton freighter. Strafing by both planes killed personnel on the ship's deck as they were preparing to man the deck guns. Lieutenant Vadnais came around again from port to starboard amidships, but missed with his two 500 pounders. However, Lieutenant Vidal scored a direct hit amidships, throwing bodies and debris 200 feet in the air, and the ship sank to the bottom in 34 seconds.

Continued reports of worthwhile shipping targets off the coast of China and the diminishing number of large merchant ships encountered along the Korean coast in the regular patrol areas prompted the decision by Commander Hicks to ferret the China coast. With reports of large shipping near Shanghai, Lieutenant Turner and Lieutenant Warren were sent to cover the Yangtze River mouth, where they conducted unsuccessful Bat attacks against a 6,000-ton attack transport and a 4,000-ton freighter.

Approaching the coast, they sighted the two ships and Lieutenant Turner released his Bat at 8,000 feet and two miles from target. The missile fell off on its own starboard wing, immediately spun to the starboard, exploding on impact with the surface. Lieutenant Warren's Bat, released from 8,000 feet and 10 miles from the target, made a wide turn to starboard before straightening out. However, it hit the water three miles from the ship.

They encountered so much shipping that four planes were dispatched the following day to the mouth of the Yangtze. The flight consisted of two sections consisting of Lieutenants Davis, Jobe, Kennedy, and Serbin. The first to arrive were

Davis and Serbin and, for the next hour, the four planes would be engaged in continuous action.

Ten minutes after noon, Davis and Serbin spotted a 3,000-ton attack transport and two small picket boats slowly moving off the coast. Lieutenant Davis began his run strafing at low level as Lieutenant Serbin prepared for a Bat attack. Davis's plane immediately took hits and was seriously damaged. Four bursts from 20mm and 40mm guns near the transport's bridge section damaged the number one and three engines, rudder controls, the radio, and the starboard fuselage. Davis's co-pilot, Ensign Chester F. Szewczyk, and the plane captain were wounded. The plane captain, William Y. Toellen, was severely wounded while bending over the pilot tightening the straps on his flak suit. Because his radio was knocked out, he could not warn the following planes of the intense defensive fire being put up by the ships. Davis immediately set course for base, where Davis made a safe landing in near zero visibility. After launching an unsuccessful Bat attack and unable to contact Davis, Serbin joined up with Jobe and Kennedy.

For the next hour, the three Privateers were in constant contact with enemy shipping. Their first target was an anchored 2,300-ton freighter. After one strafing run at 200 feet to silence the ship's AA, the planes commenced two bombing runs from 100 feet. Two near misses by 500 pound bombs started fires, and the ship listed sharply to port and began to settle when last observed.

The next targets for Jobe and Kennedy were a 4,000-ton merchantman and a picket boat. Heavily strafed by both planes, Kennedy flew along the ship from stern to bow and dropped two bombs for near misses. He began circling for a second run when Serbin told them of the two large attack transports. Preferring to save his bombs, Kennedy broke off the attack.

Fifteen minutes later, the Privateers made strafing runs on a 200-ton Lightship, four picket boats, and a 300-ton oiler. Light to moderate inaccurate AA was received during three circular strafing runs. The picket boats were strafed heavily by the three planes and were left ablaze as the planes withdrew. The oiler burst into a tower of flames as it split into two with the bow sinking rapidly, while the stern remained afloat when last observed. The attack on the oiler proved to be the last successful one conducted by Jobe and Kennedy. Jobe and Kennedy withdrew and headed for the two transports moving in line a half mile apart at 15 knots.

The pilots planned only a strafing run on the transports until certain AA was eliminated before making bomb runs. Jobe cut across the bow of the lead ship with his gunners strafing. He circled again and flew up the ship from stern to bow of the trailing ship and crossing to port of the lead ship. Kennedy, a quarter mile behind, bracketed the transport, strafing the length of the starboard side and then falling in behind Jobe as he crossed over. The lead transport turned hard to port and, as the planes came around broadside on the starboard side, opened fire with heavy accurate AA.

The first burst from the lead transport caught both planes. Jobe's plane was severely damaged, with his horizontal stabilizer and vertical stabilizer shot out and a bomb bay door blown off. With near loss of rudder control, he was forced to retire and return to base. Following close behind, a 20mm shell exploded in Lieutenant Kennedy's cockpit, killing him almost instantly and wounding his co-pilot, Ensign William E. Wassner. Although wounded and with most of his instruments shot away, Wassner made a successful crash landing at Okinawa three hours later.

On the last day of the month, the squadron received verbal orders from Commander Fleet Air Wing One to retire to Tinian for rest and repair, and the squadron was relieved by VPB-123. The maintenance problems had exceeded CASU's abilities and, by June 1, only two planes remained in a state of combat readiness. Despite enemy air attacks and primitive conditions, the men had stood up better than the planes. In only 17 days of operations from Okinawa, the squadron had sunk or damaged 64 ships.

Blond Leo Kennedy relaxing. A veteran of the squadron's first tour, Kennedy was killed when a 20mm shell exploded in the cockpit while attacking merchant shipping on 31 May 1945. *Courtesy of Oden Sheppard.*

14

Tinian and Iwo Jima

Tinian's unhurried days and diversified recreation seemed almost stateside in comparison to the tension and pressures of life at Okinawa. The CASU worked rapidly, restoring squadron planes to a state of combat readiness, and replacement personnel were received from Guam and Tinian as flying personnel relaxed and played while training Patrol Plane Pilots was the only flight demand.

Recreational facilities included all field sports, and beer was available in sufficient quantity. A squadron Basketball team of enlisted personnel subsequently traveled to Guam to beat the XXI Bomber Command's team and win the Marianas championship. In less than 10 days, the squadron felt thoroughly fit and looked forward to returning to Okinawa.

On 10 June, the squadron's immediate return to Okinawa was requested by dispatch. Four replacement Privateers were still enroute from Kaneohe and, although eleven planes were ready for combat and all crews prepared, Commander Fleet Air Wing Eighteen reported the squadron readiness date indefinitely delayed, without Commander Hicks being informed or consulted, VPB-124 replaced the squadron at Okinawa, and the days at Tinian stretched on.

On 5 June the squadron began to fly one or two daily patrols under Commander Fleet Air Wing Eighteen, which were largely "whitecap specials" across friendly waters. Only the occasional armed reconnaissance of Truk, Pagan, and Chichi Jima suggested the combat area. The month of June passed with no enemy contacts other than occasional anti-aircraft fire from by-passed islands, and combat lessons began to be forgotten and, by July, squadron enthusiasm was on the wane.

On the early morning of 3 July, Lieutenant (jg) Braddock and Lieutenant (jg) Vidal, setting out on patrol, were on the outward leg of their search when they paused at Pagan Island to practice two-plane tactics and low-level bombing. No enemy activity was observed by either plane as bombs were dropped along a runway. On the second run at 200 feet, Lieutenant Braddock's plane encountered some light anti-aircraft fire and took a hit from an enemy 13.7mm round in the bow turret, and the gunner, Robert E. Mayo, was seriously wounded. Lieutenant Braddock, because of the wounded man's condition, returned to base without attempting to locate the enemy gun position.

Increasing discontent with the inactivity and the perplexing mechanics of a squadron assigned to and reporting to one command while in actuality working under verbal directives from another command brought the squadron's future into question. However, forthcoming work of Fleet Air Wing Eighteen with the Third Fleet off Japan prevented the squadron's release. VPB-109 with VPB-121 was ordered to Iwo Jima and joined three other Privateer squadrons (102, 108, and 116) to provide fleet barrier protection.

The squadron moved to Central Field, Iwo Jima, between 8 and 10 July and, although sufficient advance notice had been given of the intended extra planes, Iwo Jima was far from ready to receive them. Living conditions, in the report of three squadron commanders, were "miserable beyond the point of justifiable excuse." The squadron, as usual, flew in its own cots, bedding, tents, and set up camp.

No water, for either drinking or bathing, was available in the living area, throughout the twenty days of the squadron's stay. Saltwater showers, a quarter of a mile away, were turned on at 1600 and off at 0900 hours. Drinking water and liquids were generally rationed in the mess-hall to one cup per individual per meal. Water was available with flight rations for flights only by a chit from the executive officer of CASUF 52. With Iwo Jima's heat and constant swirling-dust, such was hardly a liveable minimum, and only the generosity of a Naval Construction Battalion five miles distant made life tolerable.

Neither electricity or lanterns were available, and initially, sanitary facilities were utterly lacking, with only one head (capacity 8) a quarter of a mile away serving all personnel, officer and enlisted. Continued complaints to the CASU commander, Commander D.A. Mac Isaac, eased the situation somewhat on the eighth day with the construction of a new head (capacity 4) adjacent to the squadron area to serve the two hundred and thirty-three officers and men of the squadron.

After the inactive days on Tinian were the intense flight operations on Iwo Jima, averaging 111 hours for each available crew in a three week period. A plane took off every 30 minutes, and VPB-109 was placed into the role of fleet barrier between the fleet and any outgoing Japanese force. They flew special weather flights, air-sea rescue, anti-submarine patrols, and daily search and reconnaissance of the Honshu coast. Squadron aircraft were used extensively for fleet barrier duty in conjunction with the Third Fleet's strikes at Honshu on the 18th and 21st, and in the Inland Sea on the 24th and 28th. As the CASU lacked the facilities even to keep planes gassed on occasion, engine checks and maintenance were performed at Tinian, and crews were given a respite about every eight days from Iwo's squalor, but just to be flying again kept morale surprisingly high.

On one such flight, Lieutenant Thomas W. Challis and his crew were ordered to escort a photo plane to Tokyo Bay, which turned out to be uneventful, and they were on their way back to Iwo when one of the engines had to be feathered. After dumping all remaining bombs and ammunition to make the plane lighter, the crew settled back for their journey home. Wayne Turner, the primary radar operator, was tired from being on the radar and radio watch all day and decided to take a break. Herbert K. Ferguson, the 3rd radioman, was on radar when he called Turner on the intercom to come and look at the screen. He thought there was something wrong with the set because of so many blips. Turner looked and discovered that they were surrounded by airplanes. It was a flight of B-29s headed to Japan and flying at 8,000 feet. He told the pilot and he turned on the IFF and the landing lights. Turner got on radar and guided the pilot through the planes, sometimes so close that the crew could feel the B-29s' prop wash.

Contacts with the enemy, other than anti-aircraft fire from the Honshu coast, were infrequent. Therefore, the squadron took on the additional assignment of Air-Sea Rescue. Although squadron personnel had no formal training in this highly specialized field, some 18 flights were performed, resulting in the rescue of three downed airmen. One such flight was conducted by Lieutenant Chay and Lieutenant (jg) Braddock on the 26th.

View of Iwo Jima during the squadron's stay. *Courtesy of the National Archives.*

The two pilots were briefed to be on the alert for possible survivors of a Dumbo B-17 thought to be down near the far northeast corner of their search sector. Lieutenant Braddock, on Lieutenant Chay's wing at 1,500 feet, sighted an object in the water, and investigation by both planes at 400 feet showed it to be an overturned life boat of the type carried by B-17 Dumbo planes. Light blue in color, it was nearly awash with a boxed propeller, with the spilled parachute still attached and dragging in the water. A 15 minute search disclosed no survivors in the area, and full information was given to four Air-Sea Rescue planes and the search turned over to them.

After spotting the empty life boat, the two planes approached the Japanese coast of Southern Honshu and began ferreting from Nakiri to Shingu. Five 50-foot fishing boats were spotted close together inshore in a cove at Shingu Harbor, with two others 200 yards away ashore. Seeing nothing else worthy of attacking, the two Privateers headed towards the fishing boats. In one circling strafing run, accurate hits caused the boats to smoke. In hopes of better targets, the planes continued to comb the shore to Kusimoto, but heavy rain near Koza and around O-Shima reduced visibility to a minimum, and the planes turned back to Shingu for a second run on the fishing boats. As the boats were being heavily strafed by Lieutenant Chay's gunners, Braddock dropped one 250 pound bomb in the center of the group. Cascades of explosions covered the boats and tossed them around violently. Shingu Town was heavily strafed by both planes in two strafing runs as Braddock dropped a bomb from 200 feet in the village near some central docks, causing one dock and two buildings to disintegrate.

Lieutenant Braddock, leading, headed up a railroad track towards Udona and dropped his final bomb directly on the track short of a railroad tunnel between Shingu and Udano. Lieutenant Chay, following, dropped three more bombs. Two landed short of the tunnel on the tracks, while the third bomb went into the tunnel's mouth as the plane zoomed sharply up to avoid the steep cliff. The explosions caved in the tunnel mouth and tore up the tracks for an eighth of a mile. As the planes pulled up, belated intense light and medium AA was received from Shingu town, and the planes made a final deck-level run through the town, strafing gun positions before heading out to continue patrol.

Homeward bound, Lieutenant Chay, at 800 feet, sighted a yellow one-man liferaft. Almost immediately the raft's occupant attracted the pilot's attention by firing off three tracers in the air and waving a yellow poncho. Both planes dropped to 300 feet, circling and dropping float lights to mark the spot, for the rough sea made constant sight contact a near impossibility. Lieutenant Chay climbed to 2,000 feet and succeeded in contacting a lifeguard submarine. Lieutenant Chay estimated his gas was sufficient to remain on station for another two hours, and the submarine revised its estimated time of arrival. A Dumbo B-17 "Juke Box 37" intercepted the conversation and estimated he could reach the position in an hour.

While Lieutenant Chay handled communication, Lieutenant Braddock circled to the left at 300 feet while maintaining visual contact with the small life-raft. Having exhausted the float lights and dye-marker carried in the plane, Braddock's crew stripped dye-markers from their individual Mae West life-jackets and dropped them up wind from the raft for the downed aviator to float into. A yellow and red flag waved constantly from the life raft, which aided in maintaining sight contact in the rough sea. Twenty-three miles away, the submarine picked up Lieutenant Chay's plane on his radar. Chay varied his altitude between 300 and 800 feet to home in the B-17 and the submarine. The B-17 arrived, with the submarine arriving 15 minutes later, having averaged better than 20 knots. All dye marker and float lights were

One of Miss Lotta Tail's waist gunners, Roy Balke, above his tear-drop waist turret he named "My Indispensable." *Courtesy of Roy Balke.*

gone, and Braddock was dropping parachute flares when the B-17 arrived. The rescue was made by the submarine at 1630, and the pilot, Sub-Lieutenant D.W. Banks, RAF, off H.M.S. *Indefatigable*, and in the water for three and a half days, radioed his thanks. Course was set for base, and the PB4Ys made a successful landing at Iwo Jima.

After two weeks on Iwo Jima, the squadron received orders for Okinawa. The squadron's stay on the island lowered morale, and Commander Hicks grew more frustrated with the treatment his and other sister squadrons had received since Palawan. As he saw it, the squadron continued to wage a personal battle for its existence—the Battle of the Camp Area, as he called it. He found it discouraging and, on occasion, considerably more demanding than against the enemy. At three successive bases in the forward area (Palawan, Okinawa, and Iwo Jima), the squadron had built its own camp, carried in all tents, cots, and equipment in squadron planes, and set up camp with flight personnel while fulfilling a schedule of combat flights. Dining facilities and food were of poor quality in most cases, and in one instance, the water supply was insufficient even for drinking purposes. To ensure operating efficiency and basic comforts, the squadron was forced to acquire from other units almost enough supplies and gear to become self-supporting. Commander Hicks knew that in the forward area, some supplies would be difficult to obtain, however, it was quite apparent that the attitude of some Island Commands, ACORN, and CASU Commanders was that the complete comfort of their respective units preceded the needs of the squadrons they were supposed to support.

15

Finals at Okinawa

Yontan Field had been considerably altered during the squadron's two month absence. Navy Sea-Bees and Army Construction Engineers had built a surfaced air strip, parking areas, and a taxiway ran across the squadron's old living area. Living conditions improved considerably with tents having wooden or coral floors, which protected against the mud caused by frequent rain showers. Oil drum showers were available to all personnel, electricity had been installed, and Lister bags of drinking water were stationed though the camp. Less frequent air raid alerts made recreational activities such as motion pictures possible.

Land-based squadrons on Okinawa stepped up their attacks on enemy shipping in the Yellow, East China, and Japan Seas, along the coast of Japan, and in the Inland Sea. Mounting strikes and anti-shipping missions had caused a noticeable decrease in enemy shipping and were steadily cutting down on Japan's surface communications with the continent. The Chinese ports of Shanghai and Hangchow were in the process of being neutralized, as was Hong Kong and the Formosa ports in the south. The Korea-Japan shipping lanes across the Tsushima Straits were obliged to rely on heavier escort, move in smaller convoys, and proceed more and more at night.

On 30 July, Lieutenant Jobe and Lieutenant Turner, on patrol in southeast Korea, sighted a large number of enemy shipping, including a 1,900-ton freighter, which was selected as the primary target in the Tsushima Straits sector, which provided the two pilots an exceedingly busy hour of action.

As Lieutenant Turner circled the ship, his gunners laid down suppressing fire against the ship's gun crew as Lieutenant Jobe initiated a bombing run across the target's starboard bow. Lieutenant Jobe released two 500 and one 250 pound bombs, which entered the water but missed the ship by 25 feet. Swinging around for another run, Jobe dropped a 500 and a 250 pound bomb. The ship took a direct hit on the mid section, and the freighter blew up and sank rapidly.

Thirty minutes later, two 70-ton luggars were spotted abreast of each other cruising at five knots. Not wanting to waste their remaining bombs on the small ships, both Privateers made a strafing run, which resulted in both targets burning and sinking. Fifteen minutes later, two similar vessels were spotted and strafed by the planes, causing one of the luggars to blow up. Looking for bigger game, a 850-ton freighter was spotted 20 minutes later cruising at 10 knots. While Lieutenant Turner initiated a bombing run, Lieutenant Jobe's gunners kept the ship's gun crew busy with their strafing. Lieutenant Turner's first 250 pound bomb exploded in the air before striking the ship, and fragments damaged the wings and tails of both planes. Another bomb was a direct hit amidships, and the ship began to blaze before sinking. Having expended all of their bombs and most of their ammunition, the Privateers headed home.

The following day, in a daring strike, Commander Hicks and Lieutenant Hewitt, with two planes from VPB-118 and VPB-123, took off on a special strike against rail transportation and railroad facilities in Northwestern Korea. The primary target, as selected by Commander Fleet Air Wing One, was a steel 2,700-foot long, multiple span, single track bridge on the Seisin K River, just two miles north of the

Privateers flown by Lieutenants Jobe and Turner attack shipping off Korea on 30 July. *Courtesy of the National Archives.*

town of Shinanshu. The bridge works consisted of three parallel sections. A highway bridge to the east; a partially completed railroad bridge in the center, and a completed railroad bridge on the west. The primary target was the completed railroad bridge. The bridge was vital to the supply of war materials flowing south through Korea to the ports of Fusan and Kunsan and other important shipping areas. To render this important artery useless, it was necessary to cut it off by destroying the bridge.

Taking off at six a.m., and leading his planes low and outside of radar detection, Commander Hicks planned to strike the target so that retirement would be made away from the direction of the towns of Shinanshu and Anshu. The planes hit the bridge at noon, with Hicks' first 1,000 pound bomb entering the water on the starboard center of the pier for a perfect hit. The steel span momentarily lifted, covered by a geyser of water, and immediately caused the northern end of the southernmost span to drop 20 feet below the level of the tracks. A second bomb was a

Privateers flown by Lieutenants Jobe and Turner attack shipping off Korea on 30 July. *Courtesy of the National Archives.*

near miss on the second span pier. As they retired, a gun position was firing at them from between the two towns and to the north.

Return to base was started over land, looking for targets of opportunity along the railroad bed. A locomotive with 12 cars was spotted and attacked by Hicks, and was seriously damaged by bombing and strafing. A rail junction yard containing several small buildings was damaged by bombing and strafing by Lieutenant Hewitt, and a coal mine and six buildings, including a hopper elevator, were strafed by Hicks' plane and were left blazing.

Just as they were leaving the coast, four small power trawlers tied up together at a landing at the mouth of the Gaisan Ho River were strafed and bombed in passing, with bombs scoring direct hits when they landed among the moored craft, sending debris into the air.

Regular flight operations were canceled for nearly a week as a typhoon approached the Japanese coast. Instead, the squadron was ordered to conduct special weather flights to track the storm on 30 July, 1, and 3 August. Favorable weather the following week had planes from Okinawa going up in strength against Kyushu,

The 2,700-foot bridge on the Seisin K River in Korea being hit by Hicks on 31 July. *Courtesy of the National Archives.*

Southern Honshu, Korea, and over the Inland Sea, Sea of Japan, and the Yellow and East China Seas against dwindling enemy shipping.

On the 6th, Lieutenant Keeling and Lieutenant Vidal were on anti-shipping patrol off of Korea when they spotted a 2,500-ton tanker. Dropping from 1,000 feet to 200 feet altitude, the planes circled the ship to port and began strafing. Light and medium, but inaccurate AA was received during the strafing run. The search planes pulled up to 1,000 feet still circling to port as Lieutenant Keeling initiated a bombing run. Lieutenant Vidal planned to follow with a bombing run and remained a mile and a half behind Keeling.

By now the planes were being subjected to intense medium and light AA. Completing his run, Lieutenant Keeling pulled up to 500 feet with his number three engine smoking. His plane gradually nosed over in a slight turn to starboard before crashing into the water two miles west of the ship.

Following behind, Lieutenant Vidal broke off his bombing run when he observed Lieutenant Keeling in distress, and headed directly to the scene of the crash. Smoke and flames reached a height of 200 feet after the plane hit the water, and only a few pieces of debris and heavy oily smoke were visible when Vidal's plane reached the scene. An uninflated liferaft, wheel, and a large amount of dye marker was floating on the surface. Lieutenant Vidal had one of his crew members throw

Commander Hicks' hitting shipping after bombing the Seisin K bridge on 31 July. *Courtesy of the National Archives.*

Lieutenant Keeling and his crew were lost on 5 August when their plane was shot down while attacking a medium size tanker off Korea. *Courtesy of Oden Sheppard.*

out an inflated life raft and a survival kit adjacent to the crash, but no survivors were sighted. Lieutenant Vidal left the area. Lieutenant Keeling and his entire crew were listed as missing in action, one year to the day since the loss of Lieutenant Kasperson's crew on 5 August 1944.

Squadron doctrine was that coordinated attacks against heavily armed ships were considered most effective in reducing AA fire. Squadron policy has been for one plane to strafe the target ship using a circular attack, thus bringing the maximum guns to bear on the target, while the second plane would close on a straight-in bombing attack. Therefore, it was believed this AA fire would have been materially reduced on the bombing run had this type of attack been employed during this action. However, Vidal was more than a mile away and could not provide Kasperson with the needed suppressing fire.

A large power schooner under attack by Lieutenant Wilkinson and Braddock on 7 August. *Courtesy of the National Archives.*

On the morning of the 6th, Colonel Paul W. Tibbets of the 509th Composite Group took off from North Field, Tinian, in the B-29 named Enola Gay and headed for the Japanese city of Hiroshima. On board was a U-235 bomb called "Little Boy." Coming over the city at 31,600 feet, Bombardier Major Thomas Ferebee released the bomb and, at 2,000 feet, the bomb detonated over Hiroshima with a force equal to 20,000 tons of TNT.

On the 7th, Lieutenant Wilkinson and Lieutenant Braddock spotted a power oil barge of 300 tons in the Tsushima Strait. Both planes attacked at low altitude. Lieutenant Wilkinson continued to strafe while Lieutenant Braddock made two low level bombing runs. Braddock's first run was ineffective, but on his second bombing run, a 500 pound bomb hit 20 feet short and traveled underwater directly beneath the target. The explosion completely covered the ship, causing it to list to port. While both planes continued to strafe, the target rolled over and sank.

Forty minutes later, a 100-ton coastal was attacked. Strafing runs were coordinated by both planes before Lieutenant Braddock dropped a 250 pound bomb. The bomb went through the ship's superstructure and detonated in the water 15 feet beyond. Continued strafing by both planes set fire to the freighter, which soon sank.

Thirty minutes later, a heavily laden two-masted schooner approximately 125-150 feet in length was attacked and sunk. The schooner was strafed until com-

A large power schooner under attack by Lieutenants Wilkinson and Braddock on 7 August. *Courtesy of the National Archives.*

pletely riddled by the withering fire of all bearable turrets, causing it to sink in a few minutes, leaving nothing but its cargo floating on the surface. On the 9th, Major Charles W. Sweeney in the B-29 "Bockscar" dropped a plutonium bomb named "Fat Boy" on the city of Nagasaki.

On the morning of the 10th, planes flown by Lieutenant Chay and Lieutenant Moyer were on anti-shipping patrol with each plane carrying a Bat. They spotted a tanker of 2,400 tons escorted by one picket boat. Both planes immediately went to 6,000 feet to launch their Bats. Lieutenant Chay launched his, but Lieutenant Moyer's had mechanical problems and was not released. Lieutenant Chay's went over the target and exploded harmlessly. Further attack at low level was decided against due to the presence of the picket boat, and the planes continued on patrol.

An hour later, five freighters were sighted by both planes. The ships were closely disbursed over an area of two miles, making it feasible to attack all targets in consecutive runs. Fires were started on all ships by strafing, and, in passing over one ship, Lieutenant Moyer scored a direct hit from 150 feet, causing the already flaming target to sink. A second freighter was sunk, and the remaining three targets were left burning. Lieutenant Chay was forced to jettison his entire bomb load due to shortage of fuel, making another attack impossible.

On the evening of 10 August, a statement of the Japanese surrender was announced, which initiated a spontaneous and spectacular celebration, with searchlights whirling across the sky and all anti-aircraft guns firing. Men, who only two days before had been flying combat patrols, now found themselves free from the anxiety of upcoming missions. Military personnel throughout the island celebrated the news by throwing impromptu parties. However, the sounding of a red alert finally stopped the firing, but personnel who sought foxhole protection against flak continued to celebrate throughout the night.

On 15 August, orders were issued to cease attacks and carry armament for defensive purposes only. Thus, the second combat tour of VPB-109 effectively ended one year to the day of the first combat cruise of VB-109. On 16 August, in an awards ceremony at Yontan Field, Rear Admiral John D. Price, USN, officially presented the Presidential Unit Citation to the squadron for its tour of duty in the Central Pacific from 31 December 1943 to 14 August 1944. It was a fitting presentation to mark the end of hostilities with an enemy with whom the squadron had been long and intimately associated. On 24 August, nine squadron planes moved to Awase Field, Okinawa, in a non-operational capacity, thus effectively ending the operations of VPB-109.

VPB-109, in 61 days of operations in the combat zone, had destroyed 6 enemy planes in the air and one on the ground, probably destroyed one, and damaged 8, destroyed 118 ships and damaged 86, and made 46 strikes against ground installations inflicting serious damage.

Appendix A:
Tactical Organization VB-109
(31 December 1943 to 15 August 1944)

First Division: Commander Norman Miller

First Section	#1: Commander Miller	Crew 1
	#2: Lieutenant(jg)Stewart	Crew 2
	#3: Lieutenant Seabrook	Crew 3
Second Section	#4: Lt. Commander Bundy	Crew 4
	#5: Lieutenant Davis	Crew 5
	#6: Lieutenant Bridgeman	Crew 6
Third Section	#7: Lieutenant Janeshek	Crew 10
	#8: Lieutenant Jadin	Crew 11
	#9: Lieutenant Belew	Crew 12

Second Division: Lt. Commander George Hicks

Fourth Section	#10: Lt. Commander Hicks	Crew 7
	#11: Lieutenant Keeling	Crew 8
	#12: Lieutenant Mellard	Crew 9
Fifth Section	#13: Lieutenant Glenn	Crew 15
	#14: Lieutenant Jobe	Crew 16
	#15: Lieutenant Sheppard	Crew 17

Appendix B:
Japanese Naval and Merchant Shipping Losses by VB-109

The following tables represent ships attacked by the squadron. Tonnage is estimated, and discrepencies exist with ships reported sunk by the squadron with those of official sources. Ships with a (?) have not been verified as sunk by the squadron through research conducted by this author.

Date	Crew	Type	Tonnage	Status
12/31/43	Belew	Coastal	35	Damaged
1/1/44	Bundy	Freighter	2,000	Damaged
1/3	Miller	Tanker	2,000	Damaged
1/6	Mellard	Patrol Ship	300	Damaged
1/8	Miller Janeshek Jobe	Patrol Ship	200	Sunk
1/9	Hicks	Freighter	2,000	Damaged
1/9	Hicks	Freighter	2,000	Damaged
1/11	Grayson Kasperson	Cargo	2,500	Sunk
1/11	Miller	Transport	6,000	Sunk
1/11	Hicks	Transport	4,000	Sunk
1/15	Janeshek	Freighter	500	Sunk
1/15	Miller Kasperson	Freighter	500	Sunk
1/17	Seabrook	Coastal	35	Sunk
1/18	Jobe	Freighter	4,000	Damaged

1/18	Hicks	Gun Boat	800	Damaged
1/18	Hicks	Gun Boat	800	Damaged
1/19	Janeshek	Freighter	4,000	Damaged
1/23	Hicks Bridgeman	Transport	4,000	Sunk
1/23	Hicks Bridgeman	Patrol Boat	?	Damaged
1/23	Hicks Bridgeman	Patrol Boat	?	Damaged
1/25	Grayson	Cargo	2,000	Sunk?
1/25	Grayson	Gunboat	800	Damaged
1/25	Grayson	Gunboat	800	Damaged
1/25	Grayson	Gunboat	800	Damaged
1/26	Belew	Cargo	2,500	Damaged
1/26	Belew	Patrol boat	20	Damaged
1/26	Belew	Patrol boat	20	Damaged
1/27	Jadin	Cargo	700	Damaged
1/27	Jadin	Cargo	700	Damaged
2/6	Jobe	(4)Coastals	40(each)	Sunk
2/6	Jobe	(2)Coastals	35(each)	Damaged
2/9	Mellard	Supply Boat	300	Damaged
2/18	Seabrook	Freighter	200	Sunk?
2/20	Miller	Freighter	100	Damaged
2/23	Miller	Freighter	1,500	Sunk
2/23	Sheppard	Freighter	2,000	Sunk
2/24	Jobe	Freighter	500	Damaged
3/3	Jobe	Coastal	40	Sunk
3/3	Hicks	Freighter	150	Damaged
3/5	Janeshek	Coastal	100	Sunk
3/8	Bundy	Freighter	1,000	Sunk
3/8	Janeshek	Coastal	70	Sunk
3/8	Janeshek	(4)Coastals	70(each)	Damaged
3/21	Mellard	Coastal	100	Sunk
3/22	Wheaton	Freighter	300	Sunk
3/23	Glenn	Coastal	100	Damaged
3/24	Miller	Freighter	2,600	Sunk?
3/24	Miller	Freighter	250	Sunk
3/24	Miller	Freighter	250	Sunk
3/26	Jobe	Coastal	35	Damaged
3/31	Bridgeman	Submarine	1,000	Damaged
4/1	Bundy	Submarine	1,000	Damaged

4/1	Wheaton	Freighter	200	Sunk
4/2	Seabrook	Freighter	6,000	Damaged
4/2	Miller	Freighter	200	Sunk
4/2	Miller	Freighter	200	Damaged
4/4	Glenn	Coastal	50	Damaged
4/4	Miller	Submarine	1,000	Sunk
4/4	Miller	Destroyer	1,500	Sunk?
4/4	Kasperson	Coastal	100	Sunk
4/21	Miller	(6)Coastals	70(each)	Sunk
4/21	Miller	Gunboat	150	Sunk
4/21	Miller	(2)Coastals	70(each)	Damaged
4/21	Seabrook	Submarine	1,000	Damaged
4/23	Jadin	Coastal	35	Damaged
4/29	Miller	Light Cruiser	6,000	Sunk?
4/30	Kasperson	Freighter	500	Damaged
4/30	Kasperson	Gunboat	600	Damaged
5/14	Miller	Transport	5,000	Damaged
5/14	Miller	(8)Coastals	70(each)	Damaged
5/16	Miller	Tanker	10,000	Sunk?
5/16	Miller	Freighter	5,000	Sunk?
6/2	Miller	Transport	7,000	Sunk?
6/2	Miller	(5)Freighters	150(each)	Damaged
6/3	Hicks	Destroyer	1,200	Damaged
6/3	Hicks	Freighter	2,500	Damaged
6/3	Hicks	Freighter	2,500	Damaged
6/3	Hicks	Gunboat	800	Damaged
6/3	Hicks	Gunboat	800	Damaged
6/3	Hicks	Transport	7,000	Sunk?
6/4	Wheaton	Gunboat	1,300	Sunk?
6/4	Wheaton	Gunboat	1,300	Damaged
6/6	Mellard	Destroyer	1,200	Damaged
6/6	Mellard	Freighter	4,000	Damaged
6/7	Davis	Transport	4,000	Damaged
6/17	Bridgeman	Submarine	550	Sunk
6/18	Keeling	Submarine	1,000	Damaged
6/21	Belew	Submarine	1,000	Damaged
7/14	Jobe	Transport	6,000	Sunk?
7/14	Jobe	(3)Coastals	70(each)	Sunk
7/14	Miller	Destroyer	1,200	Damaged
7/14	Miller	Destroyer escort	1,000	Damaged
	Jobe			

7/14	Miller	Freighter	2,500	Damaged
7/14	Miller	(5)Coastals	70(each)	Damaged
7/14	Jobe	Freighter	3,000	Damaged
7/14	Jobe	Oiler	500	Damaged
7/14	Jobe	Oiler	500	Damaged
7/14	Jobe	(5)Coastals	70(each)	Damaged
7/18	Bridgeman	Freighter	4,000	Sunk?
7/18	Miller	(3)Coastals	70(each)	Sunk
7/18	Miller	(3)Coastals	70(each)	Damaged
7/18	Miller	(3)Coastals	70(each)	Damaged
7/18	Bridgeman	(3)Coastals	70(each)	Damaged
7/18	Jobe	Freighter	5,000	Damaged
7/18	Jobe	(3)Coastals	70(each)	Damaged
7/18	Jobe	(3)Coastals	70(each)	Damaged
7/20	Jobe	Destroyer	1,200	Sunk?
7/20	Miller	Destroyer escort	1,000	Damaged
7/20	Miller	Freighter	2,500	Damaged
7/20	Miller	Coastal	70	Damaged
7/20	Miller	(2)Coastals	70(each)	Damaged
7/20	Bridgeman	(10)Coastals	70(each)	Damaged
7/20	Janeshek	(2)Coastals	70(each)	Damaged
7/20	Janeshek	(3)Coastals	70(each)	Damaged
7/20	Jobe	(6)Coastals	70(each)	Damaged
7/27	Miller	Freighter	2,000	Sunk?
7/27	Miller	(5)LCTS	150(each)	Sunk
7/27	Miller	(7)LCTS	150(each)	Damaged
7/29	Miller	(3)Coastals	70(each)	Damaged

Appendix C:
Enemy Aircraft Engaged by -109

Enemy Aircraft Engaged by VB-109
In Air:

Date	Crew	Type	Number Engaged
3/12	Mellard	Zeke	1
5/6	Keeling	Mavis	1
6/6	Janeshek	Kate	1
6/10	Mellard	Betty	1
7/20	Miller	Rufe	1

On Ground or in Water:

Date	Crew	Type	Number Engaged
1/8	Janeshek	Mavis	2
1/8	Jobe	Emily	2
1/11	Sheppard	Zekes	
4			
7/14	Jobe	unknown land based	4
7/14	Miller	Bettys, Zekes	2, 2
7/18	Bridgeman	Petes, Emily, Rufe	2, 1, 1
7/18	Jobe	Seaplanes	3
7/20	Miller	SE seaplane, Seaplanes	1, 4
7/20	Bridgeman	Rufes	2

Enemy Aircraft Engaged by VPB-109:
In Air:

Date	Crew	Type	Number Engaged
5/2/45	Serbin	Dinah, Jake	1, 1
5/17	Warren	Jack	1
5/17	Fairbanks Warren	Jack	1
5/24	Chay	Rufe	1
5/24	Chay Hewitt	Tony	1

Destroyed on Ground or in Water:

Date	Crew	Type	Number Engaged
5/5	Jobe	Dinah	1

Appendix D:
List of Air Crews and
Individual Combat Records for VB-109

Commander Miller
Crew #1 "Thunder Mug"

Commander Norman M. Miller, USN, 36, of Winston-Salem, North Carolina. Patrol Plane Commander and Commanding Officer of VB-109.
Lieutenant (jg) Norman L. Burton, USNR, Co-pilot. Detached from crew May 1944.
Ensign James R. Park, USNR, 22, of Los Angeles, California. Co-pilot. Joined crew June 1944.
Lieutenant (jg) Robert K. Shaffer, USNR, 23, of Saginaw Michigan. Navigator.
Paul K. Ramsey, ACMM, USN, 27, of York, PA. Plane Captain and Air Gunner.
William E. Fitzgerald, ACOM, USNR, 24, of Brokklyn, New York, Air Gunner and Ordnance Chief.
Adron G. Whitson, ACRM, USNR, 26, of Blanchard, Oklahoma. Leading Chief and Radioman.
Wayne Young, ARM1c, USN, 27, of Seattle, Washington. Radioman and Air Gunner.
Henry C. NcNatt, AMM1c, USNR, 27, of Compton, California. Air Gunner and Mechanic.
Edwin L. Dorris, ARM2c, USNR, 20, Kansas City, Missouri. Radioman and Air Gunner.
Robert Gariel, AMM2c, USNR, 21, of San Antonio, Texas. Air Gunner and Mechanic.
Thomas W. Delahoussaye, AMM2c, USNR, 20, of Lafayette, Louisiana. Air Gunner and Mechanic.

Lawrence B. Johnson, AOM2c, USNR, 20, of Grampian, Pennsylvania. Air Gunner and Ordnanceman.

Bernard R. Jaskiewicz, AOM2c, USNR, 23, of Bay City, Michigan. Air Gunner and Ordnanceman.

Jack A. Simmen, AMM3c, USNR, of Pittsburg, Pennsylvania. Air Gunner and Mechanic.

Planes Destroyed

7/14: Two Bettys and two Zekes on ground at Iwo Jima.
7/20: Airborne Rufe at Chichi Jima. Fighter on ground, four seaplanes on water (probable) at Chichi Jima.

Planes Damaged

1/8: Two seaplanes on water at Wotje.
2/6: Fighter on ground at Eten, Truk.
7/14: Five planes on ground at Iwo Jima.
7/18: Five seaplanes on water at Chichi Jima.
7/29: Two fighters in air at Truk.

Ships Sunk

1/8: Patrol ship at Wotje (co-credited with Lieutenant Jobe and Lieutenant Janeshek).
1/11: 6000-ton freighter at Kwajalein (probable).
1/15: 500-ton transport at Likiep (co-credited with Lieutenant Kasperson).
2/23: 1500-ton freighter at Kusaie.
3/24: 250-ton transport near Ponape.
4/4: Destroyer at Truk.
4/21: Four coastals at Ruo.
4/21: Two coastals and a patrol gunboat at Murilo.
4/29: Light cruiser at Truk (probable).
5/16: 5000-ton transport at Truk (probable).
5/16: 10000-ton tanker at Truk (probable).
6/2: 7000-ton freighter at Truk.
7/18: Three coastals at Haha Jima.
7/27: 2000-ton transport and five LCTS at Truk.

Ships Damaged
1/3: Oiler at Taroa.
2/20: 100-ton freighter at Kusaie.

4/9: Two coastals at Ponape.
4/19: Transport at Truk.
4/21: Coastal at Ruo.
4/21: Coastal at Murilo.
5/14: 5000-ton freighter at Truk; eight coastals at Truk.
6/2: Five small transports at Truk.
7/14: Destroyer, destroyer escort, 2500-ton freighter, five coastals at Iwo Jima.
7/18: Three coastals at Chichi Jima; three coastals at Haha Jima.
7/20: Destroyer escort, medium freighter, coastal at Chichi Jima; two coastals at Haha Jima.
7/27: Seven LCTs at Truk.
7/29: Three coastals at Truk.

Attacks

1/3: Mined anchorage and strafed Taroa installations.
1/8: Mined and strafed Wotje installations.
1/11: Bombed and strafed Kwajalein installations.
1/17: Bombed Kusaie (photo escort).
1/25: Strafed Likiep installations.
2/3: Bombed and strafed Mille, Taroa, Wotje, Majuro installations.
2/8: Strafed Ebon and Ujelang installations.
2/12: Bombed and strafed Ujelang installations.
2/15: Bombed Utirik installations.
2/18: Bombed and strafed Kusaie installations.
2/20: Bombed radio station at Kusaie.
2/23: Strafed Kusaie installations.
2/28: Bombed and strafed Wake installations.
3/9: Bombed docks at Lele Harbor, Kusaie.
3/13: Bombed and strafed barracks and shops at Ponape.
3/21: Bombed and strafed Ant installations.
3/24: Bombed and strafed Pakin installations.
3/28: Bombed and strafed radio station, barracks, and hangers at Ponape.
4/2: Strafed airfields at Ponape.
4/9: Bombed and strafed airfields at Ponape.
4/19: Mined lagoon passage at Truk. Strafed airfields at Truk.
4/21: Bombed buildings at Ulul. Bombed Igup installations.
4/25: Bombed and strafed Puluwat installations.
4/29: Strafed airfields at Truk.
5/7: Bombed and strafed Ruo installations.
5/14: Bombed and strafed Puluwat installations.

5/16: Destroyed radio station at Puluwat by bombing and starfing (Lieutenant Bridgeman as co-pilot Crew #6).

5/23: Bombed and strafed housing at Puluwat. Bombed buildings at Ruo.

6/2: Strafed Moen, Dublon and Eten at Truk.

6/9: Destroyed weather station at Puluwat by bombing and strafing.

7/1: Bombed and strafed airfields at Saipan and Tinian.

7/5: Bombed and strafed airfields at Saipan and Tinian.

7/14: Bombed and strafed Iwo Jima installations.

7/18: Bombed and stafed Chichi Jima installations. Bombed and strafed Haha Jima installations.

7/20: Bombed and strafed Chichi Jima installations. Bombed and strafed Haha Jima installations. Bombed and strafed Iwo Jima installations.

7/27: Strafed Dublon, Moen, Falo and Tor installations at Truk.

7/29: Strafed Eten airfield at Truk. Bombed and strafed Ponape installations.

Special Missions

2/25: First heavy bomber landed at Majuro.

2/26: First heavy bomber landed at Kwajalein.

6/13: Operational intelligence material dropped aboard U.S.S. Rocky Mount 900 miles at sea.

7/16: Marine Battalion Commanders and Intelligence Officers of the Tinian landing force flown over the prospective beaches at minimum altitude for one hour.

Lieutenant Stewert
Crew #2

Lieutenant John E. Stewert, USN, 30, of Sharonville, Ohio. Pilot.

Lieutenant (jg) Eugene A. Terrell, USNR, 23, of Hannibal, Missouri. Co-pilot.

Ensign William I. Rarick, USNR, 24, of Eaton, Indiana. Navigator.

Marwood E. Ebert, AMM1c, USNR, 26, of Milbank, South Dakota. Plane Captain and Air Gunner.

Joma O. Allonen, ARM2c, USNR, 21, of E. Weymouth, Massachusetts. Radioman and Air Gunner.

Ovey Janies, ACM2c, USNR, 22, of Mamou, Louisiana. Air Gunner and Ordnanceman.

Miles W. Morris, AMM2c, USN, 19, of Marlin, Texas. Air Gunner and Mechanic.

Orval F. Sanderson, AOM2c, USNR, 20, of Portland, Oregon. Air Gunner and Ordnanceman.

Walter R. Stilson, ARM2c, USNR, 22, of Franklin, New York. Radioman and Air Gunner.

Jack C. Wilhite, AOM3c, USNR, 20, of Oklahoma, Oklahoma. Air Gunner and Ordnanceman.
Richard S. Levy, AMM3c, USNR, 19, of Sanford, Florida. Air Gunner and Mechanic.

Attacks

3/13: Bombed and strafed Ponape installations.
7/22: Bombed Truk (photo escort).

Special Missions

6/25: ASW and air escort U.S.S. Maryland.

Lieutenant Seabrook
Crew #3 "Mission Belle"

Lieutenant Thomas Seabrook, USN, 28, of Ridgewood, New Jersey. Pilot.
Lieutenant (jg) Clarence W. Mckee, USN, 25, of Phoenix, Arizona. Co-pilot.
Ensign Fred H. King, USNR, 23, of Fort Wayne, Indiana. Navigator.
Arthur E. Babcock, AMM1c, USNR, 23, of Adrian, Michigan. Plane Captain and Air Gunner.
George E. Holden, AMM1c, USNR, 23, of Burley, Idaho. Tail Turret Gunner.
Donald E. Houghton, AOM2c, USNR, 21, of Perry, New York. Air Gunner.
Floyd D. King, AOM2c, USNR, 26, of Newark, Ohio. Bow Turret Gunner.
Thomas J. Burns, AMM2c, USN, 21, of Sea Cliff, New York. Radioman and top Turret Gunner.
Norman A. Bye, ARM2c, USNR, 23, of Lily, South Dakota. Radioman and Top Turret Gunner.
William H. Enid Jr., AMM3c, 25 of Atlanta, Texas. Air Gunner.

Ships Sunk

1/17: 70-foot vessel at Likiep.
2/18: 400-ton freighter at Kusaie.

Ships Damaged

4/2: Ship at Minto Reef.
4/21: Submarine.

Attacks

1/9: Bombed Kwajalein (photo escort).
2/18: Bombed Kusaie installations.
2/25: Strafed Kusiae installations.
3/11: Strafed installations at Langar Island, Ponape.
3/22: Strafed Kusaie installations.
3/25: Bombed and strafed Ant installations.
3/27: Strafed Kusaie installations.
4/14: Bombed and strafed Pakin installations.
4/18: Mined passage Truk Lagoon.
8/5: Bombed and heckled Chichi Jima.

Special Missions

3/1: Photographic reconnaissance of Wake.
7/17: Fighter escort for COMINCH, CINCPAC and CTF59 from Eniwetok to Saipan.
7/18: Fighter escort for COMINCH, CINCPAC and CTF59 from Saipan to Eniwetok.
8/6: Dumbo search for Lieutenant Kasperson.

Lieutenant Commander Bundy
Crew #4 "Flying Circus"

Lieutenant Commander John F. Bundy, USN, 28, of Sioux City, Indiana. Patrol Plane Commander.
Lieutenant (jg) Robert E. Malmfeldt, USN, 23, of New Buffalo, Michigan. Co-pilot and Patrol Plane Commander.
Ensign James J. Hellesen, USNR, 24, of Chicago, Illinois. Navigator.
Bennie C. Rubing, ACOM, USN, 20, of Ellwood City, Pennsylvania. Air Gunner.
Thomas H. Combs, AMM1c, USNR, 27, of Hazard, Kentucky. Plane Captain and Air Gunner.
George R. Bowly, AMM2c, USNR, 19, of Menands, New York. Air Gunner.
Donald P. Schoener, AOM2c, USN, 20, of Rapid City, South Dakota. Air Gunner.
Frank L. Smith Jr., ARM2c, USNR, 22, of Raymond, Mississippi. Radioman and Air Gunner.
John J. Griffiths, ARM2c, USNR, 28, of Johnson City, New York. Radioman and Air Gunner.
Alexander Stasinos, AMM3c, USNR, 22, of Chicago, Illinois. Air Gunner.
Ernest Marscke Jr., AMM3c, USNR, 22, of Milwaukee, Wisconsin. Air Gunner.

Ships Sunk

1/1: 2000-ton freighter 40 miles off Jaluit.

Ships Damaged

3/8: 1000-ton freighter Lele Harbor, Kusaie.
4/1: Submarine.

Attacks

2/7: Strafed Eniwetok.
2/11: Strafed Mejit.
2/21: Bombed and destroyed buildings at Utirik.
3/8: Bombed Kusaie.
3/8: Bombed Pingelap.
3/27: Strafed Kusaie.
4/18: Bombed Truk.
6/24: Escort U.S.S. Maryland.
8/4: Bombed and heckled Iwo Jima.

Lieutenant Davis
Crew #5 "No Foolin"

Lieutenant Clifton B. Davis, USNR, 27, of Alexandria, Virginia. Patrol Plane Commander.
Lieutenant (jg) Harry B. Shepherd, USNR, 26, of Hanover, Massachusetts. Co-pilot.
Ensign Robert L. Bennett, USNR, 23, of Manton, Massachusetts. Navigator.
Orval Stewert, AMM1c, USNR, 23, of Huron, South Dakota. Plane Captain and Air Gunner.
Warren A. Williams, AOM1c, USNR, 22, of Saugus, Massachusetts. Air Gunner.
Bill E. Mincey, AMM2c, USN, 22, of Kannapolis, North Carolina. Air Ginner.
George A. Matin, AOM2c, USNR, 20, of Waukesha, Wisconsin. Air Bomber and Air Gunner.
Donald L. DeBruine, ARM2c, USNR, 22, of Sheboygan, Wisconsin. Radioman and Air Gunner.
Wilbur V. Agee, ARM2c, USNR, 24, of Whittier, California. Radioman and Air Gunner.

Francis M. Walker, AMM3c, USNR, 22, of Birmingham, Alabama. Tail Turret Gunner.
William H. Smith, AOM3c, USNR, 20, of Decatur, Illinois. Air Gunner.

Attacks

1/23: Bombed and strafed Mejit installations.
3/11: Destroyed buildings at Pingelap.
3/27: Bombed Pakin, destroying installations.
4/18: Bombed Truk.
4/27: Bombed Pakin Islands.
7/22: Bombed Truk and escorted VD-4.
8/12: Bombed airfields at Ponape.

Lieutenant Bridgeman
Crew #6 "Sky Cow" and "Climbaboard"

Lieutenant William B. Bridgeman, USNR, 28, of Pasadena, California. Patrol Plane Commander
Ensign Robert P. Lamont, USNR, 24, of Washington Depot, North Carolina. Co-pilot.Joined crew June 44.
Ensign William T. Wiley, USNR, Co-pilot. Detached from crew May 44.
Ensign Herbert H. Rittmiller, USNR, 20, of Torrance, California. Navigator.
Edwin H. Watts, AMM1c, USN, 22, of Lincoln, California. Plane Captain and Air Gunner.
Walter J. McDonald, AMM2c, USNR, 25, of Bell Gardens, California. Air Gunner.
Robert A. Tovey, AOM2c, USNR, 21, of Chicago, Illinois. Waist Gunner.
George E. Murphy, AOM2c, USNR, 22, of Milwaukee, Wisconsin. Air Bomber and Bow Turret Gunner.
Peter T. Fay, ARM2c, USNR, 20, of Atlanta, Illinois. Radioman and Air Gunner.
Howard E. Bensing, ARM2c, USNR, 22, of Louisville, Kentucky. Radioman and Top Turret Gunner.
Warren G. Griffin, AMM3c, USNR, 24, of Marietta, Oklahoma. Tail Turret Gunner.
Robert W. Carey, ARM3c, USNR, 18, of Atlanta, Georgia. Waist Gunner.

Planes Destroyed

7/18: Two Petes, one Emily, one Rufe (probable) on water at Chichi Jima.
7/20: Two Rufes (probable) on water at Chichi Jima.

Planes Damaged

7/18: Four Petes, three Rufes at Chichi Jima.
7/20: One Zeke, two Bettys, one Tess, one Pete, one Emily at Chichi Jima.

Ships Sunk

1/23: 4000-ton freighter southeast of Kwajalein (co-credit with Lieutenant Hicks).
5/16: 5000-ton freighter at Truk (probable), 10000-ton tanker at Truk (probable).
6/17: Submarine.
7/18: 4000-ton freighter off Haha Jima.

Ships Damaged

3/31: Submarine.
7/18: Three coastals at Chichi Jima.
7/20: 10 coastals at Iwo Jima.

Attacks

1/9: Bombed Kwajalein (photo escort).
2/8: Strafed Jaluit, Lae, Wotho and Bikini installations.
2/12: Strafed Rongelap, Rongerik and Alinginae installations.
2/27: Strafed Ebon installations.
3/10: Bombed and strafed Oroluk installations.
3/12: Bombed and strafed Pingelap and Rongerik installations.
3/15: Bombed and strafed Pingelap and Kusaie installations.
3/16: Bombed and strafed Ujae installations.
3/18: Bombed and strafed Pingelap installations.
3/28: Bombed and strafed Taongi installations.
4/7: Bombed and strafed Oroluk installations.
4/15: Bombed and strafed Pakin and Ant installations.
4/17: Started fires at Ulul by bombing and strafing.
5/9: Bombed and strafed Oroluk installations.
5/16: Bombed and strafed Puluwat installations (piloted by Commander Miller).
7/18: Destroyed buildings at Chichi Jima and Haha Jima by bombing and strafing.
7/20: Destroyed installations at Chichi Jima, Haha Jima and Iwo Jima by bombing and strafing.
8/12: Bombed Wake at night.

Special Missions

3/18: Photographic reconnaissance Langar Island, Ponape.
6/23: ASW and air escort U.S.S. Maryland.

Lieutenant Commander Hicks
Crew #7 "The Stork"

Lieutenant Comdr. George L. Hicks, USNR, 32, of Three Rivers, California. Patrol Plane Commander.
Lieutenant William A. Warren, USNR, 28, of St. Paul, Minnesota. Co-pilot and Patrol Plane Commander.
Ensign Dicky Wieland, USNR, 24, of Dearborn, Michigan. Navigator.
Charles A. Murphy, ACMM, USN, 24, of Watertown, Tennesee. Plane Captain and Air Gunner.
Sidney R. Metcalf, ACOM, USN, 21, of Framingham, Massachusetts. Air Gunner.
Roger W. Clemons, AMM1c, USN, 22, of Columbus, Ohio. Air Gunner.
David H. Carlson, AOM1c, USN, 22, of Everett, Washington. Air Gunner.
William B. Idleman, AOM2c, USN, 20, of Burbank, California. Air Gunner.
Donald V. Conry, ARM2c, USNR, 23, of Fort DuLac, Wisconsin. Radioman and Air Gunner
Bill N. Harris, ARM2c, USNR, 19, of Houston, Texas. Radioman and Air Gunner.
William A. McNeil, AMM3c, USNR, 20, of Springfield, Ohio. Air Gunner.
Chester E. Rosell, AMM3c, USNR, 22, of Leonardville, Kansas. Air Gunner.

Ships Sunk

1/11: 4000-ton freighter Kwajalein.
1/23: 4000-ton freighter 35 miles southeast of Kwajalein.
6/3: 7000-ton freighter 50 miles west of Truk.

Ships Damaged

1/11: Two 2000-ton Freighter at Kwajalein by strafing.
1/18: Two escort vessels 35 miles southeast of Kwajalein.
3/3: One small freighter Ponape.
3/13: One small freighter Kusaie.
6/3: One freighter, two escorts, one destroyer 50 miles west of Truk.

Planes Damaged

2/28: three fighters on ground at Wake.
3/3: One multi-engined seaplane at Ponape on water.

Attacks

1/11: Bombing and shipping strike at Kwajalein.
1/18: Kwajalein Harbor.
2/2: Bombed Rongelap.
2/6: Strafed Ebon, Ujae.
2/10: Strafed Lae, Wotho, Bikini, Ailinglapalap, Jaluit.
2/17: Bombed Uterik.
2/21: Strafed Ujae.
2/24: Strafed Rongelap, Rongerlik, Ailinginae.
2/28: Wake Island strike and photo escort VD-3.
3/3: Ponape strike at shipping.
3/26: Bombed and strafed Kusaie, strafed Pingelap.
4/12: Bombed and strafed Ant and Pakin Islands.
4/18: Truk bombed.
8/1: Bombed and heckled Iwo Jima.
8/14: Bombed Wake.

Lieutenant Coleman
Crew #8A

Lieutenant Samuel E. Coleman, USNR, of Wenatches, Washington. Patrol Plane Commander.
Lieutenant (jg) Leroy A. Shreiner, USNR, of Wenatches, Washington. Co-pilot.
Ensign Leslie E. Fontaine, USNR, of Milwaukee, Wisconsin. Navigator.
Louis E. Sandidge Jr., AMM1c, USNR, of Clinton, Mississippi. Plane Captain and Air Gunner.
Sterling T. Brown, AMM2c, USNR, of Stamps, Arkansas. Air Gunner.
James T. Heasley, AOM2c, USNR, of Detroit, Michigan. Air Gunner.
Truman Steele, AOM2c, USNR, of Fort Smith, Arkansas. Air Gunner.
Harry F. Donovan, ARM2c, USNR, of Buffalo, New York. Radioman and Air Gunner.
Daniel J. Dujak, ARM2c, USNR, of Holyoke, Massachusetts. Radioman and Air Gunner.
Lou C. Petrick, S1c, USNR, of Mt. Vernon, Indiana. Air Gunner.
John E. Tusha, S1c, USNR, of San Angelo, Texas. Air Gunner.

Lieutenant Keeling
Crew #8B

Lieutenant John D. Keeling, USNR, 25, of Scott City, Kansas. Patrol Plane Commander.
Ensign Alfred T. Peterson, USNR, 23, of Litchville, North Dakota. Co-pilot.
Ensign Willard C. Hollingsworth, USNR, 27, of Gary, Indiana. Navigator.
Robert Dale West, ARM2c, USNR, 22, of Olathe, Colorado. Radioman and Air Gunner.
Joseph W. Sarno, AMM1c, USNR, 23, of Amityville, New York. Bombadier and Air Gunner.
Donald M. Maloney, AMM2c, USN, 21, of Ferndale, Michigan. Air Gunner.
Donald R. Lursman, AMM1c, USNR, 28, of WallaWalla, Washington. Plane Captain and Air Gunner.
William F. Krier, ARM1c, USNR, 24, of Philadelphia, Pennsylvania. Radioman and Air Gunner.
Frank R. Kramer, AOM1c, USNR, of Bingen, Michigan. Air Gunner.
Frank S. Graves, AOM2c, USNR, 22, of Pekin, Indiana. Air Gunner.
Dennis E. Bornholtz, AOM1c, USNR, 23, of Sioux City, Iowa. Air Gunner.
Ships Damaged

6/18: Submarine east of Saipan.

Plane Destroyed

5/6: Mavis in air 150 miles northwest of Truk.

Attacks

3/13: Bombed and strafed Oroluk.
3/16: Bombed installations at Pakin.
8/6: Bombed Truk (Photo escort VD-4).

Lieutenant Mellard
Crew #9 "Our Baby"

Lieutenant George A. Mellard, USNR, 26, of Russell, Kansas. Patrol Plane Commander.
Lieutenant (jg) John Dooley, USNR, 28, of Boston, Massachusetts. Co-pilot.
Ensign Bruce D. DeJager, USNR, 24, of Rochester, New York. Navigator.
Andrew Halasz, AMM1c, USNR, 21, of Dorchester, Massachusetts. Plane Captain.

Robert L. Dumais, ARM2c, USNR, 29, of Brunswick, Maine. Radioman and Air Gunner.

John P. Hruska, ARM2c, USNR, 22, of Nahma, Missouri. Radioman and Air Gunner.

Thomas C. Lee, AOM1c, USNR, 29, of Louisville, Kentucky. Air Gunner.

Claude L. McWhorter, AOM2c, USNR, 20, of Danville, Illinois. Air Bomber and Air Gunner.

Evans R. Lally Jr., AMM3c, USNR, 24, of San Francisco, California. Tail Turret Gunner.

Frank P. Guarini, AMM3c, USNR, 21, of Frankfort, Illinois. Belly Turret Gunner.

Jack H. Renfro, AMM2c, USNR, 19, of Reno, Nevada. Air Gunner.

Ships Sunk

3/21: 100-ton coastal at Ant.

Ships Damaged

1/6: Patrol vessel strafed and left burning at Kwajalein.
1/6: Destroyer bombed west of Truk and large freighter or transport.

Plane Destroyed

6/10: Betty shot down east of Saipan.

Planes Damaged

3/12: Two Zeros in air at Ponape, one probable, one damaged.
4/19: Betty in air north west of Ponape.

Attacks

1/17: Bombed Kusaie, photo escort VD-3.
2/5: Strafed runway Engebi.
2/9: Strafed Wotje, damaged supply boat and supplies ashore.
2/13: Bombed and strafed Mejit, destroyed building.
2/16: Strafed Mille, Paleolap, Uterik, Mejit.
2/19: Bombed and strafed Uterik, destroyed buildings.
3/9: Bombed Kusaie, Lele Harbor, destyroyed buildings dock area.
3/16: Bombed tower Oroluk.
3/21: Bombed Ant.

4/23: Aided in rescue B-24 and PBY survivors.
6/4: Bombed and strafed Ponape, gun positions and buildings damaged.
6/24: Escort U.S.S. Maryland.
8/6: Escort VD-4 Truk, bombed Tol.

Lieutenant Commander Janeshek
Crew #10 "Come Get It"

Lieutenant Commander William Janeshek, USN, 29, of Port Washington, Wisconsin. Patrol Plane Commander.
Lieutenant (jg) Thomas C. Peebles, USNR, 23, of Newton Centre, Massachusetts. Co-pilot.
Ensign Asa L. Branstetter, 23, USNR, of Curryville, Montana. Navigator.
Albert C. Peterson, AMM1c, USN, 24, of Ft. Pierce, Florida. Plane Captain and Air Gunner.
Rolvin P. Allen, AMM2c, USNR, 22, of Cranston, Rhode Island. Waist Gunner.
Seymour Simon, ARM2c, USNR, of Golden, Colorado. Radioman and Air Gunner.
Walter G. Holmes, ARM2c, USNR, 23, of Linesville, Pennsylvania. Radioman and Air Gunner.
Joseph A. Yates III., USNR, 24, of Miami, Florida. Air Gunner.
J.C. York, AOM2c, USN, 18, of Saylor, Missouri. Air Gunner.
Jack T. Biggers, AOM3c, USNR, 18, of Inglewood, California. Air Gunner.
Joseph B. Rogers, AOM3c, USN, 23, of Dallas, Texas. Air Gunner.

Ships Sunk

1/15: 500-ton freighter 40 miles southwest of Jaluit.
3/5: Small vessel at Kusaie.

Ships Damaged

1/8: Small vessel Wotje.
1/19: 4000-ton freighter 10 miles northwest of Majuro.
3/8: Five small coastal vessels off Oroluk.
7/20: Two coastals Haha Jima, three coastals Iwo Jima.

Planes Destroyed

1/8: One multi-engined seaplane on water at Wotje.
6/6: One Kate at Truk.

Planes Damaged

7/20: Two Emilys at Chichi Jima on water.

Attacks

1/7: Bombed Wotje.
1/8: Bombed and strafed Wotje.
2/3: Strafed Eniwetok.
2/7: Strafed gas drums and personnel at Eniwetok.
2/11: Bombed and strafed Eniwetok and Ujae.
2/18: Bombed Rongelap, strafed Rongerlik, Jaluit.
2/25: Strafed Uterik, Bikar, Mejit.
3/5: Bombed and strafed gun positions, installations at Kusaie.
3/28: Bombed and strafed Kusaie.
3/30: Bombed and strafed Kusaie.
4/11: Bombed and strafed Ponape, Ujelang.
4/18: Bombed and strafed Ponape.
4/22: Bombed Napali.
5/2: Bombed and strafed Ulul.
6/1: Strafed Satawan.
7/11: Strafed Truk.
7/19: Strafed Chichi and Haha Jima.
7/20: Strafed Haha and Iwo Jima.
8/6: Bombed Wake.
8/12: Bombed Ponape.

Lieutenant Jadin
Crew #11 "Helldorado"

Lieutenant Joseph I. Jadin, USNR, 28, of Gladstone, Mississippi. Patrol Plane Commander.
Lieutenant (jg) Charles W. Tischoff, USNR, 24, of Gloucester, Massachusetts. Co-pilot.
Ensign William F. Morgan, USNR, 24, of Hollidaysburg, Pennsylvania. Navigator.
Jack H. Cosby, AMM1c, USN, 21, of Willard, Missouri. Plane Captain and Air Gunner.
Emory L. Peterman, ARM2c, USNR, 23, of Cedar Falls, Indiana. Radioman and Air Gunner.
Francis W. Farrell, AMM2c, USN, 20, of New York, New York. Air Gunner.

Amos Mollinger, ARM2c, USNR, 21, of Kalona, Indiana. Radioman and Air Gunner.

Julius H. Loeser, AOM1c, USN, 25, of Houston, Texas. Gunner.

Richard Malkosian, AOM1c, USNR, of Westboro, Massachusetts. Bow Gunner and Air Bomber.

Joseph M. McKernan, AMM3c, USNR, 20, of Chicago, Illiniois. Tail Gunner.

Cecil M. Lee, AMM3c, USNR, 20, of Calhoun City, Mississippi. Belly Gunner.

Ships Damaged

1/27: Strafed three freighters (one medium, two small) south of Eniwetok.
4/23: Small vessel Ruo.

Attacks

4/13: Bombed and strafed Pakin.
4/23: Bombed Murilo.
5/10: Bombed and strafed Hall and Murilo.
6/7: Bombed and strafed Hall.

Lieutenant Belew
Crew #12 "Climbaboard"

Lieutenant Harold E. Belew, USNR, 27, of Fresno, California. Patrol Plane Commander.

Lieutenant (jg) Robert W. Conkey, USNR, 22, of Pawtucket, Rhode Island. Co-pilot.

Ensign Alexander J. Bacon, USNR, 23, of Detroit, Michigan. Navigator.

Robert E. Spomer, AMM2c, USN, 21, of Oakland, California. Gunner

James L. Chase, ACRM(AA), USN, 24, of Miami, Florida. Radioman and Gunner.

John F. Haznar, AMM1c, USNR, 25, of Thompsonville, Connecticut. Plane Captain and Gunner.

Charles F. Kidwell, AMM3c, USNR, 24, of Venice, California. Gunner.

Walter D. Morris, AOM1c, USN, 21, of Eaton, New York. Gunner.

Claude E. Watkins, AOM2c, USNR, 21, of Wenatchee, Washington. Gunner.

Arthur R. Sherron, AMM3c, USNR, 21, of Waterloo, Indiana. Gunner.

Richard L. Duncan, ARM2c, USNR, 23, of Bedford, Indiana. Radioman and Gunner.

Ships Damaged

12/31: Small vessel out of Apamama.
1/26: Small freighter, two patrol boats.
6/21: Submarine.

Attacks

1/19: Bombed Kwajalein.
4/10: Bombed Oroluk.
4/16: Bombed Ant and Pakin.
7/22: Bombed Truk (photo escort VD-4).

Lieutenant Kasperson
Crew #13

Lieutenant Elmer H. Kasperson, USN, 30, of Arlington, Virginia. Patrol Plane Commander.
Ensign Warren A. Hindenland, USNR, 24, of Foxboro, Massachusetts. Co-pilot.
Ensign Keith E. Ellis, USNR, 24 of Landon, North Dakota. Navigator.
Joseph W. Komorowski, AMM1c, AMM1c, USNR, Plane Captain, Air Gunner.
Warren B. Simon, AMM2c, USN, Air Gunner.
Richard D. Frye, ARM2c, USNR, Radioman, Air Gunner.
Hugo L. Kluge, ARM2c, USNR, Radioman, Air Gunner.
William F. Schneider, AOM2c, USNR, Air Gunner.
Victor B. Jones, AOM2c, USN, Air Gunner.
Allen K. Stinger, AOM3c, USNR, Air Gunner.
Bobby W. Fickling, AOM3c, USNR, Air Gunner.

Ships Sunk

1/1: Small ship Likiep Atoll.
1/11: 5000-ton frieghter at Kwajalein.
4/4: Small ship Wake Island.

Ships Damaged

4/30: 1500-ton freighter on high seas.
4/30: Escort vessel on high seas.

Attacks

1/1: Bombed and strafed Taroa.
1/8: Bombed Wotje and strafed.
1/11: Attacked shipping at Kwajalein.
1/17: Bombed Kusaie.
2/3: Photo Mille-bombed Wotje and Taroa.
2/12: Bombed Ujelang.
2/15: Strafed Mejit-bombed Uterik.
2/18: Strafed and bombed Kusaie.
2/20: Strafed and bombed Kusaie.
2/27: Bombed and strafed Wake.
3/17: Attacked Jap destroyer.
3/30: Attacked Jap Freighter and escort-strafed both on 5 runs.

Lieutenant Kennedy
Crew #14

Lieutenant Leo E. Kennedy, USNR, 30, of Ethlyn, Missouri. Patrol Plane Commander.
Ensign Marcus F. Poston, USN, 27, of El Paso, Texas. Co-pilot.
Ensign Richard J. Potter, USNR, 24, of Center Conway, New Hampshire. Navigator.
William L. Willocks Jr., AMM2c, USNR, 21, of Schnectady, New York. Waist Gunner.
Troy A. McClure, AOM1c, USNR, 24, of Cloverdale, Alabama. Waist Gunner.
John O. Oates, AMM3c, USNR, 19, of Long Beach, California. Belly Turret Gunner.
William E. White, AMM1c, USNR, 19, of Danville, Georgia. Plane Captain and Gunner.
Joseph B. Edwards, ARM2c, USNR, 21, of Des Moines, Iowa. Radioman and Gunner.
Jacob E. Bryant, ARM3c, USNR, 21, of Newellton, Louisiana. Radioman and Gunner.
Garnet R. Brown, AOM2c, USNR, 22, of Jet, Oklahoma. Gunner.
Harlyn G. Bakko, AMM3c, USNR, 21, of Billings, Montana. Bow Gunner.

Attacks

8/6: Bombed Truk (Photo-escort VD-4).

Lieutenant Glenn
Crew #15 "Urge Me"

Lieutenant Oliver S. Glenn, USNR, 26, of New Orleans, Louisiana. Patrol Plane Commander.
Lieutenant (jg) John P. McKenna, USNR, 26, of Mt. Vernon, New York. Co-pilot.
Ensign Howard L. Flohra, USNR, 23, of Creston, Indiana. Navigator.
Robert M. White, ARM2c, USNR, 22, of Springfield, Massachusetts. Radioman and Gunner.
Richard H. Westmoreland, AMM2c, USNR, 21, of Wichita Falls, Texas. Plane Captain and Gunner.
Clarence O. Gibson, AOM2c, USNR, 20, of Lawrence, Indiana. Gunner
James Grieve, AOM2c, USNR, 20, of Chicago, Illinois. Gunner.
Joseph A. Mirr, AOM2c, USNR, 19, of Milwaukee, Wisconsin. Gunner.
John A. Ryll, ARM2c, USNR, 23, of North Plymouth, Massachusetts. Radioman and Gunner.
Lawrence L. Morino, AMM2c, USN, of Los Angeles, California. Gunner.

Ships Damaged

3/23: 100-ton Freighter at Ponape.
4/4: Small vessel 84 miles west of Kwajalein.

Attacks

2/14: Bombed and strafed Ujelang, Ebob, Namorik.
3/9: Bombed and strafed Oroluk.
3/19: Bombed Pingelap.
3/23: Bombed and strafed Ponape.
7/22: Bombed Truk (Photo escort VD-4).
8/6: Bombed Truk (Photo escort VD-4).

Lieutenant Jobe
Crew #16 "Consolidated's Mistake"

Lieutenant Joseph H. Jobe, USNR, 28, of Goldendale, Washington. Patrol Plane Commander.
Lieutenant (jg) Waymond T. Miller, USNR, 24, of Seymour, Texas. Co-pilot.
Ensign Oscar Juelke, USNR, 27, of Oaks, North Dakota. Navigator.
Henson Guernsey, AMM2c, USNR, 20, of Bivins, Texas. Plane Captain and Gunner.

James F. Curtis, AMM1c, USNR, 23, of Indianapolis, Indiana. Gunner.
Gustav Greve, AMM3c, USNR, 20, of Annapolis, Maryland. Gunner.
Harold J. Carter, AMM3c, USNR, 21, of Okmulgee, Oklahoma. Gunner.
Wesley L. Thompson, ARM2c, USNR, 22, of Columbus, Kentucky. Radioman and Gunner.
Armond L. Klotz, ARM2c, USNR, 30, of Vinita, Oklahoma. Radioman and Gunner.
Louis F. Paulukonis, AOM2c, USNR, 21, of Long Island, New York. Bow Turret Gunner.
Robert A. Simms, AOM2c, USNR, 20, of Buda, Illinois. Gunner.

Ships Sunk

2/6: Four small vessels by strafing at Jaluit.
3/3: small vessel Ponape.
7/20: One destroyer Chichi Jima (not confirmed by author's sources).

Ships Damaged

1/8: Small freighter at Wotje by strafing.
1/18: Large freighter at Kwajalein by strafing.
2/6: Two small vessels on beach by strafing at Jaluit.
2/24: 500-ton freighter Kusaie.
3/26: Small vessel on beach Ujelang.
7/14: 6000-ton freighter probably sunk Iwo Jima, 2000-ton freighter damaged, two oilers set afire, one destroyer escort slightly damaged, eight coastals fired.
7/19: 5000-ton freighter Chichi Jima, three+ coastals Haha Jima
7/20: Coastals Haha Jima by bombing.

Planes Destroyed

1/8: Emily at Wotje destroyed on ground.
7/14: Four planes on ground Iwo Jima.

Planes Damaged

3/3: Seaplane on water Ponape.
7/14: Five planes on ground Iwo Jima.
7/19: Five seaplanes on water Chichi Jima.

Attacks

1/8: Bombed Wotje.
1/18: Bombed Kwajalein.
2/2: Strafed Ebon, started fires.
2/6: Strafed Jaluit, damaged gun positions.
2/10: Bombed and strafed Pingelap, started fires.
2/14: Bombed and strafed Rongelap, burned down buildings.
2/14: Bombed and strafed Jaluit, damaged gun positions.
2/20: Bombed and strafed Rongelap-started two oil fires, destroyed building.
2/28: Bombed Wake (photo-escort VD-3).
3/3: Bombed and strafed Langor Island, Ponape.
3/12: Bombed and strafed Pingelap, burned buildings.
3/31: Bombed and strafed Pingelap, burned buildings.
3/31: Bombed and strafed Kusaie, started fires.
4/8: Bombed and strafed Oroluk, started fires.
4/18: Bombed Truk.
5/18: Bombed and strafed Ponape, damaged unobserved.
6/23: Escort U.S.S. Maryland.
7/14: Bombed and Strafed Iwo Jima, buildings burned and oil drunms fired.
7/19: Bombed and strafed Chichi and Haha Jima, destroyed barracks and buildings.
7/20: Bombed and strafed Chichi and Haha Jima.
8/8: Bombed airfield Ponape.

Lieutenant Sheppard
Crew #17 "Available Jones"

Lieutenant Oden E. Sheppard, USNR, 25, of Bozeman, Montana. Patrol Plane Commander.
Ensign Clifford I. Nettleton, USN, 24, of Independence, Kansas. Co-pilot.
Ensign Melvin M. Breitsprecher, USNR, 24, of Waterloo, Indiana. Navigator.
Edward M. Danilczuk, AMM1c, USN, 26, of Bridgeport, Connecticut. Gunner.
Robert C. Thompson, ARM2c, USNR, 20, of Tulsa, Oklahoma. Radioman and Gunner.
Elmer C. Webb, AMM3c, USNR, 20, of Purdow, Texas. Waist Gunner.
Robert E. Bartlett, AMM2c, USNR, 23, of Corpus Christi, Texas. Tail Gunner.
Carl R. Snyder, AOM2c, USNR, 20, of Carthage, Missouri. Belly Turret Gunner.
Howard R. Anthony, AOM3c, USNR, 21, of Ft. Worth, Texas. Gunner.
Thomas M. Loamons, ARM2c, USNR, 22, of Huntington Park, California. Radioman and Gunner.

Howard L. Haynes, AOM2c, USNR, 26, of Watertown, Tennessee. Air Bomber and Gunner.

Ships Sunk

2/23: Freighter at Kusaie.

Planes Destroyed

1/11: Two Zekes at Kwajalein on ground.

Planes Damaged

1/11: Two Zekes at Kwajalein on ground.
5/31: Irving in air.

Attacks

1/11: Bombed Kwajalein and shipping in harbor.
1/17: Bombed Kusaie (photo-escort VD-3).
2/5: Bombed Wotje.
2/23: Bombed shipping at Kusaie.
2/27: Bombed Utirik and Mehit.
3/25: Bombed Pingelap.
4/13: Bombed Ponape.
8/6: Bombed Truk (Photo-escort VD-4).
8/6: Bombed Oroluk.
8/10: Bombed airfield Ponape.

Lieutenant Weaton
Crew #18 "Sugar Queen"

Lieutenant Thomas R. Wheaton, USNR, 25, of San Diego, California. Patrol Plane Commander.
Lieutenant (jg) Ernest B. Anderson, USNR, 26, of New Haven, Connecticut. Co-pilot.

Ensign Fredrick J. Menninger Jr., USNR, 20, of Berkely, Mississippi. Navigator.
Ernest S. Hayes, AOM3c, USNR, 19, of El Cajon, California. Bow Gunner.
Vernon A. Elchert, ARM2c, USNR, 22, of Fostoria, Ohio. Radioman and Gunner.
Raymond E. McPeak, AMM1c, USN, 20, of Mt. Airy, North Carolina. Plane Captain and Gunner.
Joseph Berogi, AMM2c, USNR, 26, of Bridgeport, Connecticut. Tail Gunner
Jack R. Musburger, AOM2c, USNR, 20, of Bomidji, Minnesota. Radioman and Gunner.
J. L. Howard, ARM2c, USN, 20, of Los Angeles, California. Radioman and Gunner.
Louie J. Thomas, AOM1c, USN, 40, of Alabama City, Alabama. Air Bomber and Gunner.
Gordon V. Johnson, AOM2c, USNR, 23, of Highland Park, Illinois. Belly Turret Gunner.

Ships Sunk

3/22: Small vessel at Ponape.
6/4: Armed auxilliary 160 miles west of Truk.

Ships Damaged

6/4: Two armed auxiliaries 160 miles west of Truk.

Attacks

1/17: Bombed Kusaie (photo-escort VD-3).
1/25: Bombed and strafed Ujelang.
2/13: Bombed and strafed Eniwetok.
2/19: Bombed Utirik.
2/27: Bombed Utirik.
3/12: Bombed radio installations at Oroluk.
3/18: Bombed Pingelap.
3/22: Strafed installations at Ant.
3/28: Bombed and strafed Oroluk.
4/9: Bombed and strafed Oroluk.
8/6: Bombed Truk (photo-escort VD-4).

Appendix E:
Missions and Flying Hours
per VB-109 Patrol Plane Commander

Name	No. of Missions	Hours of Missions	Total Hours
Miller	67	741.9	885.4
Davis	60	640.1	751.8
Bridgeman	59	618.8	742.8
Belew	58	616.6	717.8
Seabrook	58	642.5	738.0
Hicks	56	579.5	702.2
Janeshek	56	591.0	716.4
Jobe	56	492.5	732.7
Jadin	55	569.1	657.6
Mellard	55	586.6	677.7
Wheaton	54	580.7	670.1
Stewart	53	539.2	629.1
Bundy	52	555.3	668.0
Sheppard	52	545.3	676.5
Glenn	41	478.3	524.7
Keeling	37	419.8	455.7
Kasperson	30	378.9	398.0
Greyson	30	283.7	346.9
Kennedy	23	259.6	277.5
Herron	18	190.1	251.9
Coleman	9	91.8	158.2
Warren	3	28.8	45.3

Appendix F:
PB4Y-1 Aircraft Assigned to VB-109

The following aircraft were assinged to VB-109 and their disposition during and after the tour is shown below. Unless specified, aircraft were transferred to Hedron FAW-14 on 9-1-44.

BUNO

32068: "Come Get It!"
32108: "Thunder Mug." Crashed on landing and surveyed on 29 July 1944.
32111
32112: "Mission Belle."
32117: Missing in Action with Lieutenant Herron and Crew.
32118: "No Foolin."
32121: "Sky Cow." Crashed by Lieutenant Kennedy on take-off and surveyed.
32130: "The Stork."
32131: "Consolidated's Mistake."
32136: "Our Baby." Destroyed on ground during air attack at Apamama.
32137: "Helldorado."
32138
32139: Missing in Action with Lieutenant Coleman and crew.
32140: "Climbaboard."
32141: Crashed by Lieutenant Herron on night landing and surveyed.
32145: "Urge Me." Lieutenant Glenn and crew assigned on 31 January.
32148: "Flying Circus." Assigned to squadron on 29 February and transferred to FAW-2 on 9-1-44.

32149: "Available Jones." Assigned to squadron on 27 January.

32241: "Sugar Queen." Assigned to squadron on 1 April and transferred to VB-116 on 8-18-44.

32263: Assigned with Lieutenant Kennedy and crew on 1 May and was lost with Lieutenant Kasperson and crew.

38779: Assigned to squadron on 30 July and transferred to VB-116 on 8-16-44.

Appendix G:
Tactical Organization VPB-109

First Division-Lieutenant Commander Hicks

First Section	#1: Lieutenant Commander Hicks	Crew 1
	#2: Lieutenant Jobe	Crew 2
	#3: LieutenantWarren	Crew 12
Second Section	#4: Lieutenant Chay	Crew 3
	#5: Lieutenant Keeling	Crew 6
	#6: Lieutenant Hewitt	Crew 13
Third Section	#7: Lieutenant Jadin	Crew 5
	#8: Lieutenant Kennedy	Crew 10
	#9: Lieutenant Wilkinson	Crew 15

Second Division-Lieutenant Commander Bundy

Fourth Section	#10: Lieutenant Cdr. Bundy	Crew 2
	#11: Lieutenant Fairbanks	Crew 7
	#12: Lieutenant Turner	Crew 11
Fifth Section	#13: Lieutenant Davis	Crew 4
	#14: Lieutenant Vadnais	Crew 9
	#15: Lieutenant Challis	Crew 14

Appendix H:
Japanese Naval and Merchant Shipping Losses by VPB-109

Date	Crew	Type	Tonnage	Status
4/23/45	Chay	Freighter	100	Damaged
4/23	Kennedy	Coastal	25	Damaged
4/24	Fairbanks	Patrol boat	100	Damaged
4/24	Fairbanks	(4)whale-boats	20(each)	Damaged
4/27	Jobe	Freighter	100	Sunk
4/27	Jobe	Cargo	30	Sunk
4/27	Jobe	Transport	5,500	Damaged
4/28	Kennedy	Cargo Barge	100	Sunk
4/28	Davis	Tug Boat	100	Sunk
4/28	Davis	Freighter	100	Sunk
4/28	Hicks	Oiler	800	Sunk?
4/28	Chay	Picket Boat	100	Sunk
4/28	Kennedy	(3)Cargo Sailboats	40(each)	Damaged
4/29	Turner	Coastal	70	Sunk
4/29	Turner	Freighter	100	Sunk
5/1	Braddock	Picket Boat	100	Sunk
5/1	Braddock	Fuel Barge	300	Sunk
5/1	Braddock	(3)luggers	30(each)	Sunk
5/1	Braddock	Freighter	300	Sunk
5/1	Davis	Cargo Boat	20	Sunk
5/1	Davis	(2)Freighters	100	Sunk
5/1	Fairbanks	River steamer	150	Sunk
5/1	Davis	(3)Freighters	100(each)	Damaged
5/1	Davis	(2)Freighters	100(each)	Damaged

5/2	Jobe	Cargo boat	20	Damaged
5/2	Kennedy	Freighter	100	Damaged
5/3	Moyer	River steamer	70	Sunk
5/3	Chay	Freighter	100	Sunk
5/3	Vadnais	(8)Freighters	100(each)	Sunk
5/3	Vadnais	(6)Cargo boats	15(each)	Sunk
5/3	Vadnais	(8)Freighters	100(each)	Sunk
5/3	Wilkinson	(3)Freighter	100(each)	Damaged
5/3	Wilkinson	River steamer	30	Damaged
5/3	Wilkinson	Cargo boat	20	Damaged
5/3	Chay	Freighter	100	Damaged
5/3	Vadnais	Schooner	250	Damaged
5/3	Vadnais	(10)Freighters	100(each)	Damaged
5/4	Davis	(7)Freighters	100(each)	Sunk
5/4	Hewitt	Freighter	300	Sunk
5/5	Jobe	(10)Freighters	100(each)	Sunk
5/5	Jobe	Cargo lugger	35	Sunk
5/5	Turner	Oiler	2,300	Damaged
5/5	Jobe	Freighter	100	Damaged
5/12	Chay	Freighter	3,000	Damaged
5/13	Hicks	Freighter	2,000	Damaged
5/13	Hicks	Transport	2,000	Damaged
5/13	Hicks	Transport	700	Damaged
5/15	Wilkinson	Transport	5,500	Damaged
5/16	Hicks	Freighter	100	Sunk
5/16	Chay	Freighter	100	Damaged
5/17	Fairbanks	Tug boat	150	Damaged
5/18	Braddock	Freighter	100	Sunk
5/18	Hewitt Serbin	Freighter	2,000	Sunk
5/18	Turner	(3)Freighters	100(each)	Damaged
5/18	Braddock	Freighter	2,000	Damaged
5/19	Jobe	Freighter	100	Sunk
5/19	Jobe	Freighter	2,000	Sunk
5/20	Hicks	Picket boat	150	Sunk
5/20	Keeling Kennedy	(2)Coastals	70(each)	Sunk
5/20	Keeling Kennedy	Freighter	2,000	Sunk
5/20	Keeling Kennedy	Cargo boat	30	Damaged
5/22	Warren Turner	Freighter	100	Sunk

5/23	Vadnais Wilkinson	Freighter	100	Sunk
5/23	Braddock	Freighter	100	Sunk
5/23	Fairbanks	(2)Trawlers	100(each)	Damaged
5/23	Fairbanks	Freighter	100	Damaged
5/24	Jobe	(2)Freighters	100(each	Sunk
5/24	Serbin	Freighter	100	Sunk
5/24	Jobe	Freighter	300	Sunk
5/25	Keeling	Transport	3,000	Sunk
5/27	Hicks	Schooner	1,200	Sunk
5/27	Hicks	Freighter	100	Sunk
5/27	Kennedy	Freighter	100	Sunk
5/27	Hicks	Freighter	150	Sunk
5/27	Kennedy	Freighter	150	Sunk
5/27	Kennedy	Freighter	100	Sunk
5/27	Hicks Kennedy	Freighter	2,000	Sunk
5/27	Kennedy	Destroyer	2,300	Sunk?
5/27	Hicks	Freighter	150	Damaged
5/27	Hicks Kennedy	Freighter	100	Damaged
5/27	Kennedy	Coastal	70	Damaged
5/27	Jadin Moyer	Freighter	2,000	Damaged
5/29	Vadnais Vidal	Freighter	2,000	Sunk
5/30	Jobe	Picket boat	150	Sunk
5/30	Jobe Kennedy	Freighter	300	Sunk
5/30	Davis	Freighter	2,000	Sunk
5/30	Davis Serbin	Freighter	2,000	Damaged
5/30	Davis Serbin	(2)Picket boats	100(each)	Damaged
5/30	Davis Jobe Kennedy Serbin	(2)Attack Transport	7,000	Damaged
5/30	Jobe Kennedy Serbin	Freighter	3,000	Damaged

5/30	Jobe Kennedy Serbin	Picket boat	180	Damaged
5/30	Jobe	Lightship	300	Damaged
5/30	Jobe	(4)Picket boats	100(each)	Damaged
5/30	Jobe	Oiler	300	Damaged
5/30	Jobe Kennedy	Lightship	300	Damaged
5/30	Jobe Kennedy	Tug boat	200	Damaged
5/30	Jobe Kennedy	(2)Picket boats	100(each)	Damaged
7/26	Chay Braddock	(3)trawlers	100(each)	Sunk
7/26	Chay Braddock	(2)Trawlers	100(each)	Damaged
7/30	Jobe	Freighter	1,900	Sunk
7/30	Turner	Freighter	850	Sunk
7/30	Jobe Turner	(4)Freighters	70(each)	Sunk
7/30	Jobe	Freighter	100	Sunk
7/30	Turner	Large Schooner	150	Sunk
7/31	Hicks	(4)Trawlers	75(each)	Sunk
7/31	Hewitt	Schooner	100	Sunk
7/31	Hewitt Hicks	(3)Trawlers	100(each)	Damaged
8/6	Jobe Hicks	Freighter	850	Sunk
8/6	Jobe Hicks	Freighter	70	Sunk
8/6	Jobe	Tug Boat	100	Sunk
8/6	Keeling Vidal	Tanker	2,500	Damaged
8/7	Braddock	Freighter	300	Sunk
8/7	Braddock	Freighter	100	Sunk
8/7	Braddock	Large Schooner	100	Sunk
8/7	Chay Moyer	(5)Trawlers	100(each)	Damaged
8/7	Wilkinson	Freighter	300	Damaged
8/7	Wilkinson	Freighter	300	Damaged
8/7	Wilkinson	Large Schooner	100	Damaged
8/10	Chay Moyer	(5)Freighters	70(each)	Sunk

Appendix I:
List of Air Crews and Records of VPB-109

Lieutentant Commander Hicks
Crew #1 "Lambaster"

Lieutenant Commander. George L. Hicks, USNR, of Oakland, California. Patrol Plane Commander.
Ensign Donald F. Hanselman, USNR, of Detroit, Michigan. Co-pilot, Navigator.
Ensign William R. Wolfran, USNR, of Pittsburgh, Pennsylvania. Co-pilot, Navigator.
Roger W. Clemons, AMM1c, USN, of Columbus, Ohio. Plane Captain and Air Gunner.
Robert O. Blake, ACRM, USN, of Glen Falls, New York. Radioman and Air Gunner.
John W. Turner, ART1c, USNR, of Wichita, Kansas. Radioman and Air Gunner.
John W. Davis, AMM2c, USN, of Litchfield, Illinois. Air Gunner.
Frank S. Graves, AOM2c, USNR, of Pekin, Indiana. Bow Turret Gunner.
John E. McLean, AMM3c, USNR, of Palestine, Texas. Air Gunner.
George R. Keeby, AMM3c, USNR, of Newton, New Jersey. Air Gunner.
Herbert M. Winter, AOM3c, USNR, of Goleta, California. Air Gunner.
Albert E. Binch Jr., ARM3c, USN, of New Hampton, New York. Radioman and Air Gunner.

Ships Sunk

4/28: Oiler at Balikpapan.
5/16: Freighter off southern Korea.

5/20: Picket boat west of Goto Retto.
5/27: Large schooner, two small freighters, stack aft. Freighter(with Lieutenant Kennedy) off southwest Korea.
7/31: Four trawlers at mouth of Gaisan Ho River.
8/6: Medium freighter, small freighter and oceangoing tug (with Lieutenant Jobe) off Korea.

Ships Damaged

5/13: Medium freighter, two freighter transports off southern Korea.
5/27: Small freighter, small freighter (with Lieutenant Kennedy) off southwest Korea. Destroyer on the high seas.

Attacks

7/31: Destroyed railroad bridge over Seisen Ko River (Korea) by bombing. Seriously damaged a railroad train, heavy equipment and installations at Shinanshu airstrip, and coal mine buildings and installations by bombing and strafing.

Special Missions

4/20: First reconnaissance of Patani Roads, Gulf of Siam
5/20: Enemy fighter decoy with 8 Army P-47s.
6/12: Recon of Truk.
7/6: Fleet barrier patrol west of Marcus.
7/9: Fleet barrier patrol northwest of Marcus.
7/15: Fleet barrier patrol east of Honshu.
7/24: Air-sea rescue off Honshu.

Lieutenant Commander Bundy (until 5 May 1945)
Crew#2A

Lieutenant Commander. John F. Bundy, USNR, of Sioux City, Iowa. Patrol Plane Commander.
Ensign Leslie L. Hunt, USNR, of Springfield, Missouri. Co-pilot and Navigator.
Ensign John F. Fuchs, USNR, of Guthrie, Minnesota. Co-pilot and Navigator.
Alvin S. O'Brien, AMMF1c, USN, of Springfield, Massachusetts. Plane Captain and Air Gunner.
Kenneth B. Collins, ACOM, USN, of Fort Myers, Florida. Air Gunner.
John J. Griffiths, ARM1c, USNR, of Johnson City, New York. Radioman and Air Gunner.

Richard S. Levy, AMM2c, USNR, of Sanford, Florida. Air Gunner.

Donald P. Shoener, AOM2c, USN, of Rapid City, South Dakota. Air Gunner.

Lester Kaufman, ART2c, USNR, of Brooklyn, New York. Radarman and Air Gunner.

George F. Charles Jr., AMM3c, USNR, of Catlettsburg, Kentucky. Air Gunner.

George H. Perdue, AMM3c, USNR, of Ceredo, West Virginia. Air Gunner.

Jackson C. Anderson, ARM3c, USNR, of Blackshear, Georgia. Radioman and Air Gunner.

Attacks

4/27: Strafed lookout towers at Mapoeti Island.

5/2: Bombed and strafed Kudat installations. Strafed Sempadi Island installations.

5/5: Strafed installations at Jesselton.

Lieutenant Turner (From 5 May 1945)
Crew #2B "Shanglai Lil"

Lieutenant Howard M. Turner Jr., USNR, of Cambridge, Massachusetts. Patrol Plane Commander.

Ensign Leslie L. Hunt, USNR, of Springfield, Missouri. Co-pilot and Navigator.

Ensign John F. Fuchs, USNR, of Guthrie, Minnesota. Co-pilot and Navigator.

Alvin S. O'Brien, AMMF1c, USN, of Springfield, Massachusetts. Plane Captain and Air Gunner.

Kenneth B. Collins, ACOM, USN, of Fort Myers, Florida. Air Gunner until 15 June 1945.

John J. Griffiths, ARM1c, USNR, of Johnson City, New York. Radioman and Air Gunner.

Richard S. Levy, AMM2c, USNR, of Sanford, Florida. Air Gunner.

Donald P. Shoener, AOM2c, USN, of Rapid City, South Dakota. Air Gunner.

Richard J. Sulewski, ARM2c, USNR, of Detroit, Michigan. AIr Gunner from 15 June 1945.

Lester Kaufman, ART2c, USNR, of Brooklyn, New York. Radarman and Air Gunner until 15 June 1945.

George F. Charles Jr., AMM3c, USNR, of Catlettsburg, Kentucky. Air Gunner.

George H. Perdue, AMM3c, USNR, of Ceredo, West Virginia. Air Gunner.

Darwin R. Teeter, AOM3c, USNR, of Hartsville, Ohio. Air Gunner from 15 June 1945.

Jackson C. Anderson, ARM3c, USNR, of Blackshear, Georgia. Radioman and Air Gunner.

Planes Damaged

5/18: Zeke in air off southern Korea (with Lieutenant (jg) Braddock).

Ships Sunk

5/22: Freighter off southern Korea (with Lieutenant Warren).
7/30: Freighter and large schooner off Korea. Four Freighters off Korea (with Lieutenant Jobe).

Ships Damaged

5/18: Three freighters off southern Korea.

Special Missions

6/22: reconnaissance of Chichi Jima.
6/28: reconnaissance of Chichi Jima.
7/6: Fleet barrier patrol west of Marcus.
7/9: Fleet barrier patrol northwest of Marcus.
7/15: Fleet barrier patrol east of Honshu.
7/21: Air-sea rescue off Honshu.
7/26: Air-sea rescue off Honshu.
8/1: Special weather flight (commended by CincPac).

Lieutenant Donald S. Chay
Crew #3

Lieutenant Donald S. Chay, USNR, of Albuquerque, New Mexico. Patrol Plane Commander.
Lieutenant (jg) Charles I. Robichaud, USNR, of Rockland, Massachusetts. Co-pilot and Navigator.
Ensign Chester L. Cline, USNR, of Centerville, Iowa. Co-pilot and Navigator.
Warren G.H. Griffin, AMM2c, USNR, of Marietta, Oklahoma. Plane Captain and Air Gunner.
Harold L. May, AOM1c, USNR, of Compton, California. Air Gunner.
Gordon D. Austad, ARM2c, USNR, of Milwaukee, Wisconsin. Radioman and Air Gunner.
George P. Haberman, ARM2c, of New York, New York. Air Gunner.
Robert W. Fritz, AMM3c, USNR, of Cincinnati, Ohio. Air Gunner.

John L. Lavoie, AMMF3c, USNR, of Auburn, Massachusetts. Radioman and Air Gunner.
Jack R. Mueller, AOM3c, USNR, of Maplewood, Missouri. Air Gunner.
James W. Elkins, ARM3c, USNR, of Mobile, Alabama. Air Gunner.
Thomas H. Pickens, S1c, USNR, of Charleston, West Virginia. Radioman and Air Gunner.

Planes Damaged

5/24: Rufe in air off Korea. Tony in air off Korea (with Lieutenant Hewitt).

Planes Damaged

5/24: Zeke in air off Korea.

Ships Sunk

4/28: Picket boat at Balikpapan.
5/3: Freighter off Makassar.
7/26: Three trawlers at Shingu (with Lieutenant (jg) Braddock).
8/10: Five small freighters in Tsushima Straits (with Lieutenant (jg) Moyer).

Ships Damaged

4/23: Small frieghter off west coast of Borneo.
5/3: Freighter at Makassar.
5/12: Large freighter off southern Korea.
5/16: Freighter off southern Korea.
7/26: Two trawlers at Shingu (with Lieutenant (jg) Braddock).
8/7: Five trawlers off Kyushu (with Lieutenant (jg) Moyer).

Attacks

4/28: Destroyed large oil storage tank at Balikpapan by bombing.
7/26: Destroyed railroad tunnel between Shingu and Udono (Honshu) by bombing, silenced three gun positions by strafing (with Lieutenant (jg) Braddock).

Special Missions

4/20: First recon of Pulo Wai, Pulo Panjang and Pulo Condore
6/16: reconnaissance of Truk.
6/23: reconnaissance of Chichi Jima.
6/30: reconnaissance of Chichi Jima.
7/8: Fleet barrier patrol west of Marcus.
7/11: Fleet barrier patrol east of Honshu.
7/16: Fleet barrier patrol east of Honshu.
7/22: Fleet barrier patrol south of Honshu.

Lieutenant Clifton B. Davis
Crew #4

Lieutenant Clifton B. Davis, USNR, of Alexandria, Virginia. Patrol Plane Commander.
Ensign Donald E. McKinley, USNR, of Glendale, California. Co-pilot and Navigator.
Ensign Chester F. Szesczyk, USNR, of Pulaski, Wisconsin. Co-pilot and Navigator.
James M. Hammock, AMM2c, USN, of Hillsboro, Texas. Plane Captain and Air Gunner.
Warren A. Williams, AOM1c, USNR, of Saugus, Masachusetts. Air Gunner.
Marvin Feinberg, AMM2c, USNR, of New York, New York. Air Gunner.
Wibur V. Agee, ARM2c, USN, of Whittier, California. Radioman and Air Gunner.
Glenn H. Jenson, AOM3c, USNR, of Las Vegas, Nevada. Air Gunner.
William A. Doelle, ARM3c, USNR, of Detroit, Michigan. Radarman and Air Gunner.
William Y. Toellen, ARM2c, USN, of Peru, Illinois. Air Gunner until 31 May 1945.
Bernard Gwinn, ARM3c, USNR, of Troy, New York. Air Gunner from 15 June 1945.
George Hausmann, S1c, USNR, of Vandalia, Illinois. Air Gunner.
Jay L. Reed II, S1c, USNR, of Long Beach, California. Air Gunner.

Ships Sunk

4/28: Large tug boat at Ular. Freighter off Kaja Wali.
5/1: Cargo ship at Padpare Bay. Two freighters at Mandar Bay.
5/4: Seven freighters at Pontianak.
5/30: Freighter off Yangtze River mouth.

Ships Damaged

5/1: Five freighters on ways at Mandar Bay.
5/30: Freighter, two picket boats off Yangtze River mouth (with Lieutenant Jobe, Lieutenant Kennedy, Lieutenant (jg) Serbin).

Attacks

4/28: Strafed towers at K. Dungun.
5/1: Destroyed buildings and gun positions at Mandar Bay by strafing.
5/4: Destroyed a shipyard and a sawmill at Pontianak by bombing and strafing.
5/30: Lighthouse at Yangtze River mouth damaged by strafing.

Special Missions

4/28: Special recon of Patani Roads, Gulf of Siam.
7/15: Fleet barrier patrol east of Honshu.
7/23: Fleet barrier patrol south of Honshu.
7/26: Fleet barrier patrol south of Honshu.

Lieutenant Joseph I. Jadin
Crew #5 "Miss Lotta Tail"

Lieutenant Joseph I. Jadin, USNR, of Gladstone, Michigan. Patrol Plane Commander.
Ensign John L. Price, USNR, of Fairland, Oklahoma. Co-pilot and Navigator.
Ensign Fred A. Beckman, USNR, of Union, Missouri. Co-pilot and Navigator.
Jack H. Cosby, AMM1c, USN, of Willard, Missouri. Plane Captain and Air Gunner.
Julius H. Loeser, ACOM, USN, of Shreveport, Louisiana. Air Gunner until 10 June.
Isadore Smith, AOMT1c, USNR, of Atlanta, Georgia. Air Gunner.
Emery L. Peterman, ARM1c, USNR, of Cedar Falls, Iowa. Radioman and Air Gunner.
Cecil M. Lee, AMM2c, USNR, of Calhoun City, Mississippi. Air Gunner.
Roy L. Balke, AMM3c, USNR, of Tigorton, Wisconsin. Air Gunner.
Edward M. Jones III, AMM3c, USNR, of Barnwell, South Carolina. Air Gunner.
Raymond A. Grover, ARM3c, USNR, of Elmira Heights, New York. Radioman and Air Gunner.
John W. Toski, ARM3c, USNR, of Pontiac, Michigan. Radioman and Air Gunner.
Kenneth B. Collins, ACOM, of Ft. Myers, Florida. (from 10 June).

Ships Damaged

5/27: Freighter off Shimono Shima (with Lieutenant (jg) Moyer).

Attacks

4/25: Bombed and strafed radar station at Cape Paroepoe.
5/2: Bombed and strafed Kudat runway.
5/27: Bombed and strafed radio and radar station at Svwanos Jima (with Lieutenant (jg) Moyer).

Special Missions

6/18: Recon of Chichi Jima.
6/21: Special weather flight.
7/2: Air-sea rescue off Honshu.
7/7: Air-sea rescue off Honshu.
7/20: Fleet barrier patrol east of Honshu.
7/23: Fleet barrier patrol south of Honshu.

Lieutenant John D. Keeling
Crew #6A "Bachelor's Delight"

Lieutenant John D. Keeling, USNR, of Scott City, Kansas. Patrol Plane Commander.
Ensign Henry Baier Jr., USNR, Seward, Kansas. Co-pilot and Navigator.
Ensign Keith W. Radcliffe, USNR, of Kirkwood, Missouri. Co-pilot and Navigator.
William L. Willocks Jr., AMM1c, USNR, of Schenectady, New York. Plane Captain and Air Gunner.
Frank R. Krier, ARM1c, USNR, of Philadelphia, Pennsylvania. Radioman and Air Gunner.
Alexander J. Boyd, ARM1c, USNR, of Pueblo, Colorado. Radioman and Air Gunner.
Melvin M. Rager, AMM2c, USNR, Johnstown, Pennsylvania. Air Gunner.
James R.T. Carswell, AFC2c, USNR, of Baltimore, Maryland. Air Gunner.
Peter G. Ilacqua, ARM2c, USNR, of Syracuse, New York. Radioman and Air Gunner.
James E. Kreiger, AMM3c, USNR, of Cincinnati, Ohio. Air Gunner.
Lawrence R. Conroy, AOM3c, USNR, of Cleveland, Ohio. Air Gunner.

Ships Sunk

5/20: Freighter transport and two coastl Freighters off southern Korea (with Lieutenant Kennedy).
5/25: Freighter transport off Korea (with Lieutenant Challis).

Ships Damaged

5/20: Cargo boat off southern Korea (with Lieutenant Kennedy).
8/5: Large tanker off Korea.

Attacks

4/27: Strafed radar tower at Kapaladoea.

Special Missions

6/26: Recon of Chichi Jima.
7/2: Recon of Chichi Jima.
7/8: Fleet barrier patrol west of Marcus.
7/11: Fleet barrier patrol east of Honshu.
7/13: Air-sea rescue off Honshu.
7/14: Air-sea rescue off Honshu.
7/19: Fleet barrier patrol east of Honshu.
7/22: Fleet barrier patrol south of Honshu.
7/24: Night tracking of unidentified convoy.
7/27: Fleet barrier patrol south of Honshu.

Lieutenant Jerrel D. Stephens
Crew #6B(from 17 August)

Lieutenant Jerrel D. Stephens, USNR, of Pasadena, California. Patrol Plane Commander.
Lieutenant (jg) Robert W. Coon, USNR, of Fort Worth, Texas. Co-pilot and Navigator.
Lieutenant (jg) John W. Morris, USNR, Elmwood Place, Oregon. Co-pilot and Navigator.
Ralph C. Brickel, ACMM, USN, of Jacumba, Georgia. Plane captain and Air Gunner.
Harold S. Jackson, S1c, USNR, of Newman, Georgia. Radioman and Air Gunner.
Thomas W. Coltrane, ARM3c, USNR, of Sophia, North Carolina. Radioman and

Air Gunner.
Carl E. Wehrley, AMM3c, USNR, of Hamilton, Oregon. Air Gunner.
Ramon L. Huff, AMM3c, USNR, of Emerson, Nebraska. Air Gunner.
Ray E. Beisswanger, S1c, USNR, of Danville, Pennsylvania. Air Gunner.
Ronald U. Dreyer, AOM3c, USNR, of Sioux Falls, North Dakota. Air Gunner.
Andrew J. Hill Jr., AOM3c, USNR, of LaGrange, Georgia. Air Gunner.
Samuel W. Lewis, ARM3c, USNR, of East Point, Georgia. Radioman and Air Gunner.

Lieutenant G.D. Fairbanks
Crew #7 "Hogan's Goat"

Lieutenant G.D. Fairbanks, USNR, of Wabasha, Minnesota. Patrol Plane Commander.
Ensign Abraham Shore, USNR, of Pittsburg, Pennsylvania. Co-pilot and Navigator.
Ensign Robert J. Groce, USNR, of Portland, Oregon. Co-pilot and Navigator.
Evans R. Lally, Jr., AMM2c, USNR, of San Francisco, California. Plane Captain and Air Gunner.
Franklin Shlyk, AMM2c, USNR, of Detroit, Michigan. Air Gunner
Marion E. Kinser, ARM2c, USNR, of Rogersville, Missouri. Radioman and Air Gunner.
Robert L. Berry, ARM2c, USNR, of Modoc, Illinois. Radioman and Air Gunner.
Dean R. Johnson, ARM2c, USNR, of Hartford, South Dakota. Radioman and Air Gunner.
Richard Jenkins, AMM3c, USNR, of Pittsburg, Pennsylvania. Air Gunner.
Alfred V. Sandquist, AMM3c, USNR, of St. Paul, Minnesota. Air Gunner.
Donald J. Hamilton, AOM3c, USNR, of Omaha, Nebraska. Air Gunner.
Kasper E. Weigant, AOM3c, USNR, of Portland, Oregon. Air Gunner.

Planes Destroyed

5/17: Jack in air off Kyushu (with Lieutenant Warren).

Ships Sunk

5/1: River Steamer at Samarinda.

Ships Damaged

4/23: Patrol boat and four cargo whaleboats off Indo-China.

5/17: Oceangoing tug off southern Korea.
5/23: Two cargo trawlers off Korea. Freighter off southern Korea.

Attacks

5/1: Bombed and strafed radar station at Mangkalihat.

Special Missions

6/19: Recon of Chichi Jima.
6/25: Recon of Chichi Jima.
7/2: Recon of Chichi Jima.
7/8: Fleet Barrier patrol west of Marcus.
7/11: Fleet Barrier patrol east of Honshu.
7/15: Air-Sea Rescue off Honshu.
7/16: Fleet Barrier patrol east of Honshu.
7/20: Fleet Barrier patrol east of Honshu.
7/23: Fleet Barrier patrol south of Honshu.
7/27: Fleet barrier patrol south of Honshu.

Lieutenant Joseph H. Jobe
Crew #8 "Consolidated's Mistake II"

Lieutenant Joseph H. Jobe, USNR, of Goldendale, Washington. Patrol Plane Commander.
Ensign Edward A. Robie, USNR, of Yorktown, Heights, New York. Co-pilot and Navigator.
Ensign Richard C. Hooper, USNR, of Philadelphia, Pennsylvania. Co-pilot and Navigator.
Lloyd B. Bowen, AMM1c, USNR, of Sunnyvale, California. Plane Captain and Air Gunner.
Wesley L. Thompson, ARM1c, USNR, of Columbus, Kentucky. Radioman and Air Gunner.
Gustav Greve, AMM2c, USNR, of Annapolis, Maryland. Air Gunner.
Robert A. Simms, AOM2c, USNR, of Buda, Illinois. Air Gunner.
Donald R. Chapman, ARM2c, USNR, of Newton, Iowa. Radioman and Air Gunner.
Sven W. Carlstrom, ARM2c, USNR, of Glen Cove, New York. Radioman and Air Gunner.
Donald M. Derham, AMM3c, USNR, of Western Point, Maryland. Air Gunner.
William H. Lehn, AOM3c, USNR, of Brandon, Minnesota. Air Gunner.

Lawrence Boucvalt, S1c, USNR, of Lutcher, Louisiana. Air Gunner.

Planes Destroyed

5/5: Dinah on ground near Pontianak.

Ships Sunk

4/27: Freighter off Temadjoe Island. Cargo vessel off Pandjang.
5/5: Ten Freighters and a cargo lugger at Pontianak.
5/19: Freighter and small Freighter off southern Korea.
5/24: Three small Freighters (one with Lieutenant (jg) Serbin) and stack-aft Freighter off southern Korea.
5/30: Picket boat, Freighter (with Lieutenant Kennedy) off Yangtze River mouth.
7/30: Freighter and small Freighter off Korea, and four Freighters off Korea (with Lieutenant Turner).
8/6: Medium Freighter, small Freighter and oceangoing tug (with Lieutenant Commander Hicks) off Korea.

Ships Damaged

4/27: Freighter transport flakship at Labuan Island.
5/2: Cargo vessel off Indo-China.
5/5: Freighter at Pontianak.
5/30: Lightship, four picket boats and a tanker off Yangtze River mouth. Lightship, oceangoing, tug, two picket boats off Yangtze River mouth (with Lieutenant Kennedy). Freighter, large picket boat off Yangtze (with Lieutenant Kennedy, Lieutenant (jg) Serbin) Two seven thousand ton attack transports in Ynagtze River (with Lieutenant Davis, Lieutenant Kennedy).

Attacks

4/27: Destroyed radio buildings at Mukan by bombing and strafing.
5/2: Strafed installations and brickyard in southwest Indo-China.
5/5: Destroyed a shipyard at Pontianak by bombing and strafing.

Special Missions

4/23: Recon of Patani Roads, Gulf of Siam.
6/18: Recon of Truk.
6/23: Recon of Chichi Jima.

7/1: Recon of Chichi Jima.
7/8: Fleet Barrier patrol west of Marcus.
7/11: Fleet Barrier patrol east of Honshu.
7/16: Fleet Barrier patrol east of Honshu.

Lieutenant Robert E. Vadnais
Crew #9

Lieutenant Robert E. Vadnais, USNR, of Portland, Oregon. Patrol Plane Commander.
Ensign Harlie A. Peterson, USNR, of Kansas City, Missouri. Co-pilot and Navigator.
Ensign George M. Torgenson, USNR, of Madison, Wisconsin. Co-pilot and Navigator.
Richard H. Smith, AMM1c, USN, Jackson, California. Plane Captain and Air Gunner.
Fred S. Lyon Jr., ARM1c, USN, Centralia, Washington. Radioman and Air Gunner.
George A. Frank, AMM2c, USNR, Wanamie, Pennsylvania. Air Gunner.
James M. Caldwell, AOM2c, USNR, Rhinelander, Wisconsin. Air Gunner.
Deloss C. Butterworth, ARM2c, USNR, Barnesboro, Pennsylvania. Radioman and Air Gunner.
Edward Dailey, AMM3c, USNR, Flandereau, South Dakota. Air Gunner.
Frederick C. Albers, AMMF3c, USNR, Rockville Center, New York. Air Gunner.
Frank T. Atkinson, AOM3c, USNR, Dubuque, Iowa. Air Gunner.
George Bachman, ARM3c, USNR, Bowdie, South Dakota. Radioman and Air Gunner.

Ships Sunk

5/3: Eight Freighters and eight Freighters on the ways, six cargo boats at Pontianak.
5/23: Freighter off southern Korea (with Lieutenant Wilkinson).
5/29: Freighter off eastern Korea (with Lieutenant (jg) Vidal).

Ships Damaged

5/3: Large schooner and ten Freighters at Pontianak.

Attacks

4/26: Destroyed lookout station at Djemadja Island by bombing.
5/3: Destroyed one shipyard and two-thirds of a second at Pontianak by bombing and strafing.

Special Missions

6/19: Recon of Chichi Jima.
6/24: Recon of Chichi Jima.
7/2: Air-Sea Rescue off Honshu.
7/7: Fleet Barrier patrol west of Marcus.
7/17: Air-Sea Rescue off Honshu.
7/18: Air-Sea Rescue off Honshu.
7/21: Fleet Barrier Patrol south of Honshu.

Lieutenant Leo E. Kennedy
Crew #10A(until 30 May)

Lieutenant Leo E. Kennedy, USNR, of Ethlyn, Missouri. Patrol Plane Commander until 30 May).
Lieutenant (jg) Albert P. Vidal, USNR, of Gainesville, Florida. Co-pilot and Navigator until 5 May 1945).
Lieutenant (jg) James D. Marshall, USNR, of Waterville, Maine. Co-pilot and Navigator from 5 May 1945).
Ensign William E. Wassmer, USNR, of Brooklyn, New York. Co-pilot and Navigator.
Harlyn G. Bakko, AMM2c, USNR, of Billings, Montana. Plane Captain and Air Gunner.
Troy A. McClure, AOM1c, USNR, of Cloverdale, Alabama. Air Gunner.
Harry L. Horton, AOMB2c, USNR, of Houston, Texas. Air Gunner.
Gerald M. Kenyon, ARM2c, USNR, of Owatonna, Minnesota. Radioman and Air Gunner.
Joseph B. Edwards, ARM2c, USNR, of DesMoines, Iowa. Radioman and Air Gunner.
John L. Butler, ARM2c, USNR, of Jamaica, New York. Radioman and Air Gunner.
John O. Oates, AMM3c, USNR, of Long Beach, California. Air Gunner (until 24 May).
Perry F. Goodson, AMM3c, USNR, of Cusseta, Alabama. Air Gunner.
William T. Pierson, S1c, USNR, of Columbus, Kentucky. Air Gunner.
Lieutenant (jg) Kenneth R. Kurz, USNR, of Quincy, Illinois. Patrol. Plane Commander (from 22 June).

Ships Sunk

4/28: Cargo vessel at Setji.

5/20: Freighter transport and two coastal Freighters off southern Korea (with Lieutenant Keeling).
5/27: Three small Freighters, stack-aft Freighter (with Lieutenant Cdr. Hicks) off southeast Korea.
5/30: Freighter off Yangtze River mouth (with Lieutenant Jobe).

Ships Damaged

4/23: Small vessel off Borneo.
4/28: Three cargo vessels at K. Merang.
5/2: Freighter off Kudat.
5/20: Cargo vessel off southern Korea (with Lieutenant Keeling).
5/27: Large schooner and small Freighter (with Lieutenant Commander. Hicks), coastal Freighter off southwest Korea.
5/30: Lightship, oceangoing tug, two picket boats off Yangtze River mouth (with Lieutenant Jobe). Freighter, picket boat off Yangtze River mouth (with Lieutenant Jobe, Lieutenant (jg) Serbin). Two attack transports off Yangtze River mouth (with Lieutenant Davis, Lieutenant Jobe).

Attacks

4/23: Strafed radar station in northwest Borneo.
5/2: Destroyed installations Kudat airfield.

Special Missions

6/25: Recon of Chichi Jima.
7/1: Recon of Chichi Jima.
7/2: Air-Sea Rescue off Honshu.
7/8: Fleet Barrier patrol west of Marcus.
7/16: Fleet Barrier Patrol east of Honshu.
7/22: Fleet Barrier patrol south of Honshu.

Lieutenant (jg) Kenneth R. Kurz
Crew #10B(from 22 June)

Lieutenant (jg) Kenneth R. Kurz, USNR, of Quincy, Illinois. Patrol Plane Commander.
Lieutenant (jg) James D. Marshall, USNR, of Waterville, Maine. Co-pilot and Navigator from 5 May 1945).

Ensign William E. Wassmer, USNR, of Brooklyn, New York. Co-pilot and Navigator.

Harlyn G. Bakko, AMM2c, USNR, of Billings, Montana. Plane Captain and Air Gunner.

Troy A. McClure, AOM1c, USNR, of Cloverdale, Alabama. Air Gunner.

Harry L. Horton, AOMB2c, USNR, of Houston, Texas. Air Gunner.

Gerald M. Kenyon, ARM2c, USNR, of Owatonna, Minnesota. Radioman and Air Gunner.

Joseph B. Edwards, ARM2c, USNR, of DesMoines, Iowa. Radioman and Air Gunner.

John L. Butler, ARM2c, USNR, of Jamaica, New York. Radioman and Air Gunner.

John O. Oates, AMM3c, USNR, of Long Beach, California. Air Gunner (until 24 May).

Perry F. Goodson, AMM3c, USNR, of Cusseta, Alabama. Air Gunner.

William T. Pierson, S1c, USNR, of Columbus, Kentucky. Air Gunner.

Special Missions

6/25: Recon of Chichi Jima.
7/1: Recon of Chichi Jima.
7/8: Fleet Barrier patrol west of Marcus.
7/16: Fleet Barrier patrol east of Honshu.
7/22: Fleet Barrier patrol south of Honshu.

Lieutenant Howard M. Turner Jr.
Crew #11A(until 5 May)

Lieutenant Howard M. Turner Jr., USNR, of Cambridge, Massachusetts. Patrol Plane Commander.

Ensign Bert O. Persons Jr., USNR, of Eldorado, Kentucky. Co-pilot and Navigator.

Ensign Lucien G. Geldreich, USNR, of Nashville, Tennessee. Co-pilot and Navigator.

Joe W. Kasperlik, AMM2c, USN, of Grand Rapids, Michigan. Plane Captain and Air Gunner.

Rufus C. Womack, AMM2c, USNR, of Phillips, Texas. Air Gunner.

Harold F. Lee, AFC2c, USNR, of Elk Mound, Wisconsin. Air Gunner.

William B. Coffey, ARM2c, USNR, of Brooklyn, New York. Radioman and Air Gunner.

Charles A. Venner III., ARM2c, USNR, of Bloomfield, New Jersey. Radioman and Air Gunner.

Stanley D. Fraser, AMM2c, USNR, of Washington, D.C. Air Gunner.
William B. Edwards, AMMF3c, USNR, of Asherville, North Carolina. Air Gunner.
Glendale D. Thannisch, AOM3c, USNR, of Harrison, Arkansas. Air Gunner.
Joseph M. McGinnis, ARM3c, USNR, of Nashville, Tennessee. Radioman and Air Gunner.

Ships Sunk

4/29: Coastal Freighter in Cape Bila Harbor.

Ships Damaged

5/5: Oiler at Parepare.

Lieutenant (jg) Albert P. Vidal
Crew #11B(from 5 May)

Lieutenant (jg) Albert P. Vidal, USNR, of Gainesville, Florida. Patrol Plane Commander.
Ensign Bert O. Persons Jr., USNR, of Eldorado, Kentucky. Co-pilot and Navigator.
Ensign Lucien G. Geldreich, USNR, of Nashville, Tennessee. Co-pilot and Navigator.
Joe W. Kasperlik, AMM2c, USN, of Grand Rapids, Michigan. Plane Captain and Air Gunner.
Rufus C. Womack, AMM2c, USNR, of Phillips, Texas. Air Gunner.
Harold F. Lee, AFC2c, USNR, of Elk Mound, Wisconsin. Air Gunner.
William B. Coffey, ARM2c, USNR, of Brooklyn, New York. Radioman and Air Gunner.
Charles A. Venner III., ARM2c, USNR, of Bloomfield, New Jersey. Radioman and Air Gunner.
Stanley D. Fraser, AMM2c, USNR, of Washington, D.C. Air Gunner.
William B. Edwards, AMMF3c, USNR, of Asherville, North Carolina. Air Gunner.
Glendale D. Thannisch, AOM3c, USNR, of Harrison, Arkansas. Air Gunner.
Joseph M. McGinnis, ARM3c, USNR, of Nashville, Tennessee. Radioman and Air Gunner.
Rudolph J. Smolar, S1c, USNR, of Tamaqua, Pennsylvania. Air Gunner from 15 June.

Ships Sunk

5/29: Freighter off eastern Korea (with Lieutenant Vadnais).

Ships Damaged

8/5: Large tanker off Korea.

Attacks

7/3: Bombed and strafed Pagan airfield installations.

Special Missions

6/10: Recon of Chichi Jima.
6/20: Recon of Chichi Jima.
6/27: Recon of Chichi Jima.
7/3: Recon of Pagan.
7/9: Fleet Barrier patrol northwest of Marcus.
7/12: Fleet Barrier Patrol east of Hokkaido.
7/15: Night anti-submarine patrol around Iwo Jima.
7/21: Barrier patrol south of Honshu.
7/27: Fleet barrier patrol south of Honshu.

Lieutenant William A Warren
Crew #12 "Blind Bomber"

Lieutenant William A Warren, USNR, of St. Paul, Minnesota. Patrol Plane Commander.
Ensign Leo F. Haas, USNR, of Tulsa, Oklahoma. Co-pilot and Navigator.
Ensign Paul E. Geyer, USNR, of Minneapolis, Minnesota. Co-pilot and Navigator.
Chester E. Rosell, AMM2c, USNR, of Leonardville, Kentucky. Plane Captain and Air Gunner.
Harold J. Carter, AMM2c, USNR, of Okmulgee, Oklahoma. Air Gunner
Floyd D. King, AOM2c, USNR, of Newark, Ohio. Air Gunner.
Richard T. Coleman, ARM2c, USNR, of Rochester, New York. Radioman and Air Gunner.
Earl W. Newton, ARM2c, USNR, of Wichita Falls, Texas. Radioman and Air Gunner.
Lowell E. Tiller, AMM3c, USNR, of Hermiston, Oregon. Air Gunner.
Val M. Higgins, AMM3c, USNR, of Iona, Minnesota. Air Gunner.
William R. Smith, AOM3c, USN, of Decatur, Illinois. Air Gunner.
Richard P. Edson, ARM3c, USNR, of Springfield, Massachusetts. Radioman and Air Gunner.

Planes Destroyed

5/17: Jack in air off Kyushu.

Planes Damaged

5/17: Jack in air off Kyushu (with Lieutenant Fairbanks).

Ships Sunk

5/22: Freighter off southern Korea (with Lieutenant Turner).

Attacks

4/25: Strafed airfield installations at Kudat.

Special Missions

6/21: Recon of Chichi Jima.
6/28: Recon of Chichi Jima.
7/6: Fleet Barrier patrol west of Marcus.
7/13: Air-Sea Rescue off Hachijo Jima.
7/19: Barrier patrol south of Honshu.
7/22: Fleet barrier patrol south of Honshu.

Lieutenant Floyd Hewitt
Crew #13 "Sleepy-Time Gal"

Lieutenant Floyd Hewitt, USNR, of Audubon, New Jersey. Patrol Plane Commander.
Ensign Andrew W. Tainter, USNR, of Eau Claire, Wisconsin. Co-pilot and Navigator.
Ensign Luther H. Lingerfelt, USNR, of Crews, Virginia. Co-pilot and Navigator.
Gordon E. Hargadine, AMM2c, USNR, of Kinsley, Kentucky. Plane Captain and Air Gunner.
Marvin R. Pearl, AMM2c, USNR, of Cleveland, Ohio. Air Gunner.
Marion W. Ritchie Jr., ARM2c, USN, of Hazard, Kentucky. Radioman and Air Gunner.
Donald O. Straub, ARM2c, USNR, of Pittsburgh, Penssylvania. Radioman and Air Gunner.
Raphael K. Mestemaker, AMM3c, USNR, of Coldwater, Ohio. Air Gunner.
William Kurz Jr., AOM3c, USNR, of Milwaukee, Wisconsin. Air Gunner.

Alfred E. Parks, AOM3c, USNR, of Somerville, Tennessee. Air Gunner.
August A. Morris, ARM3c, USNR, of Houston, Texas. Radioman and Air Gunner.
Robert S. Taylor, S1c, USNR, of Evanston, Illinois. Air Gunner.

Planes Destroyed

5/24: Tony in air off Korea (with Lieutenant Chay).

Ships Sunk

5/4: Freighter on high seas.
5/18: Freighter off southern Korea (with Lieutenant (jg) Serbin).
7/31: Schooner off Gaisan Ho River.

Attacks

4/26: Strafed radar station on Baican Island.
5/1: Bombed and strafed radar station on Tambelan Island.
7/31: Destroyed small railroad bridge on Seisen Ko River, (Korea) by bombing. Seriously damaged railroad train by bombing and strafing, heavy equipment and installations at Shinanshu airstrip, a rail junction yard and coal mine buildings and installations by strafing.

Special Missions

6/7: Recon of Truk.
6/24: Recon of Chichi Jima.
7/7: Air-Sea rescue off Honshu.
7/8: Air-Sea Rescue off Honshu.
7/11: Fleet barrier patrol east of Honshu.
7/20: Air-Sea Rescue off Honshu.

Lieutenant Thomas W. Challis Jr.
Crew #14 "Green Cherries"

Lieutenant Thomas W. Challis Jr., USNR, of St. Louis, Missouri. Patrol Plane Commander.
Ensign Herbert E. Floriani, USNR, of Lake Village, Arkansas. Co-pilot and Navigator.
Ensign James L. Ruths, USNR, of Minneapolis, Minnesota. Co-pilot and Navigator.

William H. Enid Jr., AMM2c, USNR, of Atlanta, Texas. Plane Captain and Air Gunner.
Frank L. Smith Jr., ARM1c, USNR, of Raymond, Mississippi. Radioman and Air Gunner.
Richard L. Etter, AMM2c, USN, of Waynesboro, Pennsylvania. Air Gunner.
Robert C. Harris, AMM3c, USNR, of Jackson, Mississippi. Air Gunner.
William H. Beyer, AMM3c, USNR, of Jamaica, New York. Air Gunner.
Jack T. Biggers, AOM3c, USNR, of Inglewood, California. Air Gunner.
Edwin R. Pickhardt, AOM3c, USN, of Hopkins, Minnesota. Air Gunner.
Lowell W. Turner, ARM3c, USNR, of Bennington, Indiana. Radioman and Air Gunner.
Herbert K. Ferguson, ARM3c, USNR, of Concord, North Carolina. Radioman and Air Gunner.

Ships Sunk

5/25: Freighter transport off Korea (with Lieutenant Keeling).

Attacks

4/25: Strafed radio and radio-radar stations on Tambelan Island.
4/29: Bombed and strafed radar tower and encampment on Balabalangan Island.

Special Missions

6/22: Recon of Chichi Jima.
6/30: Recon of Chichi Jima.
7/8: Fleet barrier patrol west of Marcus.
7/11: Air-Sea Rescue off Honshu.
7/19: Air-Sea rescue off Honshu.
7/22: Fleet barrier patrol south of Honshu.
7/26: Fleet barrier patrol south of Honshu.

Lieutenant Hugh M. Wilkinson Jr.
Crew #15 "Punkie"

Lieutenant Hugh M. Wilkinson Jr., USNR, of New Orleans, Louisiana. Patrol Plane Commander.
Lieutenant (jg) Edwin L. Vaughn, USNR, of Houston, Texas. Co-pilot and Navigator until 15 May 1945).

Ensign Kenneth C. Jones, USNR, of Ozone, New York. Co-pilot and Navigator from 15 May 1945.

Ensign Archie E. Davis Jr., USNR, of Rockaway, New Jersey. Co-pilot and Navigator.

Wilbert C. Leonberger, AMM2c, USNR. Plane Captain and Air Gunner until 10 June.

William R. Brady, AMM2c, USN, of Orreck, Missouri. Air Gunner.

Thomas G. Wack, AMM3c, USNR, of South Bend, Indiana. Air Gunner.

Eugene Wilder, AOM3c, USNR, of Hattiesberg, Mississippi. Air Gunner.

John A. Pollman Jr., AOM3c, USNR, of Homestead, Oklahoma. Air Gunner.

James M. Frink, AOM3c, USNR, of Bladenborg, North Carolina. Air Gunner until 10 June.

Henry H. Hennes, ARM3c, USNR, of Los Angeles, California. Radioman and Air Gunner.

Donald S. Baskin, ARM3c, USNR, of Murphysboro, Illinois. Radioman and Air Gunner.

Jay W. Mickle Jr., ARM3c, USNR, of Wichita, Kentucky. Radioman and Air Gunner.

Carlton W. Stallworth, AMM2c, USNR, of College Park, Georgia. Air Gunner from 10 June.

Richard E. Ogen, ARM3c, USN, of Redondo Beach, California. Air Gunner from 10 June.

Ships Sunk

5/23: Freighter off southern Korea (with Lieutenant Vadnais).

Ships Damaged

5/3: Three Freighters, river steamer, cargo boat at Cape Bila.
5/15: Freighter transport off Kyushu.
8/7: Freighter, small Freighter and large schooner in Tsushima Straits.

Attacks

4/30: Bombed and strafed radar installations on Pouli Obi Island.
5/2: Bombed and strafed installations at Natoena. Bombed and strafed airfield, lighthouse and buildings at South Natoena.

Special Missions

6/11: Recon of Chichi Jima.
6/20: Recon of Truk.
6/27: Recon of Chichi Jima.
7/3: Recon of Chichi Jima.
7/9: Fleet barrier patrol northwest of Marcus.
7/12: Fleet barrier patrol east of Hokkaido.
7/15: Fleet barrier patrol east of Honshu.
7/16: Fleet barrier patrol east of Honshu.
7/22: Air-Sea rescue off Honshu.
7/25: Night anti-submarine patrol around Iwo Jima.
7/30: Special weather flight.

Lieutenant (jg) Oscar S. Braddock
Crew #16

Lieutenant (jg) Oscar S. Braddock, USNR, of Jacksonville, Florida. Patrol Plane Commander.
Lieutenant (jg) Bernard C. Perkins, USNR, of Richland, Wisconsin. Co-pilot and Navigator.
Ensign Ordean S. Hockel, USNR, of Oken, Minnesota. Co-pilot and Navigator.
Charles F. Kidwell, AMM2c, USNR, of Venice, California. Plane Captain and Air Gunner.
Neil K. Campbell, ARM1c, USN, of Morton, Washington. Radioman and Air Gunner.
James F. Sizemore Jr., AMM2c, USNR, of Logan West Virginia. Air Gunner.
Henry J. Teegarden, AMM2c, USNR, of Newark, Ohio. Air Gunner.
Robert E. Mayo, ARM2c, USNR, of Millinocket, Maine. Radioman and Air Gunner until 3 July.
Charles F. Dahl, ARM2c, USNR, of Brainerd, Minnesota. Radioman and Air Gunner.
John T. Gill, AMM3c, USNR, of Luthersville, Georgia. Air Gunner.
Donald G. Schultz, AOM3c, USNR, of Topeka, Kentucky. Air Gunner.
Daniel A. Pendley, AOM3c, USNR, of Steens, Mississippi. Air Gunner.
Joseph S. Teyshak, ARM1c, USN, of Streator, Illinois. Air Gunner from 4 July.

Planes Destroyed

5/18: Zeke in air off southern Chosen (with Lieutenant Turner).

Ships Sunk

5/1: Picket boat, fuel barge and three freight luggers in Kapacas River.
5/18: Freighter off southern Korea.
5/23: Freighter off southern Korea.
7/26: Three trawlers at Shingu (with Lieutenant Chay).
8/7: Medium Freighter, small Freighter and large schooner in Tsushima Straits.

Ships Damaged

5/18: Freighter off southern Korea.
7/26: Two trawlers at Shingu (with Lieutenant Chay).

Attacks

4/23: Bombed and strafed airfield at Soebi-Ketjil.
7/3: Bombed and strafed Pagan airfield installations.
7/26: Destroyed buildings and a pier at Shingu by bombing and strafing. Silenced three gun positions by strafing (with Lieutenant Chay).

Special Missions

6/18: Special weather flight.
6/26: Recon of Chichi Jima.
6/27: Recon of Chichi Jima.
7/3: Recon of Chichi Jima.
7/9: Fleet barrier patrol northwest of Marcus. Lieutenant (jg) Robichaud, pilot.
7/12: Fleet barrier patrol east of Hokkaido.
7/16: Fleet barrier patrol east of Honshu.
7/20: Night anti-submarine patrol around Iwo Jima.
7/23: Fleet barrier patrol south of Honshu.
8/3: Special weather flight.

Lieutenant (jg) Serbin
Crew #17

Lieutenant (jg) George Serbin, USNR, of Bessemer, Michigan. Patrol Plane Commander.
Lieutenant (jg) Edwin L. Vaughn, USNR, of Houston, Texas. Co-pilot and Navigator from 15 May 1945).

Ensign Kenneth C. Jones, USNR, of Ozone, New York. Co-pilot and Navigator until 15 May 1945.
Ensign Charles A. Memish, USNR, of Whiting, Indiana. Co-pilot and Navigator.
Jack D. Tenney, AMM1c, USN, of Hood River, Oregon. Plane Captain and Air Gunner.
Richard M. Snedeker, AMM2c, USN, of Fairfield, New York. Air Gunner.
Lawrence Cordery, AOM2c, USNR, of Metuchen, New Jersey. Air Gunner (from 13 June).
William M. Goreham, ARM2c, USNR, Des Moines, Iowa. Radioman and Air Gunner.
Dallas N. Vickers, ARM2c, USNR, of Geneva, Alabama. Radioman and Air Gunner.
Donald S. Ball, AMM3c, USNR, of Encino, California. Air Gunner.
Michael J. Scully, AOM3c, USNR, of Sprinfield, Massachusetts. Air Gunner.
Bernard H. Hornish, AOM3c, USNR, of Akron, Ohio. Air Gunner (until 13 June).
James R. Asher, ARM3c, USNR, of Stafford, Kentucky. Radioman and Air Gunner.
Alton N. Druse, S1c, USNR, of Yakina, Washington. Air Gunner.

Planes Destroyed

5/2: 1 Dinah, 1 Jake in air off Indo-China.

Ships Sunk

5/18: Freighter off southern Korea (with Lieutenant Hewitt).
5/24: Freighter off southern Korea (with Lieutenant Jobe).
Ships damaged

5/30: Freighter, two picket boats off Yangtze River mouth (with Lieutenant Davis). Freighter, large picket boat in Yantgtze river (with Lieutenant Jobe, Lieutenant Kennedy).

Attacks

4/29: Bombed and strafed radar station at Daengalahan.
4/29: Destroyed supply dump on an island at Moreas Reef by strafing.
5/30: Lighthouse at Yangtze River mouth damaged by strafing (with Lieutenant Davis).

Special Missions

6/29: Reconnaissance of Chichi Jima.
7/9: Fleet barrier patrol northwest of Marcus.
7/12: Fleet barrier patrol east of Hokkaido.
7/15: Fleet barrier patrol east of Honshu.
7/19: Fleet barrier patrol east of Honshu.
7/23: Fleet barrier patrol south of Honshu.
7/26: Fleet barrier patrol south of Honshu.

Lieutenant (jg) Moyer
Crew #18

Lieutenant (jg) Russell A. Moyer, USNR, of Chippewa Falls, Wisconsin. Patrol Plane Commander.
Ensign Roderick C. Hamilton, USNR, of Wellesley, Massachusetts. Co-pilot and Navigator.
Ensign Roswell T. Fusselman, USNR, of Long Beach, California. Co-pilot and Navigator.
Gordon L. Jorgenson, AMM1c, USN, of Evansville, Wisconsin. Plane Captain and Air Gunner.
Clement L. De Marteau, ACRM, USN, of Sacremento, California. Radioman and Air Gunner.
Robert O. Wilson, AMM2c, USNR, of Chicago, Illinois. Air Gunner.
Terrel N. Deen, AOM2c, USNR, of Chattanooga, Tennessee. Air Gunner (From 15 June 1945).
Vernon C. Conner, ARM2c, USNR, of Tampa, Florida. Radioman and Air Gunner.
Kermit E. Meehan, AMM3c, USNR, Ellsworth, Wisconsin. Air Gunner.
Eugene Garrard, AOM3c, USNR, of Robinson, Illinois. Air Gunner.
Richard G. Morris, AOM3c, USNR, of Phillipsburg, New Jersey. Air Gunner.
Richard J. Sulewski, ARM3c, USNR, of Detroit, Michigan. Air Gunner (until 15 June 1945).
John W. Pearson, ARM3c, USNR, of Detroit, Michigan. Radioman and Air Gunner.

Ships Sunk

5/3: River Steamer near Tanahorogot.
8/10: Five small Freighters (with Lieutenant Chay) in Tsushima Straits.

Ships Damaged

5/27: Freighter off Shimono Shima with Lieutenant Jadin.
8/7: Five small trawlers off Kyushu (with Lieutenant Chay).

Attacks

4/28: Strafed installations and radar station on Bai Can Island.
5/3: Destroyed installations at Kudat by bombing and strafing. Destroyed a railroad engine and three cars by strafing, three oil-tank cars by bombing, and a sawmill by bombing and strafing at Tanahorogot.
5/27: Bombed and strafed radio and radar station at Suwanos Jima with Lieutenant Jadin.

Special Missions

6/15: Reconnaissance of Chichi Jima.
6/29: Reconnasissance of Chichi Jima.
7/6: Fleet barrier patrol west of Marcus.
7/10: Air-Sea Rescue off Honshu.
7/19: Fleet barrier patrol east of Honshu.

Appendix J:
Missions and Flying Hours
per VPB-109 Patrol Plane Commander

PPC	No. of Missions	Hours of Missions	Total Hours
Turner	42	289.3	306.6
Hicks	39	260.3	273.0
Chay	38	292.2	306.5
Challis	38	262.5	247.7
Moyer	38	258.4	267.9
Braddock	38	259.9	269.3
Fairbanks	37	292.0	335.2
Vadnais	37	247.3	251.6
Warren	37	251.0	272.7
Hewitt	36	238.0	263.9
Jobe	36	265.4	283.9
Wilkinson	36	284.0	295.4
Serbin	35	264.3	286.8
Keeling	34	244.8	242.1
Jadin	34	212.7	249.1
Davis	33	222.9	237.1
Vidal	31	197.5	200.2
Kennedy	25	244.8	138.8
Kure	19	118.9	127.4
Bundy	9	50.4	59.3

Appendix K:
Aircraft Assigned to VPB-109

32147: (PB4Y-1 transport plane)
59501: "Punkie."
59502: "Green Cherries."
59512
59514: "Blind Bomber."
59515: "Hogan's Goat."
59516
59518
59521: "Bachelor's Delight" Lost with Lieutenant Keeling and crew on 8-5-45.
59522: "Miss Lotta Tail."
59523
59526: Destroyed in bombing on 5-19-45.
59527
59528: "Lambaster."
59529: Destroyed in bombing on 5-24-45.
59530: Surveyed do to battle damage on 6-6-45.
59533: Destroyed in bombing on 5-24-45.
59541: Received from Fleet Air Wing Two on 22 June.
59544: Received on 22 June.
59581
59488
59613

Appendix L:
List of Personnel Killed in Action

(13 January 1944)
Lieutenant Samuel E. Coleman, USNR. Patrol Plane Commander.
Lieutenant (jg) Leroy A. Shreiner, USNR. Co-pilot.
Ensign Leslie E. Fontaine, USNR. Navigator.
Louis E. Sandidge Jr., AMM1c, USNR. Plane Captain and Air Gunner.
Sterling T. Brown, AMM2c, USNR. Air Gunner.
James T. Heasley, AOM2c, USNR. Air Gunner.
Truman Steele, AOM2c, USNR. Air Gunner.
Harry F. Donovan, ARM2c, USNR. Radioman, Air Gunner.
Daniel J. Dujak, ARM2c, USNR. Radioman, Air Gunner.
Lou C. Petrick, S1c, USNR. Air Gunner.
John E. Tusha, S1c, USNR. Air Gunner.

(13 February 1944)
Lieutenant (jg) John H. Herron, USNR. Pilot, Patrol plane commander.
Lieutenant (jg) Charles M. Henderson Jr., USNR. Co-pilot.
Ensign Nelson T. O'Bryan, USNR. Navigator.
Robert J. Bennington, AMM1c, USNR. Plane Captain, Air Gunner.
Benjamin W. Anderson, AOM(T)1c, USNR. Air Gunner.
Raymond W. Devlin, ARM2c, USNR. Radioman, Air Gunner.
Clarence H. Ziehlke, AMM3c, USN. Air Gunner.
Paul J. Graham, AOM3c, USNR. Air Gunner.
Richard C. Vancitters, AOM3c, USNR. Air Gunner.
Aern R. Durgin, S2c, USNR. Air Gunner

(5 August 1944)
Lieutenant Elmer H. Kasperson, USN, Patrol Plane Commander.
Ensign Warren A. Hindenland, USNR. Co-pilot.
Ensign Keith E. Ellis, USNR. Navigator.
Joseph W. Komorowski, AMM1c, USNR. Plane Captain, Air Gunner.
Warren B. Simon, AMM2c, USN. Air Gunner.
Richard D. Frye, ARM2c, USNR. Radioman, Air Gunner.
Hugo L. Kluge, ARM2c, USNR. Radioman, Air Gunner.
William F. Schneider, AOM2c, USNR. Air Gunner.
Victor B. Jones, AOM2c, USN. Air Gunner.
Allen K. Stinger, AOM3c, USNR. Air Gunner.
Bobby W. Fickling, AOM3c, USNR. Air Gunner.

(5 August 1945)
Lieutenant John D. Keeling, USNR. Patrol Plane Commander.
Ensign Henry Baier Jr., USNR. Co-pilot Navigator.
Ensign Keith W. Radcliffe, USNR. Co-pilot, Navigator.
William L. Willocks Jr., AMM1c, USNR. Plane Captain, Air Gunner.
Frank R. Kramer, AOM1c, USNR. Air Gunner.
William J. Krier, ARM1c, USNR. Radioman, Air Gunner.
Alexander J. Boyd, ARM1c, USNR. Radioman, Air Gunner.
Melvin M. Rager, AMM2c, USNR. Air Gunner.
James R.T. Carswell, AFC2c, USN. Air Gunner.
Peter G. Ilacqua, ARM2c, USNR. Radioman, Air Gunner.
James E. Krieger, AMM3c, USNR. Air Gunner.
Lawrence R. Conroy, AOM3c, USNR. Air Gunner.

(5 June 1944)
Hale D. Fisher, AMM1c

(5 May 1945)
Joe W. Kasperlik, AMM2c, USN, Plane Captain, Air Gunner.

(30 May 1945)
Lieutenant Leo E. Kennedy, USNR, Patrol Plane Commander.

Appendix M:
Ground Personnel

VB-109
Lieutenant Richard C. Crouch, USNR. Personnel Officer.
Lieutenant Theodore Steele, USNR. Air Combat Intellegence and Public Relations Officer.
Lieutenant William W. Robinson, USNR. Operations Officer.
Lieutenant Lyman W. Ballinger, USNR. Engineering Officer.
Lieutenant Max B. Payne, USNR. Gunnery Officer.
Chester S. Jones, CY, USNR. Yeoman.
John S. Sladech, Y1c, USN. Yeoman.

VPB-109
Lieutenant John L. Bannon, USNR. ACIO, Operations Officer.
Lieutenant Theodore Steele, USNR. ACIO, Administration Officer.
Lieutenant (jg) Leland P. Russell, USNR. Personnel Officer.
Lieutenant (jg) Robert V. Gibson, USNR. Engineering Officer.
Lieutenant (jg) William Avila, USNR. Radar and RCM Officer.
Lieutenant (jg) William L. Shaffer, USNR. Electronics Officer.
Lieutenant (jg) Calvin M. Jones, USNR. Gunnery Officer.
Lieutenant (jg) James F. Burns, USN. Radio Officer.

Notes

Introduction

[1]Steve Birdsell, *Log of the Liberators:* An Illustrated History of the B-24 (Garden City, NY: Doubleday), 128.
[2]Frederick A. Johnson, *Bombers in Blue*, (Tacoma, WA: Bomber Books).
[3]Ibid.
[4]Ibid.

Chapter One

[1]William Bridgeman and Jacqueline Hazard, *The Lonely Sky* (New York, NY: Henry Holt and Company), 20.
[2]Norman P. Miller and Hugh B. Cave. *I Took the Sky Road* (New York, NY: Dodd, Mead & Company), 87.

Chapter Two

[1]Miller, *I Took the Sky Road*, 90.
[2]Ibid.
[3]Samuel E. Morison, *History of United States Naval Operations Vol. VII: Aleutions, Gilberts, and Marshalls* (New York, NY: Little, Brown and Comapany), 213.
[4]Morison, 70-71.
[5]Morison, 230.
[6]Morison, 74.
[7]Morison, 75.
[8]Morison, 283.
[9]Edwin P. Hoyt, *How They Won the War in the Pacific* (New York, NY: Weybright and Talley), 316.
[10]Morison, 75.

Chapter Three

[1]John F. Hazaner, AMMP1c; William B. Idleman, AOM2c; and Elmer O. Ray, S2c.
[2]Ensign Amos L. Shreiner; Ensign Robert E. Malmfeldt; William F. Donovan, ARM2c; and Daniel J. Dujak, ARM2c were awarded the Navy and Marine Medal.
[3]First section consisting of Renfro, Ebright, Daley, and Wengierski from VB-108. Second Section consisting of Miller, Grayson, Hicks, and Sheppard from VB-109. Third Section consisting of Lt. Cmdr. Porter and Lt. Satterfield from VD-3.
[4]Samuel E. Morison, *History of United States Naval Operations Vol. VII: Aleutions, Gilberts, and Marshalls* (New York, NY: Little, Brown and Comapany), 214.

Chapter Four

[1]The flight consisted of three, six plane sections. First Division, First Section: Commander Stroh, VD-3; Lt. Mullron and Lt. Martin, VB-108. Second Section: Lt. (jg) Idleman, VD-3; Lt. Daley and Lt. Piper, VB-108. Second Division, Third Section: Lt. Kiem, VD-3; Lt. Rice and Lt. Webster, VB-108. Fourth Section: Lt. Satterfield, VD-3; Lt. Wengierski, VB-108; Lt. Sheppard, VB-109. Third Division, Fifth Section: Lt. Commander Porter, VD-3; Commander Miller and Lt. (jg) Herron, VB-109. Six Section: Lt. Davidson, VD-3; Lt. Mellard and Lt. Wheaton, VB-109.

Chapter Five

[1]The flight originally consisted of two sections. First Section: Miller, Hicks, and Jobe. Second Section: Lt. Muldrow, Lt. Piper, Lt. (jg) Webster, VB-108.
[2]The following sections were organized and dispatched: First Section: Hicks, VB-109 and Daley, VB-108. Second Section: Jobe and Lt. Ackerman, VB-108.

Chapter Six

[1]Hoyt, How They Won the War in the Pacific, 361.
[2]Morison, *History of United States Naval Operations Vol. VII: Aleutions, Gilberts, and Marshalls,* 307.
[3]Morison, 312.
[4]Morison, 313.
[5]Ibid.
[6]Morison, 314.
[7]Bridgeman, *The Lonely Sky*, 30-31.
[8]Members of the crew observed the numbers 12 or 112 painted on the conning tower. However, no Japanese submarine with those numbers or a combination of those numbers was reported sunk in the vicinity of the attack during this time.
[9]Morison, 317.
[10]Morison, 318.
[11]Morison, 329-330.
[12]*Ibid.*
[13]Carly Boyd and Akihiko Yoshida, *The Japanese Submarine Force and World War II* (Annapolis, Maryland; Naval Institute Press), 213.

Chapter Seven

[1]Morison, 306.

Chapter Eight

[1]Miller, *I Took the Sky Road*, 166.

Chapter Nine

[1]Morison, *History of United States Naval Operations Vol. VIII: New Guinea and the Marianas: March 1944-August 1944* (New York, NY: Little, Brown and Company), 149.
[2]Morison, 5, 8.
[3]Miller, *I Took the Sky Road*, 168.
[4]Miller, 177-178.
[5]A single engine float biplane built by the Sasebo Aircraft Company.
[6]The Nakajima A6M. A float-equipped variant of the Zeke.
[7]Kawanishi H8K2 flying boat.

Chapter Ten

[1]Tactical organization of the strike: First Division, First Section: Lt. Commander Clark, VD-4; Flying Officer Jordan, USAA 86th; Lt. Sheppard, VB-109. Second Section: Lt. Lowrie, VD-4; Lt. Cervone and Lt. Stinson, VB-116. Third Section: Lt. O'Brien, VD-4; Lt. Anderson and Lt. Groves, VB-116. Fourth Section: Lt. Mather, VD-4; Lt. Hanne, 86th; Lt. Kennedy, VB-109. Fifth Section: Lt. Wright Jr., VD-4; Lt. Keeling and Lt. Glenn, VB-109. Second Division, First Section: Lt. Tuttle, VD-4; Lt.

Robertson, 86th; Lt. Thompson, VB-116. Second Section: Lt. Hatfield, VD-4; Lt. Miller and Lt. (jg) Gomes, VB-116. Third Section: Lt. (jg) Diehl, VD-4; Lt. Wheaton and Lt. Mellard, VB-109.

Chapter Twelve

[1]Rafael Steinberg and the editors of Time-Life Books, *Return to the Philippines* (Alexandria, VA: Time-Life Books), 151-152.
[2]B.H. Liddell Hart, *History of the Second World War* (G.P. Putman's Sons: New York, NY), 688-689.

Chapter Thirteen

[1]Morison, *History of United States Naval Operations Vol. XIV: Victory in the Pacific 1945* (New York, NY: Little, Brown and Company), 270-271.
[2]D.R. Johnson, ARM3c, multiple 20mm shrapnel wounds to head and back; Ensign A. Shore, 20mm wounds to arm and back; M.E. Kinsen, 20mm wounds to right foot.
[3]Possibly the 2,278-ton Enkyo Maru which was sunk near this vicinity.
[4]Morison, *History of United States Naval Operations Vol. XIV: Victory in the Pacific 1945*, 270-271.
[5]This ship was possibly the 882-ton Taihyo Maru #2.

Bibliography

Birdsall, Steve. *Log of the Liberators:* An Illustrated History of the B-24. Garden City, NY: Doubleday., 1973.

Bridgeman, William and Jacqueline Hazard. *The Lonely Sky.* New York, NY: Henry Holt and Company., 1955.

Boyd, Carl and Akihiko Yoshida. *The Japanese Submarine Force and World War II.* Annapolis, Maryland: Naval Institute Press., 1995.

Casey, Louis S. and John Batchelor. *The Illustrated History of Seaplanes & Flying Boats.* New York, NY: Exeter Books., 1980.

Friedman, Norman. *U.S. Naval Weapons.* Naval Institute Press.

Hart, Liddell B.H. *History of the Second World War.* G.P. Putman's Sons: New York, NY., 1970.

Hoyt, Edwin P. *How They Won the War in the Pacific.* New York, NY: Weybright and Talley.

Johnson, Frederick A. *Bombers in Blue.* Tacoma, WA: Bomber Books., 1979.

Miller, Norman M and Hugh B. Cave. *I Took the Sky Road.* New York, NY: Dodd, Mead & Company., 1945.

Morison, Samuel E. *History of United States Naval Operations Vol. VII: Aleutions, Gilberts, and Marshalls.* New York, NY: Little, Brown and Company., 1990.

Morison, Samuel E. *History of United States Naval Operations Vol. VIII: New Guinea and the Marianas: March 1944-August 1944.* New York, NY: Little, Brown and Company., 1981.

Morison, Samuel E. *History of United States Naval Operations Vol. XIV: Victory in the Pacific 1945.* New York, NY: Little, Brown and Company.,(1960)

Ito, Masanori. *The End of the Japanese Imperial Navy.* New York, NY: MKacfadden-Bartell., 1962.

Steinberg, Rafael and the editors of Time-Life Books. *Return to the Philippines.* Alexandria, VA: Time-Life Books., 1978.

Joint-Navy Assessment Committee. *Japanese Naval and Merchant Shipping Losses During World War II by all Causes.*, 1947.

Notes

Notes

Notes